Making
Your
Future

In Business
- and in Other Parts of Life -

© 2015, Author: Willem N. Top
Self publishing

First edition; revision 0

Contact Information:

Email: topves@ziggo.nl

ISBN 978-90-820411-4-9

I dedicate this book to all people who wish to change their present situation and have the courage to begin their journey towards their new future.

In particular I dedicate this book to my wife Marry who, according to statistics, will still have a 20 year future after I am gone.

And certainly, I dedicate this book to our three children: Frank, Marieke and Willemijn. I hope that sometime in the future they will look at this book again and say: "Yes, he was more right than wrong: you have to make your own future".

I hope that all of you will find some inspiration in this book, some ideas, to begin your journey. Don't give up easily but be wise enough to change your objectives if and when the times comes you need to do that.

TRY TO **MAKE** YOUR FUTURE. DON'T JUST WAIT AND SEE – YOU MAY NOT LIKE WHAT'S COMING!

CONTENT

MY LOGO

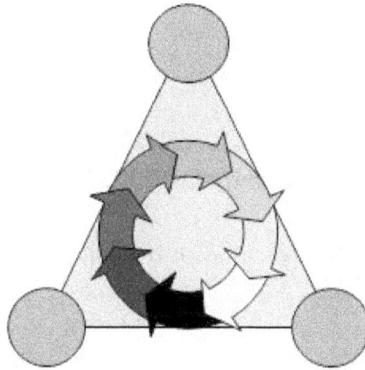

Are you wondering where the logo comes from that is shown on the cover of this book?

It is a combination of: (i) the PLATFORM MODEL that I use to show the basic ingredients for making your future, improvement or change and, (ii) the STRUCTURE that I recommend for the elements of the PLAN to go where you want to be.

In a business environment such plan may be called "management system".

The platform model:

- Three circles or columns: <u>Plan – Train – Do</u>. Know what you need to do to get where you want to be. Have the knowledge (and other resources) to do it. And: do it!
- The triangle representing the performance level carried by the three columns
- Not visible in the logo is the foundation of the platform: <u>Leadership and Motivation</u>

The element structure:

- The segmented circle in the middle representing the ever turning improvement wheel

My logo shows the basic ingredients for organizational change and improvement. These basics are applicable in business and in other aspects of life - on your way to your new future.

Peter Drucker
The best way to predict the future is to create it

Peter Drucker (1909 – 2005) – management consultant, educator and author

MAKING YOUR FUTURE

Reaching Objectives and Controlling Unwanted Events

Go hand in hand

They are the two sides of the same coin

YOU NEED A PLAN TO DO IT

Peter Drucker

What you have to do and the way you have to do it is incredibly simple.
Whether you are willing to do it, that's another matter.

Peter Drucker (1909 – 2005) – management consultant, educator and author

---

The principle of future characteristics

The past performance of an organization or unit tends to foreshadow its
future characteristics

Louis A. Allen, management consultant and writer. Founder of Louis Allen Worldwide.

In a complex situation?

Go back to the basics!

And get the results that you are looking for!

DISCLAIMER

This book provides information to help you to change, to go where you want to be. I am writing this from a business point of view. However, the ideas, principles and tools apply equally to any type of organization. They also apply to private life. The message is simple: if you want to make your future, you need a plan, carry it out and do not give up!

Since I took the business environment as the focus, the impression may be that I refer more to the making a management system than to making a plan but remember that a management system is also a plan. And, whatever I mention in this book, you need to alter it to your specific situation, to your company, to your organization, to your life.

This book includes ideas that I developed during my time as a safety management consultant, providing management system related auditing, training and consulting services to industrial clients in Europe. Ideas that have been influenced by greater spirits than I. The main tool provided is the 17-step process to make and implement a plan or management system that is effective and brings results. Results that depend on the circumstances under which the process is being put into practice as well as the intent, knowledge and motivation of all parties involved.

I would not be surprised if - after reading the book - you would say: "Hey, I could have figured that out". As a matter of fact, I hope that this will be the case because it would mean that you and I are on the same wavelength. That does not mean that it is easy to follow the 17-step process; you may even not be able to as you may not have the management or client taking the wheel driving towards the success they are looking for - with your help. However, if they do take the wheel, you are in the seat next to the driver, holding the road map.

This is not a cookbook recipe but rather a travel guide showing the road to go. There is no guarantee for success; there never is when you are working to move a company to the next performance level and beyond that. But in the book I show you the basic ingredients - you and the people you work with will have to add the flavors to make it work for you!

The contents of the book may help you to make your management system work. The success, however, will be entirely up to you and others with whom you need to work to obtain the benefits that can be the result of a management system, no matter what the objectives are.

English is not my native language. I am from The Netherlands also known as Holland and I am sure that you will find that my control over grammar is not always correct, for which I apologize. But as long as it is not "double Dutch" and I am not insulting anybody or using improper language, please consider my incorrect use of the English language as "Dutch charm".

Willem Top
The Netherlands, 2014

To set the tone:

Peter Drucker

The first duty of management is to survive and the guiding principle of business economics is not the maximization of profit – it is the avoidance of loss

In case of keen competition and low profit margins, learning from accidents can contribute more to profits than an organization's best salesperson

Management is doing things right; leadership is doing the right things.

Management by objectives works if you first think through your objectives. Ninety percent of the time you haven't.

Peter Drucker (1909 – 2005) – management consultant, educator and author

---

Louis A. Allen

Minimizing loss is as much improvement as maximization of profit

---

Louis A. Allen, management consultant and writer. Founder of Louis Allen Worldwide

NOTE: Throughout this book I am using so-called "management principles". While these can be found on the Internet and in a number of books, including those written by Frank E. Bird Jr., these principles may first have been used by Louis A. Allen. In the early 1970's the books written by Mr. Allen were of great importance to me to understand the management process.

To set the tone (continued):

Peter Drucker

The best way to predict the future is to create it

Peter Drucker (1909 – 2005) – management consultant, educator and author

---

Lord Kelvin

When you cannot measure, your knowledge is meager and unsatisfactory

William Thomson, 1st Baron Kelvin (1824 – 1907) British mathematical physicist and engineer

---

Dr. H. James Harrington

Measurement is the first step that leads to control and eventually to improvement.

If you can't measure something, you can't understand it. If you can't understand it, you can't control it. If you can't control it, you can't improve it

H. J. Harrington (1929), American author, engineer, entrepreneur and consultant

---

When making your plan to make your future, it helps if you are able to measure: (i) where you want to be, (ii) where you are now, (iii) what you need to do to get where you want to be and (iv) the results of what you are doing compared to where you want to be.

PLEASE NOTE. Measurement does not have to be in absolute terms. That will not always be possible when measuring management related aspects. Measurements can be subjective against references and criteria but when those references/ criteria are agreed upon and accepted by knowledgeable people these measurements will be less subjective. You will find some examples of subjective measurement in appendices F and H (pages 267 and 298 respectively).

FOR WHOM THIS BOOK IS

Do you want your future to be different from your present situation?

Or are you:

- Interested to improve your organization or company as a manager?
- Working as an internal consultant with the task to help your management?
- An external consultant hired to assist your customer to reach their objective(s)?

Then this book is for you.

Mind you, I address you – the reader – with "you" realizing that your interest may vary depending on your role in the improvement process. Your role and interests as a manager may not be the same as your role and interests as a consultant. When I refer to your management system or your plan, it may not actually be yours but rather that of your management or your customer if you are a consultant. Please keep that in mind.

What Future?

Of course, the future maybe tomorrow or next month, next year or 5 or more years from now. Am I talking about all these futures? Well, yes. But this book is really more about futures that are further away, maybe 3 or 5 or more years away. However, the principles in this book apply to any future and in all cases you need to:

- Have an objective – where you want to go or be
- Make a plan – how to go there from where you are now
- Set priorities – first things first to build on initial success
- Involve all people that need to be part of your plan and future
- Have the resources to do what you want – time, money, knowledge
- Periodically check if you are doing what you need to do
- Periodically check if you are coming closer to where you want to be
- Keep on doing this till you are where you want to be

In business, if you want to reach objectives and have to involve (many) people, it may take more time. If you want to be a doctor or a lawyer or travel around the world, that may also take a lot of time. However, in business or private life, on your own or with others, the approach is basically still the same.

Even if you have a short time objective - such as having a vacation with family or friends three months from now - the above process still applies. You will have to agree with you family or friends that they too want to do this and you will have to agree on where you all will spend that vacation.

In other parts of life

While I am writing this book mainly for application in (industrial) organizations, the principles and tools provided will serve equally well in private life. The message is simply this: if you want to be or go somewhere, if you want to make your future better or different: make a plan. Basically it is that simple. You need to do what is in your plan and keep doing that and adapt whenever necessary until you are where you want to be. After that: keep working to stay there or go to the next future.

Peter Drucker said this: "What you have to do and the way you have to do it is incredibly simple. Whether you are willing to do it, that's another matter." Think about all those New-Year plans and you understand what he means.

I will try to relate the business concepts to private life where communication normally is limited to a few people only. I will do this where I think it is appropriate and you will find my attempts in text boxes like this. I hope it helps to make the bridge between business life and private life.

Improvement is the theme throughout this book. Improvement, change, is part of the future building on the past, taking action today. Improving is THE way to survive and probably the ONLY way.

The principle of future characteristics

The past performance of an organization or unit tends to foreshadow its future characteristics

---

Louis A. Allen, management consultant and writer. Founder of Louis Allen Worldwide.

The above principle simply means that if you don't do anything, your future will be the same as the past or today. It may even be worse, because if you don't do something, other people will and the environment in which you live will never be the same. Unless you start today, your tomorrow will most likely be the same as yesterday. If you want the future to be YOUR future: "The best way to predict the future is to create it", also from Mr. Drucker. Your future starts today or whenever you make the decision to begin your journey.

Doing "something" will not be enough. You need to do the "right things" and you must do them the "right way". If you want positive change you have to undertake specific activities in a specific way.

> If you really want (to do) something, you will find a way.
>
> If you don't, you will find an excuse.

E.J. Rohn (1930 –2009) was an American entrepreneur, author and motivational speaker

If you really want to be where you want to be, go for it but it may need all of you, more than 100%. If you want to have a successful business 3 or 5 years from now, it may just take 24/7 and all of your energy and attention. When I started on my own as a safety management consultant in 1985, my working days started at seven in the morning and went on to eleven or later at night. Seven days per week and 365 days per year. Hard to say how long that went on. After initial success I sold my firm in 1987. I bought it back again early 1989 as success was falling and employed two people and that took quite a bit of my time and attention. I think in 1990 I was able to be more relaxed. In 1991, after some successful years and with five consultants, I sold my firm again and for the last time. So, my own experience is like this: to become successful, give it all your time and attention and when success is there, you may be able to relax but do not become complacent as that will be the first step towards failure. Success needs attention too!

THE BASIC PRINCIPLES FOR SUCCESS ARE SIMPLE, BUT ….
YOU HAVE TO WORK TO GET IT

IF IT WOULD BE EASY TO HAVE SUCCESS, EVERYONE WOULD HAVE IT

If you don't really want to do what is necessary to make your future, this book may not be for you.

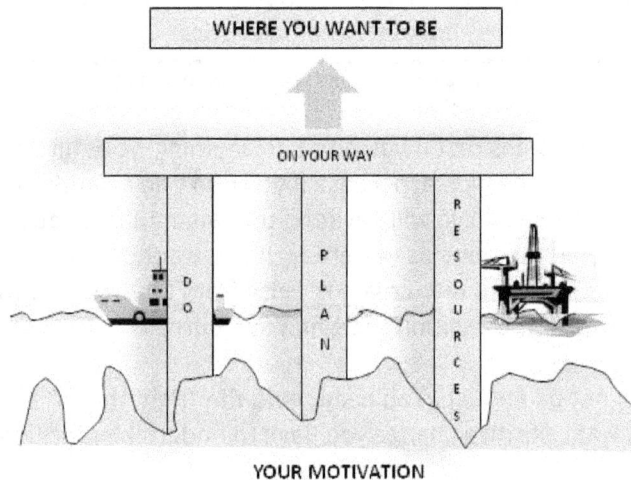

Picture 0.01 – The essentials to make your future

In other parts of life

What is important is that you first determine where you want to be in the future, next year, two years from now, or further away. If your final objective is far away, try to be realistic and have shorter term goals on your way to the end objective. Reaching short term goals may help you to remain motivated on your way to success. They also provide you with milestones, measuring points while you are en route.

Should you have monetary objectives?

You may, but I rather consider money as a measure of success, as the outcome of what you are doing. When I set up my consulting company in 1985, money was not really the objective although, of course, I needed the money to live. But other than that, I saw the income more as a measure of success of what I was doing. Money was the final indicator that I was doing the right things, that people were buying my services. But be careful, success can blind you and complacency may just be around the corner.

Already as a young boy, our son very much liked drawing. He also liked computer games. So before he finished secondary school, he decided that he wanted to make a living as an artist, a concept artist. That was his final, more distant, objective. His shorter term goal was to learn the necessary drawing skills and after visiting art school open days in Breda and Rotterdam during several years and after graduating from secondary school, he entered into the IGAD (International Game Architecture and Design) program at one of the higher educational institutes in The Netherlands. Shortly after the first year of the four year program, he found that this was not his cup of tea; he really wanted to do more art work, more drawing than the program offered and he left the study mid second year. He then went on to learn the craft of painting as it was done many years ago in a guild-like relation between master and apprentice. In 2013 and after 3 years of drawing and painting at the Atelier Stockholm in Sweden, he was ready to start his career to be a painter. Had he reached his final objective? Far from that. But he had obtained his shorter term objective: to gain the knowledge and skills necessary to start his career as a painter and make his living from making and selling his work.

So, with his those skills, he is ready to start the next phase of his plan to become a painter and make a living. His plan to reach his final objective, a plan that will be there for the rest of his life. That plan basically has two main routes: (i) work in commission, for example making portraits, and (ii) free work including still lives and sell that to whoever wants to buy it. These routes also represent two different target groups that at least partly need to be approached differently. However there is one common denominator: he has to make his existence and his work known to both groups of potential buyers.

To get group (i) clients he needs to make his presence known to those people who may have paintings made in commission, like portraits. This can, for example, be done though mailings to certain trade or income groups: notaries, lawyers, medical specialist, religious profession, nobility, architects, the military etc. Or just put flyers into mailboxes of the bigger houses in the area. One of the important things he did was to make free portraits of people with important networks with potential clients. That may create the snowball effect that he is looking for.

So there you have 3 ways to market approach: direct mail, house-to-house distribution and free portraits.

To get group (ii) customers he also needs to make his work known to potential buyers, art lovers. His own work including traditional painting such as: models, still lives and landscapes or, less traditional, the works that come out of his own imagination. Basically that includes two product "lines" he has to make known to the market through art galleries and participating in exhibitions and competitions such as the BP Portrait Award. And that gives three channels along which he is able to promote his work. So he needs to make paintings to offer a good selection to potential buyers, visit art galleries and talk to the gallery owners to interest them showing his paintings in their shops.

For both groups (i) and (ii) he made a website showing his works. He needs flyers or a brochure, mailings lists and other things. Brochure, flyers and mailing lists are all relevant to get people interested to visit his website to learn about him and his work.

Well, it is not my intention to go into much detail here but you can already see what would be included in his plan to make his future. It takes work to get there including work that has little to do with making paintings; necessary work, certainly at the beginning of his career. He needs to do what needs to be done and evaluate what he is doing and if that brings the results that he is looking for. And he needs to keep doing that and not give up! His success will be measured by the number of paintings that people buy and that translates into the amount of money he will generate from what he makes.

Why did I write the above? Maybe an attempt to show by example the vital aspects of making your future: the objective, the resources (skills/knowledge) and do what you must do and keep on doing while measuring progress towards your goals. These are all aspects of making your future.

One way to make your plan may be to do some mind-mapping; your objective at the center and everything that is needed to get there around it – all the way down to where you are now: your starting points. You can draw your mind-map on paper or use available software. Mind-mapping was presented in the 1974 BBC series "Use your head" by Tony Buzan. If you want to know more about mind-mapping, use the Internet. For a simple mind-map example see picture 2.16 on page 133.

Making your plan is one thing, doing what you put in it is something else. Normally success does not come easy – it takes a good plan, time, persistence, stamina, endurance, determination, patience .... don't give up easily - failing is the easy way out and you will never be where you want to be.

INTRODUCTION

I first published this book in 2013 with the title: "How to Build a Management System that Works – Guide to Management Success". I picked that title because of my background having worked in the area of (safety and risk) management consulting as well as in certification. In those areas it is not uncommon to talk about a "management system" as the vehicle, the plan, to reach certain objectives. I wrote this book mainly with industrial organizations in mind; that is where my experience was for over 40 years.

A year later, after writing my second book "Risk Management, Safety and Control of Loss – Protecting your Organization – an Introduction", I decided I had to make some text changes to the "How to Build" book. When doing that I also had a second look at the title and came to the conclusion that this would not excite many people. So, after some thinking, I figured that the essence of my book is to go from A to B, from present to future, from where you are now to where you really want to be. After all, a management system is no more than a plan to reach objectives. To reach objectives is not only a business matter but is relevant in all aspects of life.

So that is where the new title came from: "Making Your Future – In Business and in Other Parts of Your Life". The main focus is on business, on organizations where you would have to work with other people. But in private life you also have to work with others to make the future that you want together with your family, your friends, your neighbors. The principles and ideas in this book apply to business, to your private life and to you as a single human being. If you understand the approach as far it concerns your company or organization, you should also be able to work it out in private life. As Peter Drucker put it: "What you have to do and the way you have to do it is incredibly simple. Whether you are willing to do it, that's another matter." Doing it may not be so easy but remember: the principles are simple.

Following Mr. Drucker I added: "If it becomes complex or complicated, go back to the basics." If you do not get results, ask yourselves: What are the essential things to do and have these be done properly?; Has my plan been made involving the people that need to be involved to get results?; Does my plan contain the proper activities and have the necessary resources been made available – time, knowledge, money? Leadership? Motivation?

I like to believe that the even the start of complex processes should contain no more than 3 to 5 essential aspects. People should agree on those first; if they do not, they will probably never agree on the detail later on. I use that principle in this book and the three essentials are: plan – train – do. When you add leadership, you will have four essentials and when adding the objective you have 5 prerequisites; all included in the 17-step improvement process that you will find in this book. Once you agree on the essentials, you can move on to find out that it will become more complex or complicated further down the road. If you have too many essentials at the start, people – including you – may lose focus and motivation.

Leadership

By far the most important ingredient when making your future is the desire, motivation and will to move from where you are to a better tomorrow. That ingredient is very much related to people, to individuals that see the need to shape a better future. For themselves, their family, their organizations.

Within organizations – companies, any type of organization – that will to change starts with the woman or man at the top and from there that leadership should go all the way down to the level where the real action takes place.

Anush Kostanyan - Leadership Professional, Huffington Post Blogger and Writer – recently wrote:

"10 Principles of Effective and Authentic Leadership"

There is a great amount of definitions and theories about effective leadership. Each leader chooses their unique formula of success, but still there are keys to authentic leadership that can't be ignored. Below are 10 important principles each leader should know.

1.   *Leadership Is Behavior, Not Position*

Leaders are the ones who take responsibility for making decisions and bringing change. Leaders are the ones who empower people to discover and use their greatest potential. The executive position on someone's visit card won't do all of these. People are the ones to choose their leader. And how will they do that? They will judge by behavior, attitude and actions. If you want to be a leader, then act like a leader and shape a better reality.

2.   *The Best Way of Influence Is Setting an Example*

Each leader wants to get the best out of their team. Excellence orientation is great, as there is always need for development. But here is the simple truth. Instead of telling your team members what to do, show it to them by your own example. They are following you each and every moment. Practice what you preach, and the results will astonish you. Especially during hard times, when chances to give up are very big, you should be the one who faces obstacles with confidence and determination towards success. Be sure, that they will do the same and stand by your side.

3.   *Leading Means Making an Impact*

Think about the greatest leaders in history. What was the one thing they had in common? Yes, they all made an impact. Leadership is not just setting goals and effectively achieving them with your team. Leadership is not just brilliant public speaking and great communication skills. If you want to be an authentic leader, you should have your unique contribution to the welfare of the society. You should make a positive change.

4. *Leadership is Chasing Vision, Not Money*

Without a vision, your activities are meaningless. Each person can be very busy implementing various tasks, but the key is devoting your efforts and time to the realization of your vision. Vision is what inspires people to take action and go forward. Discover your unique vision and coordinate all your activities towards it. Inspire each and every member of your team with that vision.

5. *Actions Speak Louder Than Words*

It's not a secret that much talking and less acting has nothing to do with effectiveness. What people see affects them many times greater than what they hear. So, choose actions. Don't waste your and other people's time on endless conversations about your plans. Just realize those plans and be sure that everyone will see it.

6. *Flexibility May Refer to Behavior, Not Values*

Depending on circumstances you may choose a different style of leadership or communication. Flexibility is a truly effective trait, if it doesn't affect your values. Each and every decision of yours, no matter the situation, must be based on your value system. As long as your actions are value-driven, you will have the trust and respect of people around you.

7. *Leadership is All About People*

Could you be a leader in an empty room by having profound goals and skills? Of course, not. Leading means communicating, influencing and engaging. Communication skills are the foundation of effective leadership. Constantly improve your relationships with people, and the amazing results won't make you wait.

8. *It Is Fine To Admit Mistakes*

If everything has always been done perfectly, we would have somehow lost the ability to analyze and improve. Mistakes are proof that you are doing something. You won't become a worse leader if you admit your mistakes. By doing that, you will show that you are wise enough to learn from your experience.

9.   *Unity Is Strength*

Team is somehow the most important resource for each leader. Embrace your team and devote your energy to care about its unity each and every day. As long as your team is splendid, nothing can stay on your way to success. Make sure that all people in your team consider themselves as members of a strong, unified family.

10.   *There Is Always Room for Growth*

Remember, satisfaction should be a short-term feeling. Life would become useless without ongoing improvement. This doesn't mean that you shouldn't appreciate what you have. This means that you should be thankful for everything you have achieved, but still try to do a little more for this world.

Other leadership related articles by Anush Kostanyan - Leadership Professional, Huffington Post Blogger and Writer- can be found at www.huffingtonpost.com/anush-kostanyan. Another of her articles that you may find interesting is "15 Effective Ways to Motivate Your Team".

The 10 principles mentioned above reflect the more positive personal behavioural issues of a leader.

Interesting also is the video "What is the biggest mistake a leader can make", insights from "Imagining the future of leadership", a Harvard Business School Symposium. Below you find the keywords I took from the brief presentations provided by 9 different participants:

1. Self interest first
2. Arrogance, hubris
3. Betraying trust
4. Knowing it all
5. Not living up to values
6. No self doubt
7. Not stepping back
8. All about me
9. No self reflection

Note that there is one issue that is mentioned more frequently: lack of self doubt (numbers 2, 4, 6, 7, and 9), the arrogance, I know it all. Actually all points mentioned above indicate a "self-centred" attitude, putting oneself in the first place. That cannot be - a leader leads people and has to take their interest and concerns at heart. A leader that does not do that is not a leader; he or she may be the boss, but not a leader. You cannot be leader when putting your own interest first. Interesting in this respect also is the January 2014 article that I refer to on page 28 which was based on an interview of Mr. Manfred Kets de Vries of INSEAD.

Making your future is making your life, yours and that of others. Privately as well as in business. To be successful, you not only need the will to do what is required to make your future, you also need a plan involving those others. This book is about making that plan .... and then some.

LEADERSHIP ≈ PLAN ≈ MANAGEMENT SYSTEM

Making your future includes: (i) knowing what to do to reach your objective, and (ii) taking care of those events that are in the way of getting there; positive actions and controlling – eliminating and reducing - those things that will keep you from where you want to be.

YOUR PLAN

Reaching Objectives
and
Controlling Unwanted Events

Your plan needs both!

To go where you want to be you need: (i) to know where you want to go, (ii) what to do to get there, (iii) the knowledge and resources to do what is needed, (iv) do what needs to be done, (v) change what you are doing when needed and (vi) keep on doing until results are there.

The main issue in my book is making the plan – or management system – that will get you from present to future. That subject will be discussed in chapter II. Chapters I and III are providing information that I found relevant and are supporting the main subject.

A Management System is a PLAN:

"This is where we want to be and the way we will get there"

Making this plan to reach objectives, includes:

(i) process, (ii) content and (iii) structure

I tried to be as generic as possible. However, my background is related to safety management, safety management systems, -training and -audits. So you will recognize that in the text. I used to work with the International Safety Rating System (ISRS) and predecessors between 1974 and 1991. The ISRS was and is a (safety) management audit tool and can also be used as a reference for building a (safety) management system.

Management Success ≈ Management System Success

The basic ingredients for management system success are few and the principles involved can be applied to all sorts of management systems, irrespective their objectives.

While this book contains the basics to make a management system work and to move an organization from A to B and beyond, I am certainly not saying that changing an organization is an easy job. It could be relatively easy to set up a "management system" but to make it work may be a different matter because that will involve people and sometimes many. Those people may be the main barrier to success. But, people also are the main source of success and the process described in this book may help you to get their involvement, cooperation and support.

Anyway, it may help to keep in mind to go back to the basics when in a difficult situation. Those basics include only a few items as I try to convey through this book. I will provide you with these basics for success that can only come from "doing the right things, the right way" and keep on doing them. Obviously when on your way to success, you may need to adapt what you are doing as circumstances always change; if not by you then by someone else.

Doing the right things means to carry out activities, contained in "(management) activity areas", to obtain and maintain success. To secure ongoing success, these activities cannot be done just today or this week or this year; they may have to be done "forever". And they have to be evaluated and improved based on results, as long as the organization exists. Combined, the activity areas form the management system or plan.

This book

This book has the following chapters:

    I.   Management and Management Success (pages 40 – 96)
    II.   Making the Management System, the Plan (pages 97 – 188)
    III.   Improving the Management System (pages 189 – 212)

Chapter I should be seen as an introduction to chapters II and III. Chapter I includes information concerning the subject of management, risk management, the management system and the cause - consequence sequence relating the management system to (unwanted) events that may be barriers to reaching the system's objective(s).

Chapter III is about improving and maintaining the management system once it is being implemented. Main items offered for this purpose are: (i) the audit and (ii) learning from unwanted events through investigation and cause analysis.

Subjects in chapters I and III are not discussed in too much detail but sufficiently to understand their purpose.

The essence of this book is contained in chapter II, including the basics to make a management system work:

1. The <u>process</u> to make a management system or plan that will bring results
2. The <u>contents</u> of that management system
3. The <u>structure</u> that, in principle, has to be present in each activity area or element that is part of the management system

Of these three items, the first one is most important; the other two items are actually part of the process. These items are part of the basics that I present in this book and which come from my experience and ideas during more than 45 years in the area of safety and risk management.

I have repeated text at several places in this book where I found that it might help for proper understanding without having to go back in the book to look for the background information.

Will the ideas in this book work for you? Well, you will be the judge. If they work, they work because you understand what I am saying, you adapt and improve the ideas and use them as your own so they will work for you. And if you find that others disagree with you, challenge them to come up with a better approach. But try to stick to the basics and do not get lost in the complexity that others may present to shoot down the process that will benefit all.

Basically simple

Once you have decided that you want to go somewhere or be somewhere, you probably want to know where you are but you certainly have to know where you want to go or be and what you have to do to get there. And when you are on your way, you want to establish from time to time if you are doing the right things and if you are progressing towards your goal. And you may have to adjust what you are doing on your way to success. Basically this is simple, is it not?

Whether you have only one activity (area) or many, they all should have a structure to allow success. A structure that will help you and your colleagues to do what must be done, why, when, where, by whom and how and to periodically assess if those activities are done as they should and bring the results expected. Simple is it not?

The combination of management activity areas to reach the objective is what I would call a "management system" which may include many activity areas or "elements" or only a few; each containing activities embedded in the element structure.

While the management system has its activity areas to reach the "overall" objective, each element of the system has its own specific activities and its own specific objective.

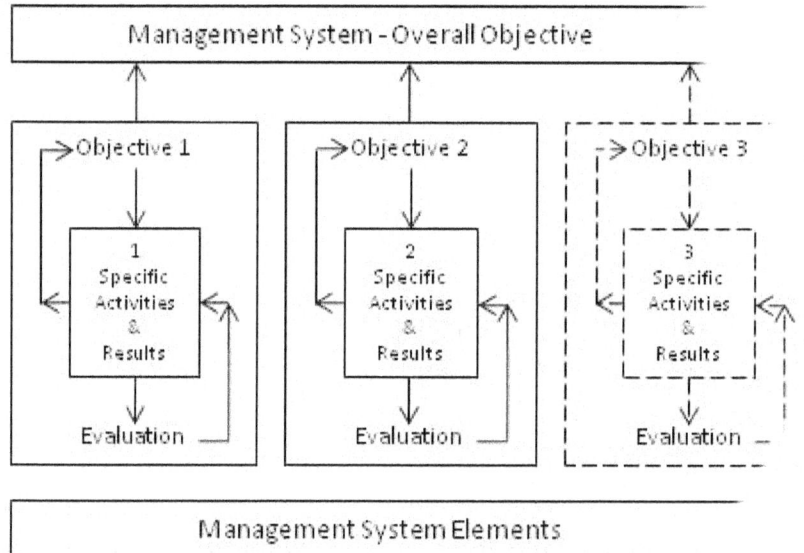

Picture 0.02 - Management system and elements – activities, results and objectives

In practice: more complex

I said "simple", but in an organization it may be more complex as you have to deal with people and that may make execution of your plan a bit more complicated, sometimes more than just a bit. Because those people often have other thoughts, other objectives and other priorities. They may bring in all kinds of arguments why things cannot be done, or cannot be done THAT way. They may have a vested interest in what is already there and what you want to change.

The Principle Emotional Ownership (2)

The more ownership people have in the way a present situation has developed, the more difficult it is to change

---

There may be limited resources to do things, external restrictions etcetera. Many things that may divert you from the objective: to make your management system work, to get results from your plan!

It does not matter what you want to improve:

- Safety & Health?
- Quality?
- Environment?
- Cost Control?
- Sustainable Profits?
- Stakeholder Relations?
- Something else?

Whatever you want to make better, you need to undertake well identified activities that will bring you towards your objectives and you need to structure those in a certain way to make sure that those activities are properly carried out and evaluated. You need to follow a certain process to make it work - it does not really matter whether you are on your own or someone in an organization; the process is basically the same! But in an organization it takes more attention, more communication, more time etc. And you need to take that into account; improvement may not happen overnight or easy. In an organization there may also be more chances for failure as you may have to work with many people. But those people may also be your guarantee for success, provided you use the process to get their involvement, support and commitment.

Following the 17-step process may help you to get the involvement and cooperation of people, reducing the resistance to change and facilitating the execution of your plan. Of course following this process should be done open and honest; no hidden agenda's!

The principle of resistance to change

The greater the departure of any planned change from the accepted ways of the past, the greater the potential resistance by the people involved

---

Whatever you do, take a step back once in a while; painters do that when creating their art and I know that from my son who is on his way to become the famous painter we hope he one day will be. Doubt is the beginning of wisdom, necessary for improvement and to stay away from complacency. Keep asking questions: What have I done and how? Can I do it better?

Don't stand so close to the trees!

You may not see the forest anymore

In any case, knowing the basics will help you to see the forest where others may be too close and only see trees. Whether you are working as a consultant (internal or external to the organization), it does not make a difference: in a complex situation, go back to the basics! Go back to the three items that will guide you, your company or your client towards success: (i) process, (ii) content, and (iii) structure.

> **In a complex situation?**
>
> **Go back to the basics!**
>
> And get the results that you are looking for!

If the objective is important enough to you and the other people then together you will do what needs to be done. If it is only something "nice to have", think twice before you start or make "nice to have" part of something that is really important. If only "nice to have" you may be tempted to give up easily and that may make the next change more difficult or even impossible.

> **Success**
>
> Success is neither magical nor mysterious. Success is the natural consequence of consistently applying the basic fundamentals.

E.J. Rohn (1930 –2009) was an American entrepreneur, author and motivational speaker

Some of the models, methods and ideas in this book are well-known in business areas such as safety, quality, environment, risk management. Some of the models and ideas are my own and may be somewhat different from those that are considered common knowledge.

TERMINOLOGY USED

In this section I describe the meaning of some of the terms that I use in this book. If you have other descriptions of the terms used, please use those; the important thing for me is that you understand what I am talking about.

MANAGEMENT

There are various definitions of "management". I do not wish to get very scientific about this. You may have heard this: "management is to obtain results through and with others". But you need to add something to this. These results have to be obtained within certain restrictions: without unnecessary losses and with the least possible efforts and use of resources. "Unnecessary" and "least possible" depend on circumstances, culture, personal believes, etc.

Louis A. Allen gave some body to "management" by listing the following main functions:

- Planning
- Organizing
- Leading
- Controlling

While these functions are actually inseparable, the "controlling" function is of particular importance within the context of this book and includes:

- Establishing performance standards
- Comparing actual performance against standards
- Taking corrective action when necessary

I think it was Frank E. Bird, Jr. who extended the above three issues giving us the acronym ISMEC:

- Identification of areas of management activities or "elements" to be part of your plan; the content of the "standing plan" or "management system"
- Standards or criteria for element activities: what, when, whom, how
- Measuring performance
- Evaluating or assessing performance against standards set
- Correcting in case of deviations, commending if none

When looking at "performance", consider input and output. This also comes back in the structure that I recommend for management system elements. So add two things to the above:

- When setting standards, also set <u>objectives</u> to be obtained by the whole management system as well as those of the contributing elements
- When evaluating, also look at <u>results</u> versus objectives set

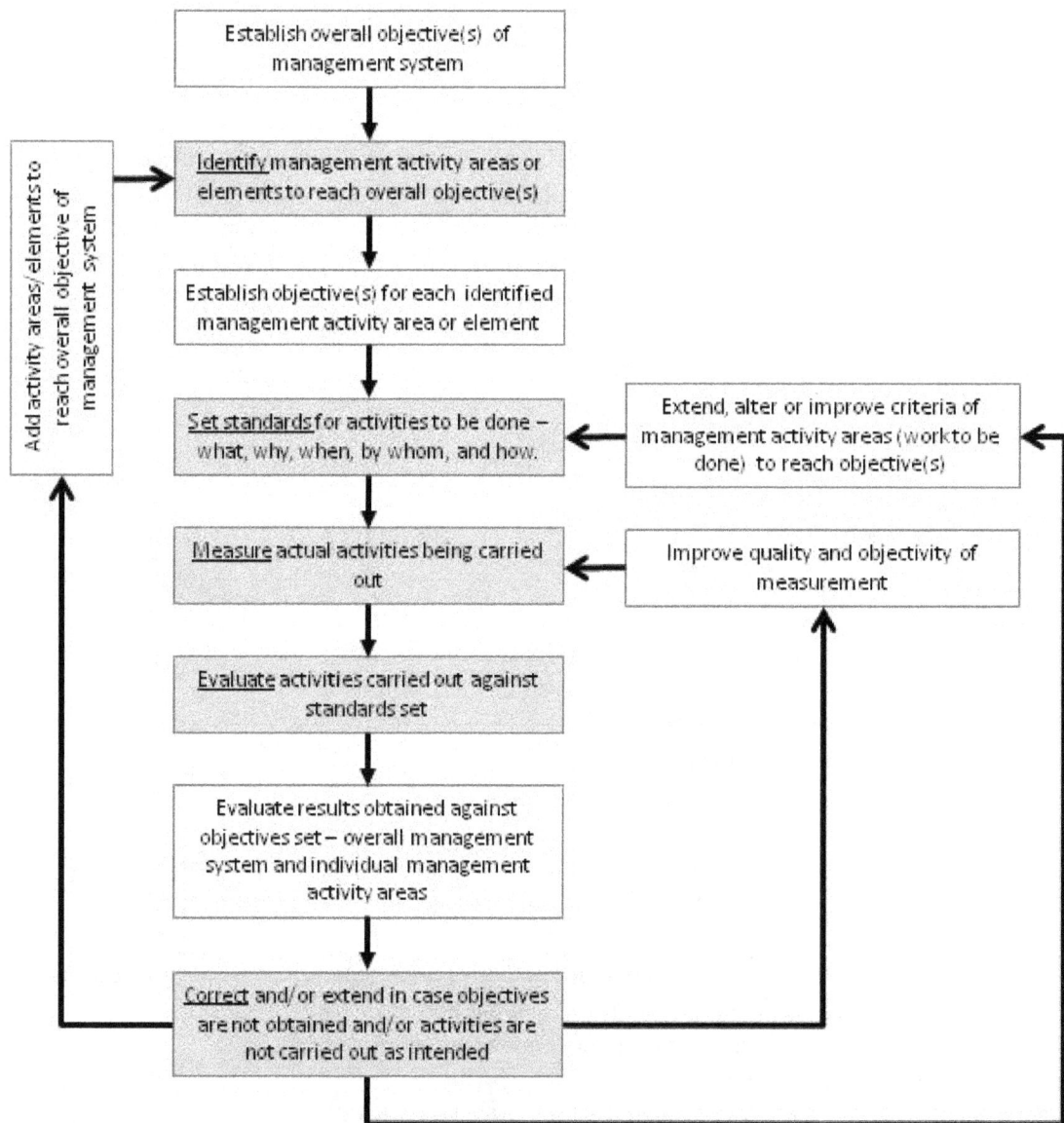

Establish overall objective(s) of management system

Identify management activity areas or elements to reach overall objective(s)

Establish objective(s) for each identified management activity area or element

Set standards for activities to be done – what, why, when, by whom, and how.

Extend, alter or improve criteria of management activity areas (work to be done) to reach objective(s)

Measure actual activities being carried out

Improve quality and objectivity of measurement

Evaluate activities carried out against standards set

Evaluate results obtained against objectives set – overall management system and individual management activity areas

Correct and/or extend in case objectives are not obtained and/or activities are not carried out as intended

Add activity areas/elements to reach overall objective of management system

Picture 0.03 – The management loop including ISMEC

As desired, please search the Internet for other descriptions of management and its functions; I am sure you will find plenty.

"Management" and "managers" are not synonymous. The <u>function</u> of management, as described above can, and should, be carried out by many in an organization, including operational personnel and is part of each job; from top to bottom.

One of the main aspects of the management function is to control loss

To know problems in advance

To control unwanted events and their consequences

To close the gap between "practice" and "theory"

Between "how it is (done)" and "how it should be (done)"

Please note that I refer to the management <u>function</u> that exists at all levels in the organization. It is not a prerogative of those we call "managers"; it is also part of operational work. Top-down AND Bottom-up is the key for (management) success. The degree of freedom in decision-making varies and is normally more limited at the operational level, at the "point of control". Downsizing – taking out management levels between top and bottom of the organization – requires a well-built management system to allow the necessary degree of "people empowerment". To enable "management" at the point where the action takes place, the "point of control".

The principle of point of control

The greatest potential for control tends to exist at the point where the action takes place

---

Louis A. Allen, management consultant and writer. Founder of Louis Allen Worldwide.

MANAGER

A Manager is a person responsible for planning, coaching and directing the work of others, monitoring their work, taking corrective action when necessary and commending for a job well done as the case may be.

A manager per se is not an entrepreneur, not a leader, not a risk taker. A manager is first of all an administrator. It is the manager's job to "keep the show on the road". Entrepreneurs are, first and foremost, ideas people, people who take (commercial) risks while leading others towards success. If a manager is a risk taker, he or she may be the source of an accident or other unwanted event waiting to happen.

> **Peter Drucker**
>
> Management is doing things right; leadership is doing the right things.

Peter Drucker (1909 – 2005) – management consultant, educator and author

Depending on his or her role in an organization, these two different and sometimes conflicting roles – management and leadership - may have to be combined in one person. There is a risk: if that person is primarily an entrepreneur dealing with the external world, he or she may forget to pay sufficient attention to the "world within", to the "control" of what takes place in the organization and how.

Two "types" of leadership – external and internal – are required to assure that commercial success will not be diluted by unwanted events and their consequences (losses) and that internal success will not be wasted by accepting unnecessary external risks. Risk management should consider both aspects and the same problem solving approach applies to both.

Allow me a brief sidestep following the article "Leaders are often self-destructive" that was published in Elsevier magazine on January 4, 2014 providing an interesting view on leaders and leadership. The article was based on an interview with Mr. Manfred Kets de Vries, Professor of Leadership Development at INSEAD, one of the world's leading graduate business schools.

From the article (free translation):

Mr. Kets de Vries has given courses on leadership for top managers including intensive group sessions based on socio-psychoanalysis. He dissects his students psychologically, and then confronts them with shortcomings, pitfalls and challenges. Being a certified psychoanalyst he cannot reveal who have been on the couch, but: "The count is well over a thousand. Many former students are top CEO's and ministers. "

His impression? "They - the leaders - are above average often neurotic, and especially narcissistic. They often surround themselves with the wrong people and are very susceptible to group thinking. Besides, they are often driven by greed and they have no contact with the reality."

Mr. Kets de Vries continues: "I regularly come across leaders who are self-destructive. After seven years in the same place they get bored. Then they can do weird things that do not serve the interests of the company. They want, for example, all kinds of takeovers, while all the statistics show that the majority of them failed. Or they keep themselves occupied with external affairs, such as their image. Not that that's necessarily unimportant, but there must also be someone running the business."

"After about seven years a leader has to go. This applies to many organizations, perhaps only except family businesses. It is really dangerous if someone is proclaimed for example Businessman of the Year. That is often a sign that he is too busy with other things than the core of his business and often this is the beginning of hubris." (hubris = arrogance, haughtiness).

"Of course there are many good, inspiring leaders", he says."Leaders like that almost always have the four H's: hope, humility, humanity and humor. They are able to give people hope of improvement, and to this end turn to humility, humanity and humor. They allow themselves to be less influenced by greed."

I like to add one word that goes very well together with the four H's that Mr. Kets de Vries mentions and that is "care". Leaders should care about the stakeholders of the organization that they are leading and in the first place, they should care about the people that make the organization but can also break it if neglected.

The principle below often applies to managers and supervisors as many of them are selected based on their technical qualifications and experience.

The Principle of Technical Priority

When called upon to perform both management work and technical work during the same time period, managers tend to give priority to technical work

---

Their functioning as a manager may be helped quite a bit when management systems are set up with their cooperation and consent to provide the margins in which they are expected to function. The management system will indicate what they need to do, why, when and how to reach objectives and limit, often unnecessary, losses. The management system includes how to do the right things right.

The management FUNCTION,

is not a just prerogative of those people we usually call "managers".

The function of management is present at all levels in the organization and within all functions and disciplines.

The degree of freedom to make decisions varies. The degree of freedom to decide parallels the responsibilities for the functioning of the organization and for the well-being of its stakeholders.

Leadership and management

Without even trying to be scientific or complete, some more words about leadership and management and about leaders and managers. I think there often is a misunderstanding about the two "areas". We may tend to refer to managers as leaders and we may refer to people at the top of organizations as leaders. In both instances we may be right but we also may be wrong.

Leadership and management are both activities. Leadership and management are both required to be successful.

Leaders and managers are roles or positions. Managers are not necessarily leaders and "leaders" are not necessarily managers or leaders. Top people of an organization are not necessarily LEADERS either.

Leadership provides objectives and direction to make companies and organizations successful. Leadership is related to doing the right things to reach those objectives. Leadership is freedom to decide which, at the same time, carries the responsibility that goes with it. Leadership is synonymous to involving people in making and carrying out a plan that will produce desired results. For that you need a process that starts at the top of the organization and goes all the way down creating two-way communication channels and using the knowledge and expertise that is available at all levels.

Leaders are people that provide leadership. No leadership, no leaders, no objectives, no plan, no future. Everyone can be a leader in his or her own environment – in business and in other parts of life.

Management is doing the right things the right way; to produce results that lead to objectives set. Management is also controlling unwanted events that are in the way of reaching those objectives. The management function exists at all levels in the organization; people manage their affairs within the margins provided by the plan or management system that follows the leadership at the top.

Managers are people in positions to work with others to reach the objectives. In one way or another, everyone is a manager in his or her own environment, life and within the limitations that we all have; even without a clear plan towards the future. Only some of us are called "managers"; others just do what they need to do to "manage".

Freedom to decide varies and will normally be more limited at the operational level and more extended at higher levels in the organization. This is why management almost always needs to contain some leadership aspects and managers need to have at least some leadership qualifications. If not for anything else, because there is always some room for decisions-making. At operational levels the freedom to decide will be further reduced even to the extent that it may be limited to just following rules and procedures as may be the case in high hazardous operations.

We may all be leaders in one aspect of life and followers in another aspect; followers at work and leaders at home.

Leadership and management are hand-in-glove; one cannot really exist without the other. But in practice that may be slightly not so - leadership cannot exist without management but management can exists where there is no or very little leadership. In the latter case, one may wonder: where will management bring us when the leadership is not there?

Desired behavior and culture of people and organization will be molded from the top down following the process to involve all in making the future. That requires leadership and management; in business as well as in other parts of life.

MANAGEMENT ACTIVITY AREA

A management activity area is a part of a management system containing activities that belong together to reach the specific objective of the activity area contributing to the overall objective of the system. I also refer to activity areas as "elements" and I use both terms to mean the same. One management activity area or element would be "learning from what goes wrong" or you may just call it "accident investigation" if you would want to limit the activity to just the control of accidents. Other management activity areas would include: purchasing, design, training, hiring and placement of personnel, change management and inspections. Management system elements or "activity areas" make the content of the management system.

Management activity areas or elements should each have their own specific objective and specific activities. Element objectives should not be the same as the overall management system objective.

ELEMENT

I use the term "element" also to mean "management activity area" and vice versa.

Management system elements, management activity areas and standing plans are very similar. The only difference that I could see is that the words are different – but they mean the same, at least within the context of this book. If you would like to differentiate between those terms, just go ahead and use whatever suits your situation best.

MANAGEMENT ACTIVITIES

Management activities are part of a management activity area or element and indicate WHAT shall be done, WHY, by WHOM and WHEN. For example: while a management activity area would be "to learn from what goes wrong", management activities would include: reporting unwanted events, registration of those, cause analysis, remedial action development, action follow-up and designation of people to be involved.

The "HOW to carry out" activities is, in principle, part of the activity area. However, for practical reasons, I think it is better to only refer to them in the element. Description of how to carry out these activities can be extensive and subject to more frequent change and should better be in separate documents. For example, in the system element "learning from unwanted events" you may include a reference to the related protocol while the protocol itself will be a separate document. The same is true for design activities, purchasing, etcetera. That way you can keep the management system overview limited to a "what, why, when, where and by whom" manual with related "how to" details separated in other documents.

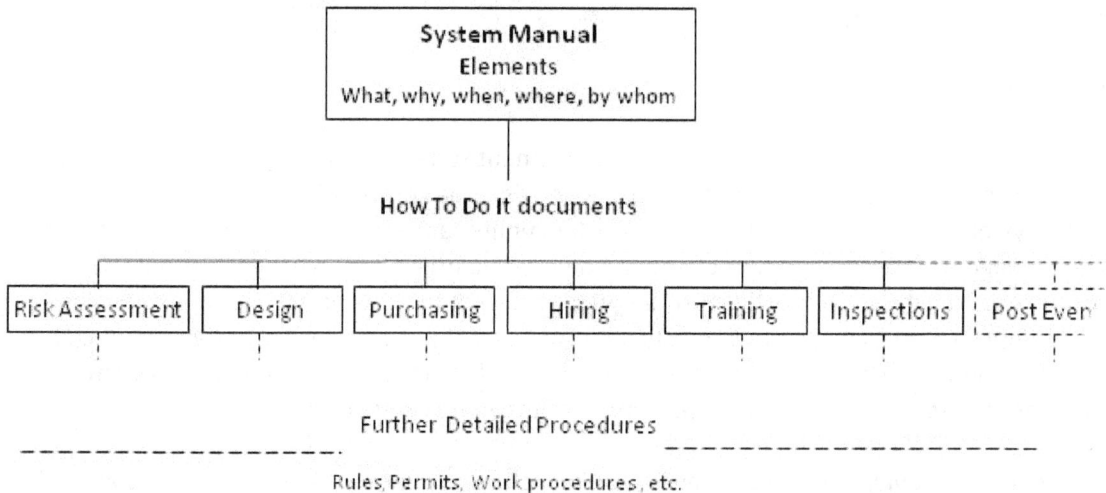

Picture 0.04 – Basic management system structure

CONTENT OF A MANAGEMENT SYSTEM

The content of a management system includes the activity areas or "elements" that together are necessary to reach the overall objective(s) of the system. The content will vary depending on the objective(s) but each management system is likely to have a number of similar activity areas. Activity areas or elements and their specific activities can be selected from external reference sources including legislation, industry standards, certification norms, etc.

In principle, a management system should have the following types of elements:

- As many elements as needed to reach the system objective(s) including specific activities to reach the (element) objective(s)
- One or more elements to detect deviations before they develop into unwanted events
- An element including activities to cope with emergency situations – what to do if things go wrong
- An element to learn from unwanted events – learning from what goes wrong

STRUCTURE OF MANAGEMENT SYSTEM ELEMENTS

This structure should be present in each of the elements of a management system and stimulate the implementation of element activities as well as the periodic assessment of their execution and results. The reason why I say that the structure should be in each of the elements is that each element is considered important to reach the overall objective of the management system. Therefore each element should contribute and should have its own specific objectives which should not be similar to the overall objective of the management system.

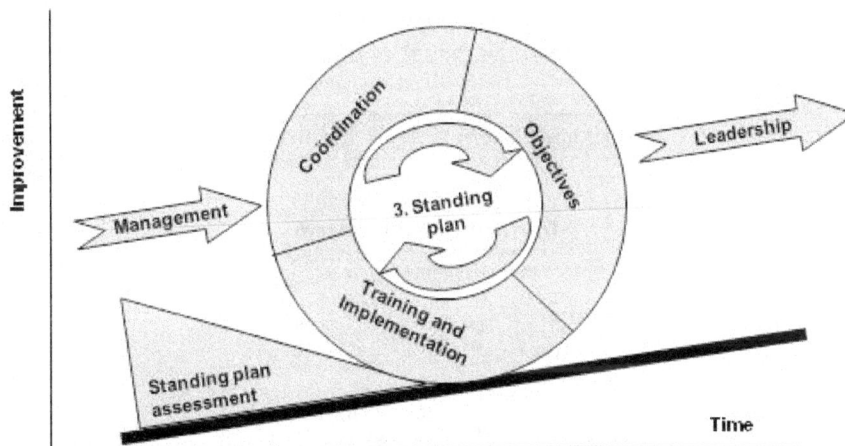

Picture 0.05 – The improvement "wheel" – plan, activities, structure and leadership

17-STEP PROCESS

The process that I developed during my consulting work to assist companies to improve their performance. When I was working as a safety consultant, I developed the process for the purpose of setting up an effective safety management system. However, the process that I describe in more detail in this book is generic and can be used to set up a management system for whatever purpose. As the name indicates, the process to build an effective management system includes 17 steps. If you feel that is too much, or not enough, just make alterations but be careful not to leave out steps that are important for reaching success.

Peter Drucker said: "Leadership is doing the right things, management is doing those right". The 17-step process combines leadership and management through all levels of the organization, from top management to operational levels and back. The plan or management system that is the essence of the 17-step process is the vehicle to do this and provides the up and down communication channels necessary to reach and maintain desired results.

OBJECTIVE

This is where you want to go or be; where your plan or management system will bring you. Could be anything that you want it to be. To get there, to reach your objective, you need a plan, the resources to carry it out, the motivation and the persistence and endurance to keep doing what you must do. And after that? Right, keep on doing what you are doing and do it better.

MANAGEMENT SYSTEM

A combination of management activity areas or "elements" containing activities directed at obtaining a more general (strategic) objective or set of objectives.

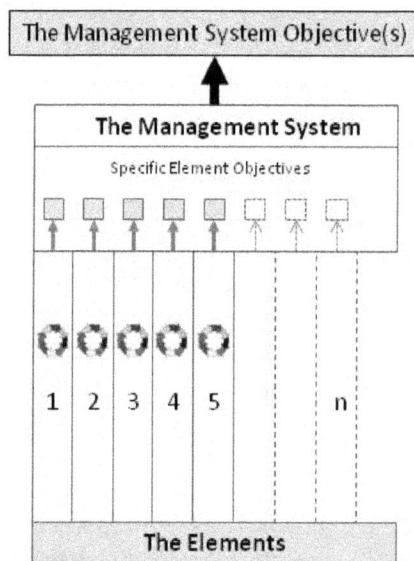

Picture 0.06 – Management system elements contributing to the overall objective

An organization could have more than one management system, each with their own objectives. There could be systems for the management of risk, quality, environment, safety and health, product safety, cost, or any combination of those and other business areas.

Although those different management systems address different objectives, they normally will share a number of management activity areas including, but not limited to: design, purchasing, hiring and placement of personnel, training/instruction, maintenance and inspection, change management, work procedures and rules, learning from what goes wrong, emergency preparedness.

A management system should also be directed at the elimination, reduction and control of unwanted events that are in the way of reaching the objective of the management system.

Through this combination of reaching objectives and controlling unwanted events the end result of management system application will be better organizational performance with fewer (unnecessary) losses, in short: a better organization.

I would consider a management system to be a MANAGEMENT SYSTEM if it meets at least the following criteria:

- There is a more or less clear objective to which the combined management activity areas or "elements" are directed – the overall system objective.
- There is enough content - a sufficient number of relevant elements to reach the overall management system objective.
- Each element contains a structure to stimulate implementation of the specific element activities to reach the specific element objectives.

Just a note of caution here. The term "management system" is often related to certification such as for ISO 9000, ISO 14000 and OHSAS 18000. You should realize that a certification management system is set up with the objective to obtain a certificate. The management system or plan that is the main subject of this book has the objective to make your future better. Getting better and getting a certificate may not be the same; as a matter of fact getting a certificate may give the impression of improvement while, in practice, it may be sending the wrong message. After the certificate has been obtained, people may just go back to business as usual and the improvement momentum that might have been there may be lost.

Standing Plan

This is an ongoing plan to arrive at a more general goal/objective, with ongoing allocation of resources and without a specified (limited) time period. A standing plan is used to reach more strategic objectives. A standing plan normally will be there for the duration of the undertaking and apply to the entire organization or a major part thereof.

If the name "program" or "work process" is better understood by people in your organization, then use that name instead of "standing plan".

Within the context of this book, I consider a "standing plan" similar to a "management system".

If you want, you may also consider the management system elements as standing plans that are part of the management system as both are plans and both are there for an extended period of time; probably for the duration of the company or organization. That way, a management system may have several or many standing (sub-) plans and in that case a standing plan is similar to a management activity area or element. Your choice, I do not like to be limited too much by definitions but if you are working in a company or with a client you may need to determine what is what. If not for anything else: it helps communication if you agree on terminology.

Single-use Plan

This is a onetime plan to address with a specified budget and to be executed within a pre-determined time period. Single-use plans or "projects" are used to cope with specific problems or reach specific objectives. These projects may lead to issues that should be considered for inclusion in one or more elements of the management system; to prevent re-occurrence of the same or similar problems in the future or to maintain performance at a desired level.

UNWANTED EVENT

An unwanted event is any event that is in the way of obtaining desired objectives and which could or does produce loss. In principle any type of loss, you can have your pick:

- Harm to people
- Property damage
- Unplanned production interruption
- Loss of customers
- Harm to the environment
- Product loss
- Quality loss
- Liability claims
- Loss of information
- Loss of key people
- Delivery problems
- Theft
- Etcetera

Now, you may say: "these are all different losses". But think about it - are they really? Not if you would consider where these losses are coming from: the basic or "root" causes. You will find that many of these different losses share the same origins: design of product or installations/work environment, purchasing of equipment or services, hiring of people, training, inspection of installations or work environment, identification of risk or potential problems, lack of learning from what goes wrong, rules or work permits, communication, etcetera. These "activity areas" are not only basic causes from which losses develop; they are also the basic causes of success.

Often, management systems are directed at a single objective and control of related type of (unwanted) events. Quality systems are to control product quality issues and customer complaints; environmental systems are there to control environmental emissions and incidents; safety systems are there to control injuries and other accidents. And so on. But they all address largely the same issues when considering the basic or root causes of (unwanted) events that are barriers to reaching desired goals. With little more effort those specific management systems, containing root cause related activity areas, may also be used to limit other loss producing events coming from the same causes. Thus becoming more valuable to the organization. And when you do so, would that not lead to integration of management systems?

One example: I have been involved in setting up a safety certification scheme in The Netherlands. Although the scheme exists since 1994 and now includes over 14.000 or so certificates, its focus is still primarily on injury related accidents causing days away from work. With a (minor) shift in focus, a system set up in a company to obtain the safety certificate could also address other type of losses thus becoming more valuable to the company.

Some people may call the loss producing event an "unplanned" event. Certainly most people or organizations do not plan to have mishaps, errors, accidents etc. But are they really "unplanned" if there are gaps in the management system allowing those events to take place and undermine the objective of the system? Or if people do not learn from what happened before or even do not have a proper system to do that? They may not plan for those events but certainly do not do the necessary to control them either.

Throughout this book, I really do not make much or any difference between an unwanted event and an accident, an incident, damage or loss. The reasoning behind this is that the outcome of the unwanted event often determines whether we talk about a near-miss or close call, an injury type accident, an environmental problem, a property loss or a quality issue. The outcome often depends on the circumstances that exist when the event occurs. In principle the unwanted event should be the focus and most of those events share the same or similar basic causes that root in the management system. So keep this in mind: when I mention "unwanted event", I also mean accident, incident etc. and, of course, an accident or an incident is also an "unwanted event".

HAZARD

A source of risk.

RISK

Risk = potential loss, any type of loss. Measured in terms of (i) frequency of occurrence (of the unwanted event leading to loss) and (ii) (potential) consequences or loss that can be expected to result from the unwanted event.

INCIDENT

Within the context of this book an incident is the same as the unwanted event: an event that could or does produce loss. If you see an incident as an event without visible loss - a "close call" - that is fine. Use a risk classification method to determine if such incidents need attention.

Near Miss

An unwanted event not resulting in (visible) loss.

ACCIDENT

An accident is the (visible) result, or loss, of an unwanted event. If to you an accident is limited to an injury with lost time, that is fine but you may be missing a lot of opportunities to learn from and become better in what you are doing. Again, a risk classification method may help you to determine how much attention the accident should receive.

LOSS

Anything that you would consider a loss: human suffering, monetary loss, loss of customers or market, company image, environmental damage, theft, etcetera.

RISK MANAGEMENT

The control of risk. In essence this is problem solving. Risk management consists basically of two areas: loss control and risk financing.

LOSS CONTROL MANAGEMENT

The control of loss, any loss and you may determine what that means in your organization. "Control" is the combination of (i) eliminating the risk, (ii) reducing the event frequency and, (iii) limiting the event consequences. Loss control = cost control.

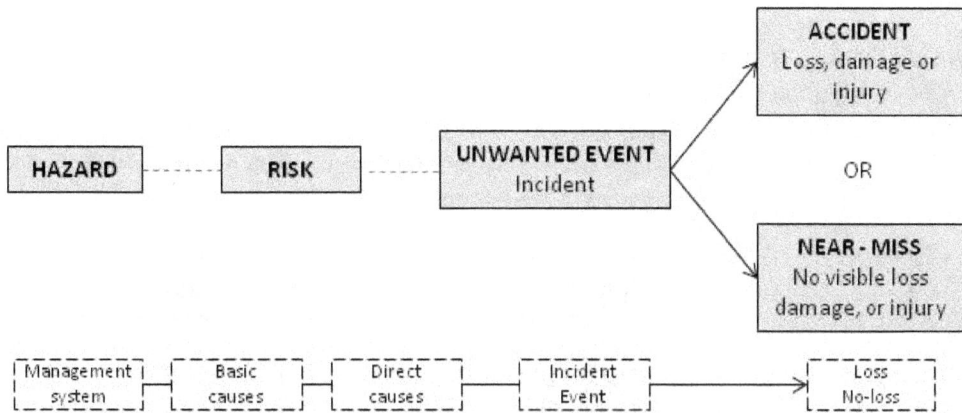

Picture 0.07 – The hazard – loss relationship

CHAPTER I   MANAGEMENT AND MANAGEMENT SUCCESS

"Making your future – in business" has everything to do with the management function: to make things work, reach objectives, targets, goals. For this, "management" activities need to be carried out and communicated to all concerned, within the organization and external as required or desired. Management activity areas or "elements" and their activities are part of a "management system", an ongoing plan, to reach objectives.

> ### Management System Success ≈ Organizational Success

As a management system will be there for the entire duration of an undertaking, project, company or organization, it probably should be put in writing for reference and communication purposes. It is only when a company is very small that it might not be necessary to put things in writing, either on paper or electronically. However, if that company wants to have a certificate, the system should probably have to be in writing to make it verifiable.

In other parts of life

In private life you would not normally talk about "management". However, the functions still will be there: to accomplish what you want with the help of others. Most effectively in terms of time, money and effort and without unnecessary interruption and loss. Would that make you a manager or a leader? Yes, I think so but you may not be called that way. Would sound a bit odd if your team consists of your family members. You also would not be talking about a "management system" but probably refer to it as your plan or our plan. Depending on the situation, your plan may not be there forever but will be there for a shorter period of time which may vary between a couple of weeks and several years. When only for a couple of weeks, your plan may even not be in writing but for plans that take (much) longer, I would advise to have it on paper or electronically so you can share it with others and refer to it when discussing progress and consider any changes that may be necessary.

The detail of a management system and related instructions and procedures will depend on aspects such as:

- The complexity of your organization and its processes
- The (internal and external) risks to which your organization is exposed
- The media sensitiveness of your organization
- The level of professionalism, training and experience of your personnel
- External requirements such as legislation or certification

Top-management leads the organization towards objectives through activities within activity areas, the elements of the "management" system. These elements are the channels through which management makes sure that the organization is going into the right direction. These channels are two-way communication channels, from the top down and from the bottom up.

THE MANAGEMENT GAP

One of the vital aspects of the management function is to control loss

To know problems in advance

To control unwanted events and their consequences

To close the gap between "practice" and "theory"

Between "what & how it is (done)" and "what & how it should be (done)"

There are plenty of books written about management and I used to have a few of those which I started to buy and read from the early seventies on. I did that because, as a chemical and industrial engineer by education, I had little idea about what "management" represented as that was not taught in college. However, I found out that there were quite a number of similarities between the process of management and what I had learned about chemical engineering, particular where it concerned process control. I kept buying these management books for a number of years but, after a while, only reading few chapters of new books to find out that it often was the same thing all over again; the main difference was in the cover and the title.

Finally, in 2004 and close to official retirement, I gave all my books away to two younger people in Belgium starting as independent consultants. I remember a number of those books and sometimes I may regret that I gave them away: "Professional Management" by Allen – which I recently bought again through the Internet - and "Beyond the Quick Fix" by Kilmann. The books written by quality guru Crosby such as "Quality is Free" and "Quality without Tears" were interesting and others were also funny such as "The One-minute Manager" by Blanchard and Johnson and The "59 Second Employee" by Andre & Ward, staying ahead of the one-minute manager. The Peter Principle ("rising to the level of incompetence"), Parkinson's law ("divide and rule"), "Managing for Results" by Drucker, "Managerial Breakthrough" by Juran, "The Practice of Management" also by Drucker, "The Human Side of the Enterprise" by McGregor and "Theory Z" by Ouchi, books written by Likert, Maslow, Argyris, Herzberg, Kepner & Tregoe, and others. And of course books on safety and risk management as I have been working in that area since 1968.

In case you wonder: is my memory so good that I remember those books? At age 74? To be honest: my computer has the memory and I use desktop search software to find what is on it. See appendix K on page 342 showing the English books I used to have.

> **Management is reaching objectives**
>
> Without unnecessary cost and loss
>
> You need a plan to do that
>
> A plan that is supported by all involved

Anyway, if you want to learn more about management and its functions, buy yourself some good books on the subject if you feel that is necessary. Don't forget that when you are dealing with management systems, you are also dealing with management and managers; knowing a bit of their world would not harm, would it? By the way, I like to think that this book is kind of a short course in management ….. and leadership. But of course, I am biased, am I not?

> **THE MANAGEMENT GAP**
>
> The gap between "what is" and "what should be"
>
> The gap in which problems and unwanted events happen:
> errors, mistakes, accidents, failures, losses, downgrading incidents,
> whatever you may want to call them.
>
> They eat away your profit!

Management: "to obtain results (through and) with others without unnecessary losses and with the least possible efforts and use of resources".

The role of management - in particular top-management - is to lead the organization into the desired direction and obtain desired results in each business area. They hardly can do this alone and need to lead and support the work of others in reaching objectives.

A management system is THE vehicle, along which leadership can flow down the organization, provided it:

- Is set up using a well defined process to include people from all organizational levels
- Has adequate content to reach the objective(s)
- Is structured to stimulate implementation and obtain results

Management System	Basic Causes	Direct Causes	Event Facts/Contact	Results Losses

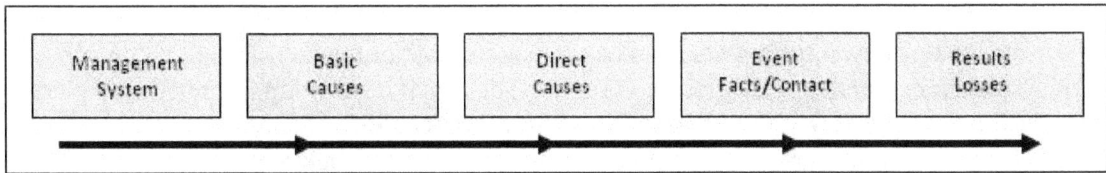

Picture 1.01 – The cause – consequence process

The above picture shows the relation between the management system and the (unwanted) event that may or may not produce loss. It is a simplified model originally coming from H.W. Heinrich and later adapted by Frank E. Bird, Jr., also a well-known safety leader introducing the management system as the source of events, either good or bad.

The model presented above can be considered in two ways:

- Negatively with unwanted events and losses at the end
- Positively with but positive results at the end

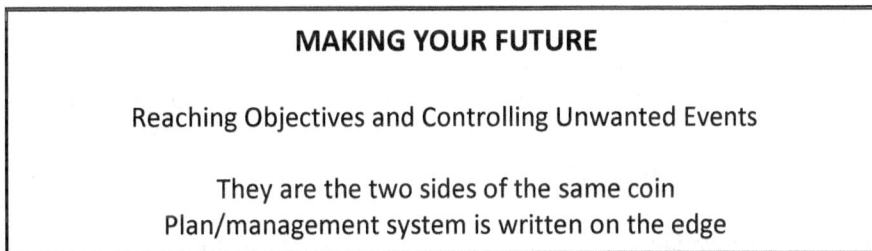

MAKING YOUR FUTURE

Reaching Objectives and Controlling Unwanted Events

They are the two sides of the same coin
Plan/management system is written on the edge

1.1   PHILOSOPHY - BASIS FOR MANAGEMENT SUCCESS

The philosophy behind "Making your future – in business" is relatively simple. In essence it comes down to doing the right things the right way.

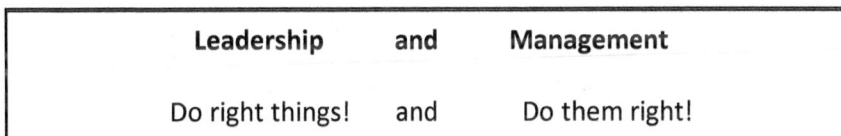

Leadership	**and**	**Management**
Do right things!	and	Do them right!

Leadership: doing right things to reach (strategic) objectives. Management: doing those things right while controlling unwanted events.

Controlling unwanted events and losses that keep you away from your success requires:

1. Preventing unwanted events from happening through problem/risk elimination and reduction; purchasing of goods and services; design of installation, product, workplace; hiring and placement of people; management of change
2. Early detection of deviations from accepted standards through audits, inspections, observations, incident recall and accident imaging and taking corrective actions as needed
3. Limiting (possible) consequences of unwanted events through emergency preparedness and a post event or post emergency plan (PEP)
4. Learning from those events to carry out remedial actions to eliminate or reduce future occurrence of same or similar events and their consequences

Basically this is simple: if you want to be somewhere, you need to do something. Or rather: you need to carry out well-defined activities in a well-defined manner by well-trained people. Results can only be obtained if you:

*   Know where you want to be or at least have some idea about it
*   Know more or less where you are
*   Establish objectives and a time path
*   Find out what needs to be done, why, when, where, by whom and how, to reach objectives
*   Provide the environment that stimulates cooperation of all involved to reach desired goals
*   Provide the knowledge, skills and resources to do what must be done
*   Make sure that what needs to be done is done properly and that results are being obtained
*   Do it better and over again if results are less than expected
*   Keep on doing and improve as appropriate even if results are what they should be: continuous improvement.
*   Be aware of complacency

> **If everything appears to go well ...**
>
> you've obviously overlooked something

You need these ingredients for success:

*   MOTIVATION and LEADERSHIP to move from where you are now to a better future
*   a PLAN or "management system" containing what needs to be done, why, by whom, when, where and how

- Resources including knowledgeable, TRAINED, people to assure they can do what needs to be done
- DO what is in the plan; including periodic assessments to assure that the plan is properly carried out and results are being obtained

These four ingredients are visualized in the platform model that I developed during the late eighties of last century – more about that later.

1.1.1 Combination of top-down AND bottom-up: management philosophy in action

Any major change or improvement in an organization is best done through a combination of top-down and bottom-up activity in which the appropriate people will play their specific roles. Bottom-up cooperation is obtained by top-down leadership. Such dual approach is in line with business excellence practices in approaches and models such as employee empowerment, TQM (Total Quality Management) and that of the EFQM (European Foundation of Quality Management). The combination of top-down and bottom-up forms the basis to get desired behavior and obtain a culture in which the right things are done the right way. A culture in which learning from past, present and future (accident imaging) will be a way of work and life.

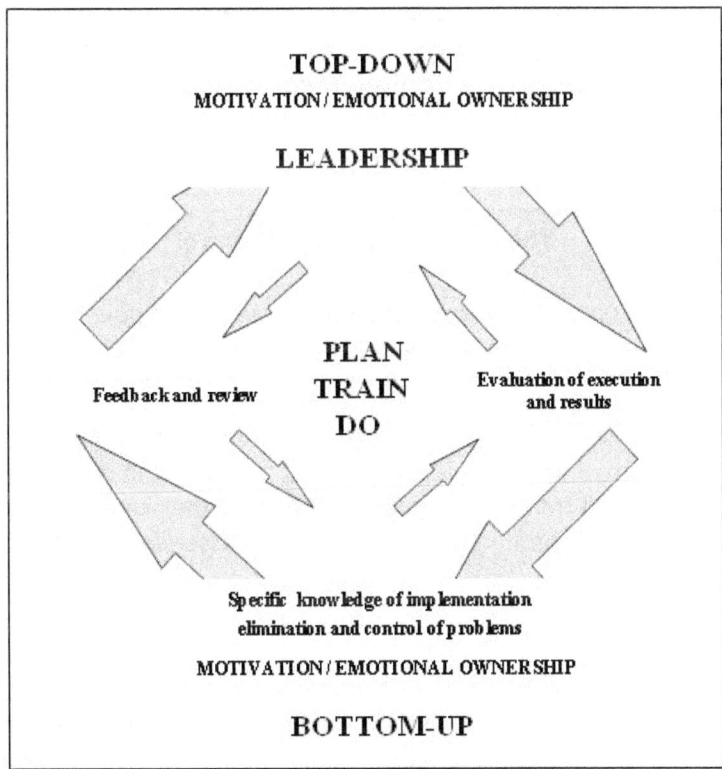

Picture 1.02 – Combination of top-down and bottom-up; basis for ongoing success

The simple "philosophy" is that, if you want to be somewhere, you will have to work at it. Often things that come by themselves are things you may not want such as unhappiness, illness, pain, sadness, poverty, accidents, and losses. If you do not want those, you have to work at it, even though it may be difficult and you may not be successful in the beginning. The same is true for bottom-up involvement; if it comes by itself you may not want it. But if you want to benefit from the knowledge, experience and cooperation that is available throughout the organization, you have to work at getting it; ask for it, let your actions show that you want it, walk the talk - you have to earn it!

The principle of participation

Motivation to accomplish results tends to increase as people are given opportunity to participate in matters affecting those results

---

If top-down "leadership" comes by itself, you should be aware: that may be a ticket to disaster. Successful top-down leadership needs to be motivated, desired, visible and ….. planned.

To remain successful reaching objectives and controlling unwanted events you need a plan, a "management system" containing all necessary activity areas and their activities. You need to set it up and maintain it such that it will be effectively used. By people who have control over activities and over unwanted events, their (direct) causes and their consequences. People at the point control.

The principle of point of control

The greatest potential for control tends to exist at the point where the action takes place

---

The "point of control" varies depending on the activity. If the activity is design then the point of control will be in the design office. If it relates to buying products and services, it probably will be the purchasing department. If training is concerned it may be the personnel unit or human resource office. And, yes, if it is production, construction or assembling that may be the production or service department.

To become and remain successful boils down to:

- Leadership from the top down to initiate and lead the top-down and bottom-up efforts
- A process – like the 17-step process discussed later on - to set up, execute, maintain and improve the management system with the involvement of all concerned
- A management system with the proper content and the right structure

The 17-step process builds upon a combination of top-down and bottom-up participation. In fact the process is a guide to get the involvement of people at all necessary levels in the organization when preparing, making, executing and improving the activities towards success.

Leadership

Does it come natural? Can it be learned? I do not want to spend much time on this but I like to believe that the answer to both questions is "yes". To some it comes natural but then, they still have to know what it means in an organization. It means more than charisma; you would have to do certain things in a certain way. Peter Drucker: "leadership is doing the right things". So either way the leader has to do identifiable things and as such leadership can also be learned. Leadership does not focus on the person but rather on what that person does to involve others on the way to success. Leadership can be practiced when you know what to do. When you combine the 10 leadership principles mentioned by Anush Kostanyan (page 16) with the 17-step process and the principles mention in this book, you should come a long way on the leadership path. Also learn what not to be or do as a leader – look at the 9 points on page 18, coming from a Harvard Business Publishing video, and the interview with Mr. Kets de Vries mentioned on page 28.

This book addresses the issues relevant to leadership in practice:

- Organizational aspects relevant to the operation of a management system
- The basic model on which the improvement process is based
- The description of the improvement process and the rating tool that I set up for it
- Examples of what could be the content of a management system
- The description of the structure that the management system elements should have to stimulate implementation and improvement
- Main means to maintain and improve the management system

1.2   CULTURE CHANGE

Culture - good or bad, you always have one

You always have a culture in your organization. You may not like it but you have one. It may just have grown over the years, all by itself, maybe simply because people were busy doing other things and ignored the small symptoms of changing behaviors and culture. If that happens the culture may not be the one that you want, underlining what I said before: what comes by itself may not be what you want.

Culture just may sneak in over a long period; it just grows slowly and nobody may even notice. It is like the boiling frog story metaphor pointing at the inability or unwillingness of people to react to changes that occur gradually.

I am not sure if the frogs will actually stay in the water when that is heated slowly. Fact is that, if you want the culture you want, you will have to work at it and be aware of small changes indicating that culture may be going the wrong way. Getting and keeping good results or a desired culture requires work and doing the right things the right way.

The principle of future characteristics

The past performance of an organization or unit tends to foreshadow
its future characteristics

Situations where a negative culture developed over a long period of time are difficult for the consultant to work with. Maybe even impossible, unless the management of the company is set to change and willing to go all the way, leading the change process. But what do you do if half of the managers do not show up for a meeting that was planned well in advance?

In my consulting work, I also had contacts with companies that had grown into a culture that was far from desirable. I remember two chemical companies that actually came to us - I was working for a consulting company then - because they had problems with the authorities; one because of environmental issues, the other because of the high accident frequency rate.

I do not know what happened to the company with the environmental problems (the one where the managers did not show up) but the one with the high accident rate does not exist anymore. It was broken up and partly sold. The remaining company that survived had to report fatal accidents in 2009 and was subject to losing its operating license because of environmental problems. In November 2012 the company was declared bankrupt. (This is the chemical company mentioned in chapter 2.8, point 2 on page 184.)

1.2.1   17-steps to positive culture change – a travel guide

The 17-step process that is described and detailed in this book is the pathway via which you may be able to work at the culture in your organization. The management system – which is the core of the 17-step process - may be then directed at "getting a better culture". That may be a bit vague and I would suggest selecting an objective that would be more identifiable. I consider culture as a result, a "byproduct", of what you do and it really does not matter too much which objective you select. A good one may be one close to people and their working environment. So safety and health - in a broad sense - may be a good choice and it would not be difficult to include quality and environment as these also relate to the work that people do, the products and equipment they work with and the environment in which they do their work.

The 17-step process includes the steps for culture change and should be a good tool in the hands of a knowledgeable consultant; it could be the basis for an agreement between the consultant and the client looking for change.

As the 17-step process invites people from all levels to participate in the development, execution and improvement of the management system, it is the pathway to culture change from the top down AND from the bottom up.

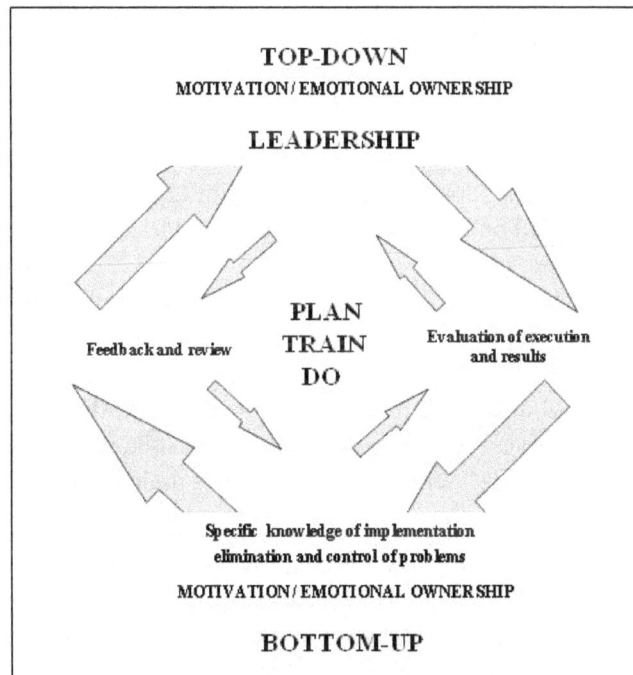

Picture 1.03 – Culture: the result of top-down and bottom-up cooperation

Not a psychologist

I am not a psychologist; I have been educated as a chemical and industrial engineer. However, when going through life, you are bound to pick up something about people, what they feel and think and do and why that is so. And, since we at least share some of this, take a look at yourselves and asked: what and why? And keep doing that – it may lead to understanding, improvement and wisdom. Reading some books about human behavior may also help.

Anyway, I think that behavior comes from attitude and that you can, within certain margins, influence the attitude of people by influencing their behavior. I also think that the combined behavior of people, "the way we work here", is synonymous with the culture of the organization.

Working as a safety management consultant, behavior has had my interest for a long time and in 2000 I came very close to setting myself up as a safe behavior consultant which, after some considerations, commercially and otherwise, I decided not to do.

The 17-step process provides plenty of opportunities to influence behavior and thus culture.

The Principle Emotional ownership (1)

People tend to be more willing to participate in planed change when they have (had) an opportunity to participate and influence the process leading to change

---

There are some items you may want to look at which I made for one reason or another; these are available on my website www.topves.nl. Select "Culture Change" under "Management Success" in the navigation menu on the left side of the screen to find the following:

Behavior measurement – a chapter that I wrote in 1996 for the book "Safety Performance Measurement", published by the European Process Safety Centre (EPSC).

Behavior program - the layout of a presentation that I once gave at the start of a safe behavior management process in a chemical company in Belgium. This followed an internal investigation made by that organization showing "behavior" as one of the main accident causes.

The principle of behavior reinforcement

Any behavior will sharply increase in probability if it is immediately followed by some event that satisfies a need.

How to make rules is a guide to make rules, procedures or work instructions with a high acceptance and compliance rate. Rules etc. relate to behavior and, if made well, may help to get desired behavior and thus influence culture - see also appendix D on page 238.

The principle of deviation from normal behavior

The more a rule or procedure deviates from normal behavior, the more effort is required to obtain compliance with the rule or procedure concerned.

Loss Control Maturity Profile - a helpful instrument which I used in management training. Purpose of this profile was to get opinions of those who were in a position to influence the safety culture in their organization. I put value factors on the columns ranging from 1, on the left "Uncertainty", to 5, on the right "Certainty". That gave me the opportunity to get an average (quantitative) indication of how a group of people felt about the subject. If you want, you can repeat this process at various managerial/supervisory, operational and other levels to see what the differences of opinion are.

Use of the maturity profile may help to start the discussion that is necessary to agree on the present situation and begin the process of change in which the 17-step process could show the way. The maturity profile (appendix B on page 224) was made by Frank E. Bird, Jr. based on the Quality Maturity Grid made by Philip Crosby.

The Principle Emotional Ownership (2)

The more ownership people have in the way a present situation has developed, the more difficult it is to change

Opinion Surveys - will also help to obtain a picture of how people think about an aspect of the organization. I used to carry out opinion surveys prior to doing safety management audits using the ISRS – the International Safety Rating System. These opinion surveys were directed at three organizational levels: (i) top- and middle management, (ii) supervision, and (iii) operational personnel. Opinion surveys are part of the 17-step process; they may help to loosen up the organization towards desired change. See an example of (i) - appendix C, page 228. At the time I was using these surveys there was no Internet, so surveys were done using paper questionnaires. Nowadays, these surveys can be done online, using programs such as CheckMarket or Survey Monkey and making execution a lot easier and more accessible.

Culture Element of a safety management audit system. I used to work with an internationally known safety audit system between 1975 and 1991. The document provided through my website was a personal attempt to include some culture related issues in the audit system as I felt that those concerns should have their place when carrying out an audit.

Culture is often related to behavior and I know that there are these BBS (Behavior Based Safety) programs to correct undesired behavior in companies. While I can agree with at least some of the basics, I am not in favor of observation programs that often focus on the behavior of people on the shop floor.

Attention to behavior often starts after it is noticed that behavior is less than what it should be and the undesired behavior is seen as the problem that needs to be attacked. But think again: where does the shop floor behavior come from? Did it just get there by itself? Is shop floor behavior not a reflection of the upstream – management – behavior and the end-product of a process that has been allowed to take place over time? If so, would it then be wise to focus on the end of the process? Or should you rather look at the source to correct the undesired behavior that comes out at the end? I am pretty sure that we would agree to work at the source and then see if the behavior at the end will improve. The advantage, when we do this right, is that we will change the behavior from top to bottom rather than just changing the behavior at the sharp end of the organization.

Am I saying that you should not look at the undesired shop floor behavior? No, I don't. But if you focus on that, you may be focusing on the wrong thing. It should be sufficient to notice that the behavior is not what you want and then start working on what is causing it. And when you are doing that of course you need to see if the outcome is what you want: desired behavior.

I think identifying undesired behavior should be part of direct supervision's routine: to see how people do things, notice deviations from "the right way", find out the possible causes, and take action which may involve higher management to take care of root cause related issues. If you have to include all levels of the organization to correct behavior problems at the shop floor level that may indicate that the problem actually developed over a longer period of time. It also may indicate that your "system" is not working that well, maybe because it was not set up properly.

The better approach should be to set up, execute, maintain and improve a plan or "management system" from the start of an organization. With the cooperation of those who have to do the work. As part of that process, people will agree on how the work needs to be done without unwanted events and leading to desired behavior and culture. Why wait setting up a management system that will help you to get that behavior and culture?

Anyway, work at improving what you are putting into your (management) system and involve people at all levels when doing so. It will take effort and time depending how far your culture went off-track. But if you do it right you will get not only desired behavior but also the culture that comes along with it. If that does not happen that you may not be doing the right things the right way, so try again and do better!

The 17-step process discussed later on is the pathway to get what you want; starting at the top and involving all organizational levels to reach mutual results and benefits:

- Desired behavior
- Desired culture
- Reaching company objectives
- Controlling undesired, downgrading, events
- Optimizing (sustainable) profit

Peter Drucker

The best way to predict the future is to create it

Peter Drucker (1909 – 2005) – management consultant, educator and author

By the way, why attention to <u>safety</u> related behavior and not in a more general sense? Why sub-optimize? Could we not just refer to desired and undesired behavior instead of focusing on a sub-aspect? Why separate safety behavior from quality behavior or behavior in other areas? Behavior has to do with what people do and how, irrespective of specific issues. And solutions to behavioral issues are basically the same anyway.

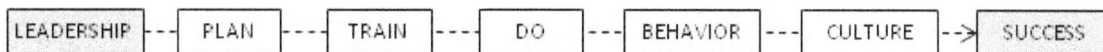

LEADERSHIP	PLAN	TRAIN	DO	BEHAVIOR	CULTURE	SUCCESS

Picture 1.04 – From leadership to success

1.3   THE MANAGEMENT SYSTEM

A management system is a set of (management) activity areas or "elements" that combined have the purpose of reaching a certain (overall) objective. Or: a management system is a plan – or a set of (sub) plans – to go where you want to be. That could be in the area of safety, quality or environment, any combination of those or other business areas.

The management system or plan is at the extreme left of the cause – consequence process shown in picture 1.01 on page 43. It is the product of leadership and a tool of management.

A management system could be set up to improve, to get a certain certificate - such as ISO 9000 or OHSAS 18000 – or to comply with legislation. A management system should include the control of unwanted events that undermine the objective of the system.

> A management system involves: (i) moving towards objectives while, (ii) controlling unwanted events that may keep you from reaching those.
>
> You have to do both and at the same time.

Reaching a desired objective and controlling unwanted events are actually two sides of the same coin as reaching a certain objective would include the elimination and/or reduction of events that undermine obtaining the objective. A management system includes both aspects.

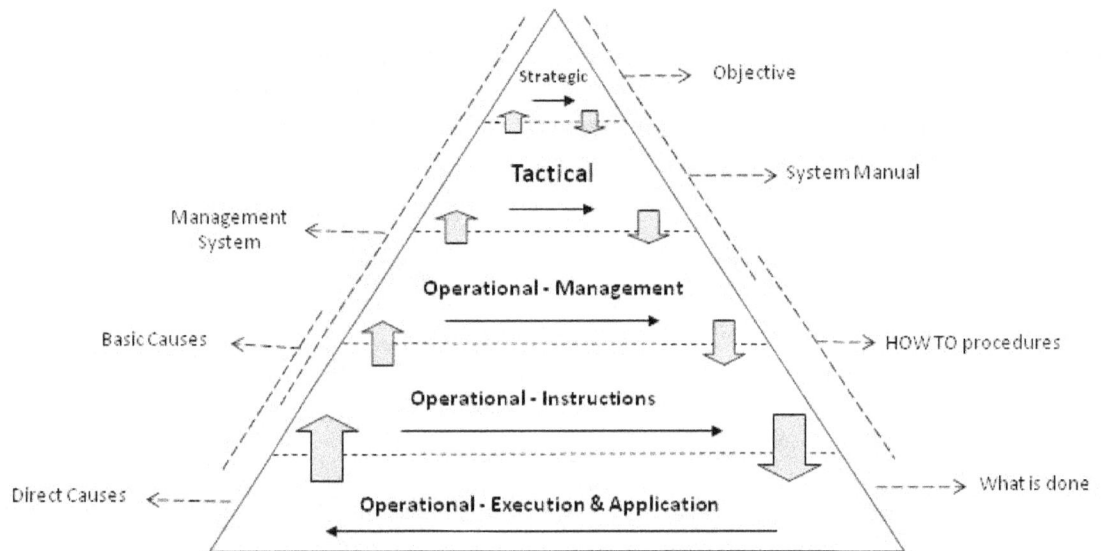

Picture 1.05 – The multi-layer management system from strategy to operations

The above picture shows a simplified diagram indicating several levels of management- and operational activity going from the top of the organization down to the operational levels and from the operational levels back up to the top. Dotted lines between the levels indicate no clear separation; those levels overlap and extend into one another.

To me, the management system starts on the strategic level at the very top of the organization and extends downward into the operational instructions level. The core of the management system – how I see it - is the system manual incorporating the strategic and tactical levels. Below that come how to do the work procedures, both managerial as well as operational. These "how to" procedures are the guidelines and instructions regarding how the work should be done and include the basic causes shown in the model on picture 1.01 page 43. The lowest levels also include the level where the action takes place; the "point of control" where the work actually is done. That is also the level of the direct causes, the errors, mishaps and unwanted events which may or may not result in loss.

Put this way, the system manual is the top document – the leadership document - giving direction to everything that comes below. If done well, the manual will remain rather static while the documents at lower levels will be adapted based on work practice including changing conditions both within the organization and externally.

Note the communication between the various levels indicated by the arrows going from the top down on one side and going up from the operational level on the other side.

The management system manual contains the activity areas or "elements", each of those with the specific activities to reach the specific element objective. Together these element objectives accumulate into the overall objective of the management system at the very top of the triangle, the "strategic" level.

The elements contain the "WHAT shall be done, WHY, by WHOM, WHEN and WHERE ". HOW the activities are to be carried out comes on the level of Operational Management; this is not included in this book. The "Operational Instructions", the work- or task procedures and instructions, are not part of this book either.

Preferably, management system elements should contain references to separate documents explaining the detail of HOW element activities should be carried out. That way execution details can be changed based on experience without the need to alter the basis of the management system contained in the manual at the tactical/strategic level.

The Management System - source of all good and bad?

I described a management system as: "A combination of management activity areas or elements directed at obtaining a broad or more general objective."

Once set up and running, a major effort of a management system will be directed at the control of unwanted events that undermine the system. By doing so, the result will be better organizational performance with fewer (unnecessary) losses, in short: a better organization.

> **Management System Success ≈ Management Success**

The management system includes:

- Management activity areas or "elements" - main building blocks of the system necessary to obtain the overall system objective(s)
- Management activities - specific activities, contained in individual elements, to reach the specific element objective(s)

Behind this is that reaching system objectives depends on meeting element objectives. And those will be obtained through execution of the activiteis contained in the elements. Basis for the success of the management system are the element activities and for this reason these activities should be embedded in a (generic) structure representing the "improvement loop".

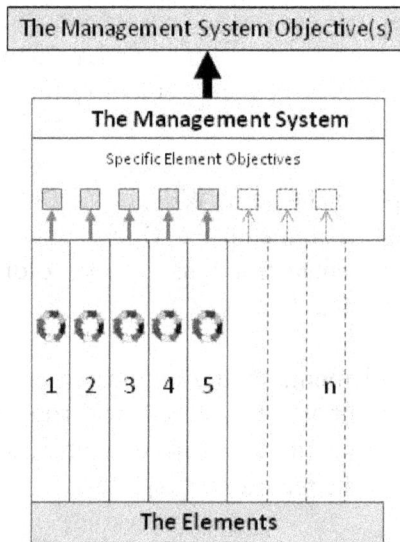

Picture 1.06 – System elements, the basis for overall system success

I introduced the concept of elements having their own specific objectives and generic structure in 1993 when I was heading a small international team to develop a process industry version of an internationally well-known safety audit reference. The original reference had about twenty elements each with their own specific activities but without specific element objectives. It also did not have the generic element "improvement loop" stimulating activities to be carried out. For various, non-essential, reasons the process industry version with its generic element structure was not accepted by the company that I was working for at that time.

Having separate objectives for each element has distinct advantages over having only one objective for the whole management system:

1. It will have a much greater influence on the whole organization. Instead of one (overall) objective, you will have as many of 10 or 20 or more – one for each element in the system.
2. If you have only one objective for the entire management system and not able to get to that objective, it may be hard to determine why not. With 10 or 20 "sub-objectives" you will be in a much better position to find out why you are not getting the overall system results that you are looking for.

Because elements and their objectives are so important, they all need to have the structure to stimulate execution of activities and periodic assessment of those and their results compared to element objectives. If you feel that an element does not need this structure then maybe you should consider removing the element from the system. No structure needed = not important.

The Management System - source of all good and all bad!

The importance of the management system in controlling unwanted events is visualized in picture 1.07. This picture represents the incident causation or event sequence that comes from the work and thinking of Heinrich and Bird; I have added some of my own thoughts.

While the model highlights control of unwanted events, it also stands for the process to reach objectives. Remember: reaching objectives and controlling unwanted events go hand in hand; they are two sides of the same coin.

The basic idea behind the model is that the management system, containing the management activity areas or "elements", creates the basic causes leading to the direct causes (acts and conditions) that result in accidents, incidents or other type of unwanted events. Those may or may not result in initial loss, depending on circumstances and barriers that may or may not be present. The final loss then depends on the effectiveness of the emergency remedial actions taken. PEP stands for Post Event or Post Emergency Plan including actions to reduce various (material or immaterial, direct or indirect) losses that may result from the incident or unwanted event, including business interruption or consequential losses.

I trust that you realize that practice does not necessarily follow the sequence given in the model. The model is only an attempt to put a real life situation into boxes; in practice the boxes overlap and extend into one another.

People related issues are vital to the total sequence. That is why they are mentioned along the entire sequence. These issues are either permanent or temporary. They may be deficient (or "sub-standard") or they may be proper (or "standard"). If they are permanently deficient they lead to imperfect organizational and production systems, imperfect technical systems and sub-standard behavior of managers, supervision, staff and operational employees. Deficiencies are "built-in" and the only thing one needs to do is to wait and see that risks materialize into losses.

If the people issues are temporarily deficient, they should be seen as deviations from an otherwise "standard" way of doing things. If these deviations are not spotted early enough or if no action is taken following their recognition, losses may occur. No action taken may turn temporary deficiencies into permanent deficiencies, into "basic causes" in technical or procedural controls.

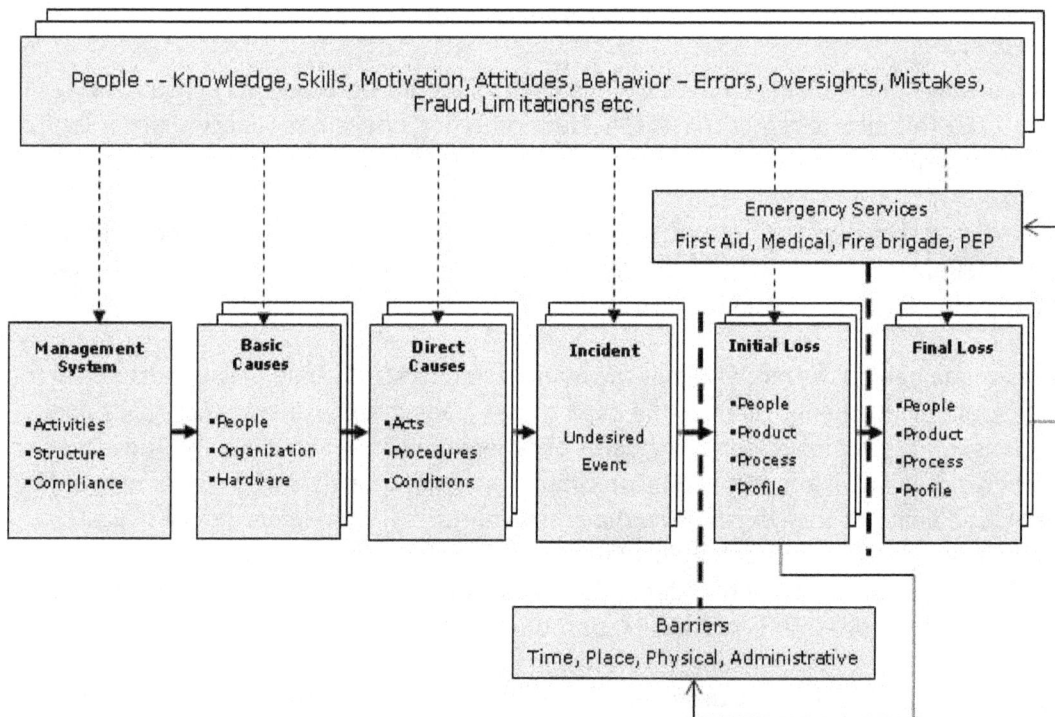

Picture 1.07 - modification of the Bird model – Total Operation Performance

Cause-consequence models may give the impression that only one person may be involved in causing the unwanted event: the person committing the substandard act preceding the event. In practice, however, a number of people, including those further "upstream" (to the left in the sequence), may have played their role in creating the environment and circumstances allowing the incident to occur. For example, it may be the act of the person, directly involved in the execution of the work that triggered the event resulting in loss. However, that person may not have been trained properly (= act of supervision/management) to do the work or it may have been the purchaser who did not buy the right equipment (= act of staff person) or the designer who did not design the work environment properly (= act of staff person). Or it may have been the top manager (= act of manager) who did not make sure that the purchaser was buying the right stuff or the designer was following state of the art design criteria including ergonomics.

The principle of shared responsibility

Accidents and other unwanted events are almost always the result of work done by many people at different levels in the organization and at different times. They all share responsibility for the consequences.

I provided multiple layers throughout the sequence (with the exception of the management system box) to indicate that there is often more than one issue involved and almost always more than one person. This shared responsibility can also be concluded from the "management system triangle" (picture 1.05 on page 54 showing the interrelationship between the top of the triangle and the lower levels; from top managers to the "point of control" people.

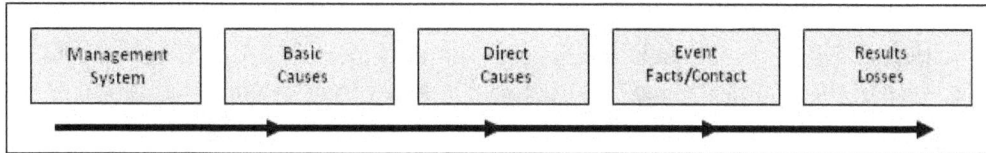

Management System	Basic Causes	Direct Causes	Event Facts/Contact	Results Losses

The above, more simplified, 2-D version of the model can be read in negative way in the sense that all, or some, "phases" are below standard to produce loss at the end. Alternatively, the model can also be put in a positive mode to produce success in the end box. To arrive at that desired situation, all phases in the model must be positive to create an organization that knows its risk and has taken suitable actions to control them. On top of that, the organization will have installed appropriate instruments to uncover deviations from the "standard" (= right) situation in order to take actions before those deviations can result in undesired events and loss. In that case, the term "Abnormal Situation Management (ASM)" may apply.

The Management System: "Source of all good and all bad?" You can answer that for yourselves but I think the answer, in principle, must be affirmative. But is it the management SYSTEM? Ask yourselves: "Who initiates the management system?" and "How is or was it set up and improved to include all in the organization?"

Read the cause-consequence model from left to right and you have the sequence to control potential problem on your way to success. If you read the model from right to left you have the process to learn from what went wrong while on your way to success.

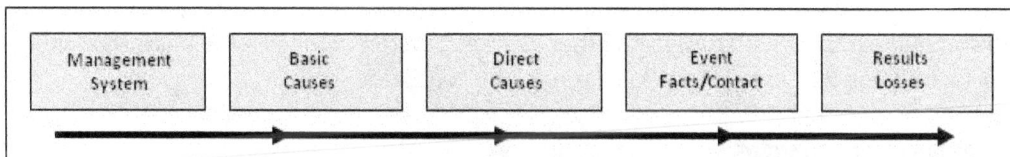

Management System	Basic Causes	Direct Causes	Event Facts/Contact	Results Losses

Picture 1.08A - Pro-active problem solving: from cause to consequence:

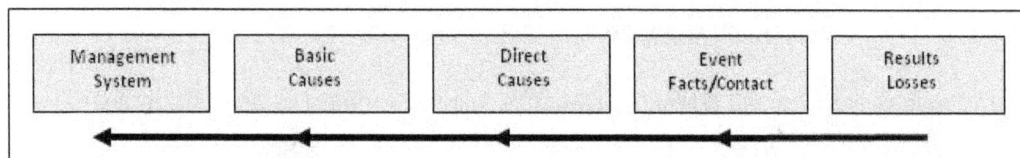

Management System	Basic Causes	Direct Causes	Event Facts/Contact	Results Losses

Picture 1.08B - Re-active problem solving: from consequence to cause:

The management system is important and what really makes it a system of management or "management tool" includes these two things:

- The "content" - the management activities areas or "elements" included in the system
- The "structure" in which the element activities are embedded to make sure that work is done and results obtained

To be effective, activities contained in the system elements must be properly carried out. To assist this, each of these areas should be structured in a way to drive implementation as well as improvement of activities vital to obtaining the element objectives. This (generic) structure includes:

- Management statement – why the element is required and what the objective is
- Element coordination – responsibilities assigned to assure proper functioning of element
- Identification of element activities – what needs to be done, when, by whom, how
- Periodic assessment of activities – to verify that activities are carried out as intended
- Periodic evaluation of results obtained compared to element objectives set
- Periodic review and improvement of element activities

Oh, yes, also important - and maybe most important - is the process along which the management system is made. So that all levels in the organization will be involved to make implementation of the system or plan easier and successful.

The Principle Emotional ownership (1)

People tend to be more willing to participate in planned change when they have an opportunity to participate and influence the process leading to change

---

I raised some questions in relation to the management system and gave my answers – go to appendix A on page 220 to see if we may agree.

1.4   PROBLEM SOLVING

Problem solving is an essential part of the management function and should be one of the top priorities of every manager and supervisor, in fact of everyone in the organization.

Problem solving goes into two ways: (i) pro-active, looking forward to prevent undesired events and consequences and, (ii) re-active, looking backward from the unwanted event and its consequences to learn from what has gone wrong, all the way upstream to the management system.

Problem solving is the basis for all business areas, whether that concerns internal matters such as safety, risk management, cost control, quality, environment or external issues such as product safety, environment, market and marketing, etc. THE basic questions are: what can go wrong in what we are doing? What did go wrong? And, of course, what can we learn from it?

How can you become a top quality organization? By controlling the unwanted events that form barriers to reaching your desired level of performance – in any area; by solving problems, pro-active and re-active. Preferably pro-active, pre-event, so measures can be taken at the earliest stages, before events materialize in loss.

**The quality of a management team
is determined by:**

1. Knowing in advance what problems may occur in their organization or unit
2. The number and size of problems that may occur
3. Knowing what the causes of those problems could be
4. Knowing what to do to remedy the causes at the earliest stages
5. Knowing what actions to take to minimize negative consequences

A quality management team should only have known problems with limited consequences

---

Philip B. Crosby (1926 – 2001) - US quality consultant, business philosopher and author

1.4.1   The problem solving sequence

Problem solving includes the following steps:

1. Identification of the (potential) problem: What is the problem? What can be the problem? What is wrong? What can go wrong? What has gone wrong?
2. Evaluation of the problem: How large is it? How large could it be?
3. Cause analyses of the problem: What are the reasons why this problem exists or can occur?
4. Establishing alternatives for dealing with the problem: What can be done to eliminate the problem and its consequences? If that is not possible, reduce it? What can be done to prevent the problem from happening again?
5. Selection of best alternatives: Which action or combination of actions will provide the desired results with the least effort and use of resources (time, money, etc.)?
6. Execution of selected actions
7. Assessment to see that the selected actions are carried out and corrected if not done

properly
8. Evaluation of results and correction of actions (more or different) if desired results are not being obtained
9. Continuous investigation and analysis of deviations, losses, damages, accidents, etcetera that nevertheless may occur leading to possible further correction of actions

The picture below schematically illustrates the problem solving sequence.

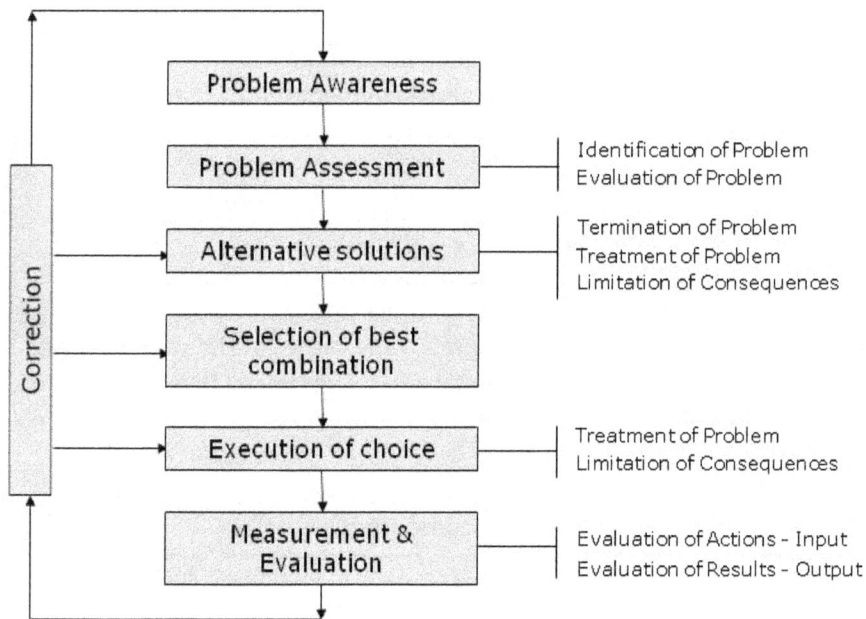

Picture 1.09 – Problem solving sequence

1.5   RISK MANAGEMENT

Managing risks follows the same sequence as solving problems; present and future, actual and potential. In particular, risk management is looking ahead at what can happen tomorrow, next year or further into the future. The process is the same, only the word has changed and "problem" has become "risk".

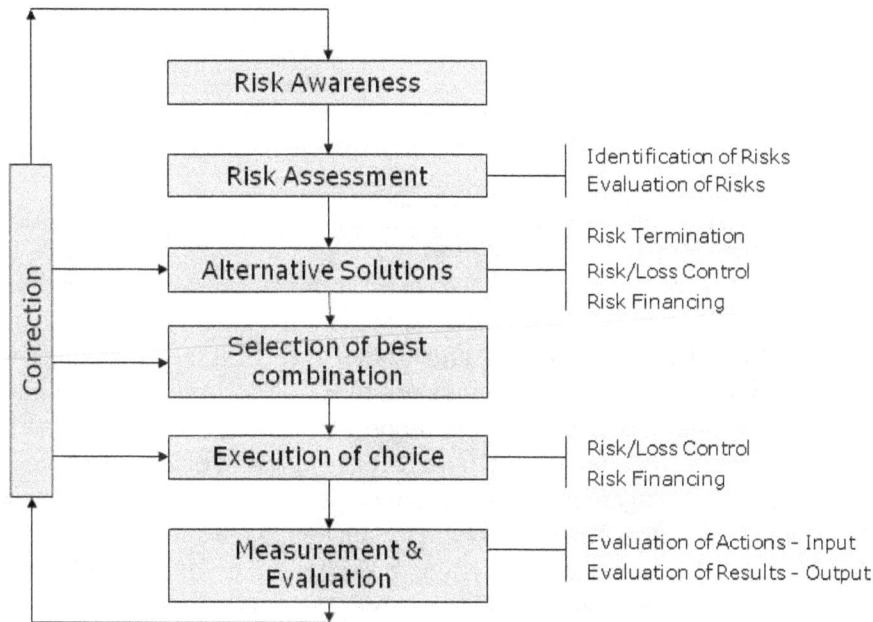

```
                    ┌─────────────────────┐
                    │   Risk Awareness    │
                    └─────────────────────┘
                              │
          ┌───────────────────┴────┐       Identification of Risks
  C       │   Risk Assessment      │─────   Evaluation of Risks
  o       └────────────────────────┘
  r                   │                      Risk Termination
  r       ┌───────────┴────────────┐         Risk/Loss Control
  e       │  Alternative Solutions │─────    Risk Financing
  c       └────────────────────────┘
  t                   │
  i       ┌───────────┴────────────┐
  o       │   Selection of best    │
  n       │     combination        │
          └────────────────────────┘
                      │
          ┌───────────┴────────────┐         Risk/Loss Control
          │   Execution of choice  │─────    Risk Financing
          └────────────────────────┘
                      │
          ┌───────────┴────────────┐         Evaluation of Actions - Input
          │    Measurement &       │─────    Evaluation of Results - Output
          │     Evaluation         │
          └────────────────────────┘
```

Picture 1.10 – Risk management process

If you want to manage something, you first want to know what it is. So, in case of Risk Management, you first want to know what the risks are. You also want to know how large they are, or rather: can be, so you can prioritize them for further processing. The first step then will be the identification and evaluation of risk. After that, Risk Management can grossly be divided into two main areas: (i) risk control and, (ii) risk financing.

Control of risk includes the elimination of risks and, if that is not possible, the reduction including event frequency as well as type and size of consequences. Control of risk has an important influence on the financing of risk irrespective of whether that will be out-of-pocket, through insurance or otherwise.

```
                    ┌────────────────────────────┐
                    │      RISK MANAGEMENT        │
                    │  Identification and Evaluation│
                    │         of Risk             │
                    └────────────────────────────┘
                          │
           ┌──────────────┴──────────────┐
           ▼                             ▼
   ┌──────────────────┐        ┌──────────────────┐
   │   Risk Control   │───────▶│      Risk        │
   │Elimination/Reduction│      │    Financing     │
   └──────────────────┘        └──────────────────┘
        │
   ┌────┴────┐
   ▼         ▼
┌──────────────┐   ┌──────────────┐
│Organizational│──▶│   Technical  │
└──────────────┘   └──────────────┘
```

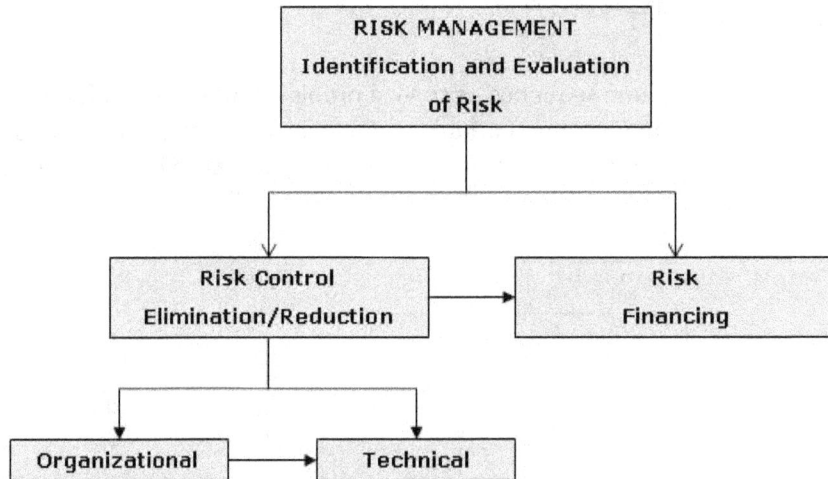

Picture 1.11 - Schematic presentation of risk management main functions

Risk control can be divided into two areas: (i) organizational and, (ii) technical. Preference will often be given to technical (hardware) solutions since those - if done well - do not normally depend on the direct influence of people. Organizational measures, apart from work procedures, administrative controls and decision making, include: designing and building technical systems, maintenance and change management to keep them in safe operating conditions. Organizational issues are the heart of risk management. They are included in management activity areas brought together in the (risk) management system to keep technical and procedural systems working without unwanted events and unnecessary loss. The "organizational" part is the risk management system or -plan.

The Risk Management process is very similar to the problem solving sequence. Risk is a potential problem, something that can happen in the future. If the risk materializes then we have a loss. The difference between risk and loss is the time factor: if the hazard is there, the risk will materialize sooner or later via an unwanted event and presenting itself as a loss; type and the extent often depending on the circumstances that exist when the event occurs. Murphy's Law popular version: "If anything can go wrong, it will" or "What can happen, will happen".

┌───┐
│   **Control of Risk ≈ Control of Loss = Loss Control ≈ Cost Control**   │
└───┘

1.5.1 **Risk management** – a problem solving process

In the problem solving sequence, replace the words "problem" by "risk" and you have the risk management process to include:

1. RISK IDENTIFICATION

Is there a hazard? If so, there normally is also a risk; all you need is an activity that could lead to loss. A <u>qualitative</u> assessment of risk: what can go wrong?

2. RISK EVALUATION

When there is a hazard, what are the activities that can cause an unwanted event transferring hazard into loss? How often do these activities occur? What is the chance that the unwanted event will take place? What can the consequences be? A <u>quantitative</u> assessment of risk: how often and how large?

To prioritize risks for further processing, risk assessment/-classification is used to compare various situations based on their anticipated risk level.

Is the risk small enough to be ignored? Even under different circumstances? If not - go to step 3 and be careful not to ignore risks with very low frequencies but potentially serious or catastrophic consequences. Those still may need attention, even when the classification shows a very low risk level.

3. RISK CONTROL

1. Can the risk be eliminated? If so, that may be the preferred option.
2. If not, we will have to live with it and take action to reduce the risk to an acceptable level.
3. Cause analysis - what are the possible causes that may transfer the hazard into risk and lead to the event that may produce unwanted consequences in terms of monetary, human, environmental or business loss?
4. What are the event frequencies and potential consequences related to the possible causes?
5. Establish alternatives to control risk, based on risk level prioritization; a combination of technical and organizational measures - prevention (directed at event frequency) and limitation of consequences, including risk financing.
6. Choice of best combination of technical, organizational and risk financing measures. *Identification* of what needs to be done and setting *Standards* or criteria for these control activities. This leads to making a PLAN as the first basic step of the platform model that will be discussed later.

7. Carry out the selected control measures/activities by people who know what and how to do; the other two basic steps of the platform model: TRAIN and DO.

8. Periodic evaluation of the control activities - *Measurement* and *Evaluation* of activities carried out. Are activities carried out as planned?

9. *Correction* if control activities are not carried out properly. Loop back to 7.

10. Evaluation of results; if control activities are properly carried out, do they produce desired results? If not, altering or extending of activities may be required or other/additional measures may have to be introduced. Loop back to 5/6.

11. Learn from what goes wrong and feed that learning experience back into the process. Loop back to 1.

The above sequence represents a process with several loops depending on implementation of choices and results obtained.

You may have noted that the risk management or problem solving process described above includes the basic PLATFORM model (PLAN-TRAIN-DO) and the management control function steps *ISMEC*.

The acronym ISMEC, by the way, is very similar to Deming's circle: Plan – Do – Check – Act and was introduced by Frank E. Bird, Jr. during the early/mid seventies of last century.

Ideally, any activity we undertake should start with hazard identification and risk assessment and then develops from there.

The process above is based on:

1. Need for activities to be carried out (steps 3.1 – 3.4)
2. Development of control activities (3.5 – 3.6)
3. Execution of those activities (3.7)
4. Periodic evaluation of execution and results (3.8 – 3.10)
5. Learn from what goes wrong (3.11)

In the 17-step process for management system development and application, the above process (1 – 5) parallels the structure (chapter 2.6, page 163) that should be present in each of the system elements. That structure starts with a need assessment for the activity area concerned and ends with the periodic evaluation of activities and their results.

I also visualized the risk management process in a different way, as an event tree:

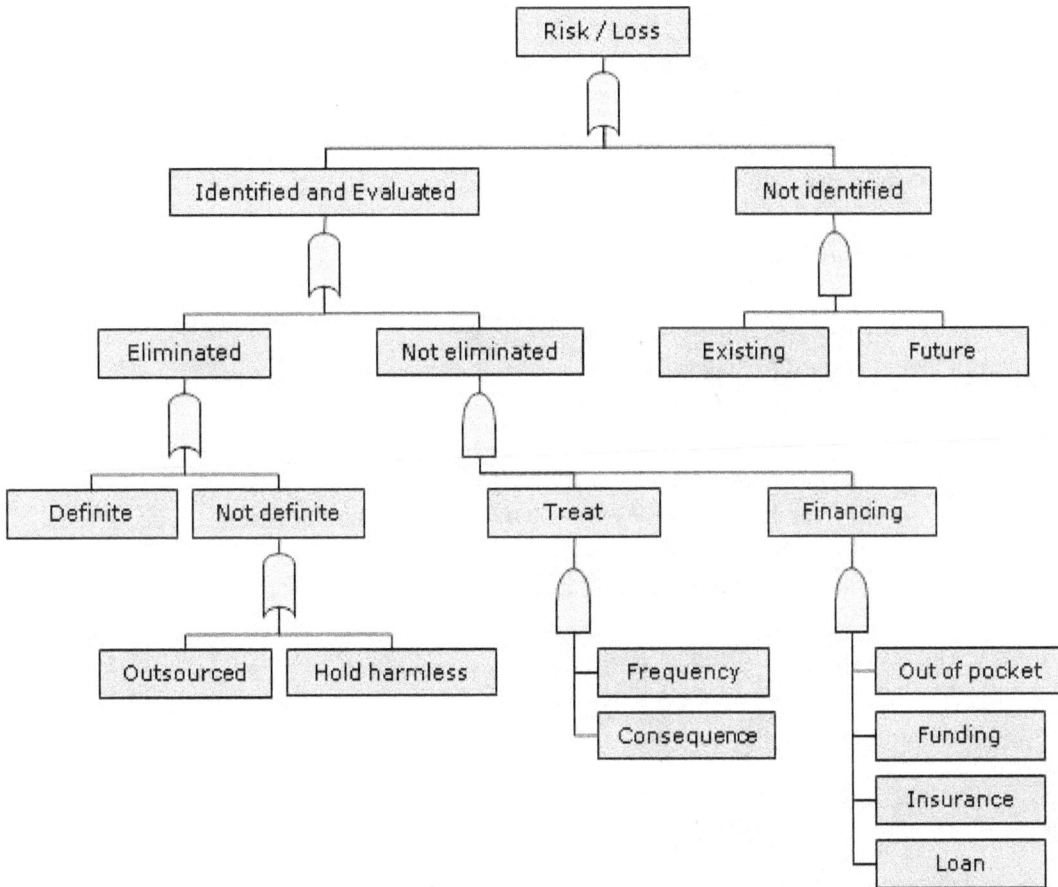

Picture 1.12 – The risk management process presented as an event tree

1.5.2 Risk identification – what the future problems can be (qualitative risk assessment)

Risk Identification - (potential) problem identification - is the first step to control events that may lead to undesired consequences or loss. Events that may keep you away from reaching your objectives/goals.

I will not go into much detail here; I am not a risk specialist and apart from that, the techniques and tools to use depend to a great extent on your situation and the processes of your organization. Risk identification and evaluation is also not a main subject of my book.

Management

is

RISK IDENTIFICATION

(knowing what future problems can be)

There are many techniques/tools available for risk identification and you may want to use one or several depending on the type of industry in which you are working.

To mention a few techniques/tools:

- Hazard and Operability (HAZOP) studies
- Preliminary Hazard Analysis (PHA)
- Failure Mode and Effect Analysis (FMEA)
- Event Tree Analysis (ETA)
- Fault Tree Analysis (FTA)
- Management Oversight and Risk Tree (MORT) and related documents

There are other risk identification methods that are more part of general operations, such as:

- Task Risk Analysis
- Incident Recall
- Accident Imaging

Task Risk Analysis

Task Risk Analysis or TRA, also called Critical Task Analysis, is a general technique and can be used on operational jobs as well as non-operational, technical as well as non-technical.

The technique is basically what has been known as Job Safety Analysis (JSA) for decennia. In practice, however, JSA was/is often limited to safety (injury) related risks only. Which is an opportunity missed because, if you go through the process, you may as well look for other risks associated with the same task or job.

TRA is more than analysis alone as is shown below; the actual analysis is one of the first steps in a sequence to deal with task related potential problems.

A simple (qualitative) list of potentially critical operational tasks may also help to identify risks:

Working on/in/under/over/above/with:
Height
Moving equipment
Chemicals
Enclosed space
Open flame
Water or other liquids
Extreme temperatures
High value equipment
High voltage installations
Heavy equipment
Explosives
Transportation equipment
Hoisting/lifting equipment
Production critical equipment
Flammable materials, liquids, gases
Quality critical processes
Equipment under vacuum
Equipment under high pressure
Environmentally unfriendly conditions
- Add to list as appropriate -

Picture 1.13 – Simple list of activities containing risk

A more extensive risk identification checklist - which may be a good start to identify risks - can be found in books, such as:

- "The Property Damage Accident – the Neglected Part of Safety" (1997) by Frank Bird, Jr. and George L. Germain
- "Safety, Health, Environment and Quality – Guide to Management Risk" (2011) by David Bird, George Germain and Carel Labuschagne
- "Safety, Health and Environmental management – A Practitioner's Guide" (1997) by George L. Germain, Robert M. Arnold, Jr., J. Richard Rowan and J.R. Roane

1.5.3 Risk evaluation/-classification – how large future problems can be (quantitative risk assessment)

Risk evaluation/- classification, is important as tool to quantify risks; to compare and prioritize risks for further treatment. And to obtain attention and involvement of higher management levels to develop, resource, and implement actions to eliminate, reduce or control risk.

```
                        Management
                            is
                    RISK CLASSIFICATION
           (knowing how large future problems can be)
```

The basic questions, using risk classification in a pre-event process, are:

1. How often can the unwanted event occur, turning hazard into consequences?
2. What and how large could these consequences be?

Risk classification is also an important post-event tool as part of inspection/observations and of the investigation of accidents, near-miss incidents and other unwanted events. Questions to ask are similar to those above.

```
              The principle of dimensional value

      The degree of management attention is directly related to the size of
                            the problem
```

Determining the potential loss is the objective of risk evaluation/-classification. The outcome of the process helps to determine such issues as:

- Setting priorities to deal with identified risks
- Whether a team approach should be used - highly recommended - to contribute to risk control and unwanted event investigation
- Which persons should be on the team - operational, management, staff, others
- The management level of the team chairperson
- Selecting risk control alternatives and making resources available
- Assigning responsibilities to make sure that remedial measures will be done correctly and in time

Two important methods to quantify or classify risks are:

- Risk matrix
- Fine/Kinney

In principle, these methods are the same, both combining frequency of occurrence (of the unwanted event preceding the loss) with the potential size of loss. The main difference is that the Fine/Kinney method combines an exposure factor with a likelihood factor to arrive at the frequency. So, if you want, the matrix is 2-dimensional while Fine/Kinney has 3 dimensions.

1.5.3.1 Risk Matrix

Risk Classification using a matrix combines two factors:

- Failure rate - the frequency of occurrence of the event that could lead to loss
- Potential (possible) consequences

A risk matrix could be a simple 3 x 3 matrix (using frequency values such as: low, average, high and potential loss values such as: minor, serious, catastrophic) or be more complex such as the 5 x 5 matrix shown below and to be further explained in an accident investigation protocol. (See appendix J on page 331 for a protocol example.)

Potential Consequence

Failure Rate	A	B	C	D	E	
5	0	0	0	0	0	0
4	0	0	0	1	0	1
3	0	0	0	0	0	0
2	1	0	0	0	0	1
1	0	0	0	0	0	0
	1	0	0	1	0	2

Picture 1.14 – Risk matrix example

The numbers on the left side of the matrix represent the failure rate values, from lowest 1 to highest 5. At the top the letters indicate the potential loss level from A being the lowest to E being the highest. The combination of failure rate and potential consequences can result in risk classification values such as 2A and 4D. The numbers in, below and to the right of the matrix refer to the number of risks in the database, their classification, failure rate and potential consequence values. Total number of risk classified events in the example above is 2.

1.5.3.2 Fine / Kinney

While the matrix in the figure above shows a 2-dimensional approach, the method originally published in 1971 by W. Fine (later publication in 1976 by G.H.F. Kinney) is 3-dimensional. It combines:

- Failure rate
    - o Exposure (E) - the frequency of the activity from which the unwanted event may result. How often will the activity take place?
    - o Probability (P) or likelihood of the occurrence of the unwanted event during the activity. How often will the unwanted event occur when the activity takes place?
- Consequences (C) - the possible consequences of the unwanted event.

The three aspects E, P and C are provided with value descriptions and value factors allowing the calculation of a numeric risk score: R = E x P x C. The method provides risk acceptance/rejection descriptions related to the numerical risk score and a cost justification factor to be considered when looking at remedial actions.

The Fine/Kinney method has an advantage over the risk matrix as it divides the failure rate into two factors; the method forces the user to consider one more aspect.

1.5.3.3. Task Risk Analysis

Task Risk Analysis is a general good method to identify risk as it focuses on the work that needs to be done. Risk related aspects to be considered include: products, tools and installations, human capabilities/limitations and conditions under which tasks are to be carried out, normally as well as in abnormal situations. Through these aspects the task risk analysis has direct connections with design, purchasing, personnel hiring and placement, training, etcetera; all elements of a management system.

Carrying out task risk analyses should always involve the people expected to do the work.

A good starting point to identify risks is to list all functions in your organization, operational and non-operational to include: supervision, management, specialist and operating personnel.

The Task Risk Analysis process involves the following steps:

- Listing of all functions in the organization
- Determination of tasks per function and include decision-making as applicable
- Identification of risks involved when executing tasks – use risk classification
- Determination of main steps of a "critical" task considering:
    - o Possible elimination of risk

- o Risk reduction measures
  - o Control measures, often leading to task or work procedures
- Training of people, using established work procedures; include performance observation
- Periodic observation or discussion of the execution of (critical) tasks
- Feedback from accidents, incidents and other unwanted events

The last two points are important to: (i) improve work and decision-making procedures including adaptation because of introduction of new tools, changes in the working environment, etc. and, (ii) add tasks to the critical task list for further processing.

Risk Identification - keep on doing

Risk identification is seldom, if ever, 100% complete. The process needs to be completed by:

- Repeat the process of risk identification/-evaluation
  - o Using different tools to carry out the process
  - o Have the process carried out by different people
- Use information from accidents, incidents and other unwanted events, through:
  - o Accident or unwanted event investigation
  - o Incident recall
  - o Inspections
  - o Accident imaging

1.5.4   ISO 31000 (2009) - "Risk management, Principles and guidelines"

Some interesting quotes from ISO 31000:

QUOTE
- Risk management creates and protects value.
  - o Risk management contributes to the demonstrable achievement of objectives and improvement of performance in, for example, human health and safety, security, legal and regulatory compliance, public acceptance, environmental protection, product quality, project management, efficiency in operations, governance and reputation.
- Risk management is an integral part of all organizational processes.
  - o Risk management is not a stand-alone activity that is separate from the main activities and processes of the organization. Risk management is part of the responsibilities of management and an integral part of all organizational processes, including strategic planning and all project and change management processes.
- Risk management is part of decision making.
  - o Risk management helps decision makers make informed choices, prioritize actions and distinguish among alternative courses of action.
END QUOTE

In its introduction ISO 31000 (2009) provides a broader base when stating:

QUOTE
When implemented and maintained in accordance with this International Standard, the management of risk enables an organization to, for example:

- Increase the likelihood of achieving objectives
- Encourage proactive management
- Be aware of the need to identify and treat risk throughout the organization
- Improve the identification of opportunities and threats
- Comply with relevant legal and regulatory requirements and international norms
- Improve mandatory and voluntary reporting
- Improve governance
- Improve stakeholder confidence and trust
- Establish a reliable basis for decision making and planning
- Improve controls
- Effectively allocate and use resources for risk treatment
- Improve operational effectiveness and efficiency
- Enhance health and safety performance, as well as environmental protection
- Improve loss prevention and incident management
- Minimize losses
- Improve organizational learning, and
- Improve organizational resilience

END QUOTE

1.6   UNWANTED EVENTS – barriers to obtaining success

While the objective of your plan or management system will be to obtain success, real life does not necessarily follow the path you designed and unwanted events happen. Things go wrong or other than intended and they may keep you from where you want to be. If possible those unwanted vents should be avoided but practice often proves otherwise: what can happen, will happen. The "good" thing is that you may be able to learn from what goes wrong so they may help you to become better. Provided they do not put you out of business first! In any case, you need to know where these events come from and how you can control them.

1.6.1   Cause – Consequence model: from management system to results

Below is the simplified 2-D model showing the relation between the management system and the (unwanted) event. Simplified but including the main phases of the sequence that lead to loss; from the management system on the left to the consequences on the right.

The "domino" model shows the cause - consequence process and can be read going "downstream" indicating the role of the management system to:

- Reach objectives
- Control unwanted events and their consequences

Leadership in Action = Management System

The model can also be read from the other end to use the process to learn from what goes wrong, with the loss or unwanted event as a starting point and going "upstream".

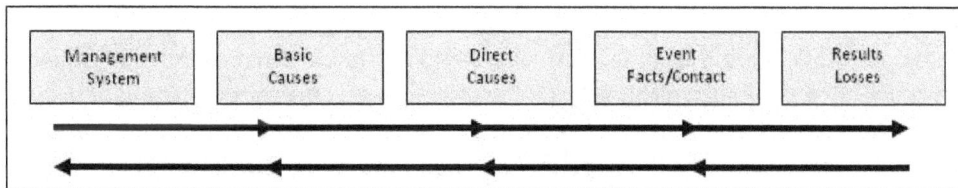

Picture 1.15 – The important role of the management system to bring success – or loss

The model was originally developed as an accident causation model by W.H. Heinrich during the thirties of last century. At that time "Management System" was labeled "Ancestry - Social Environment" while "Basic Causes" was called "Fault of Person". Not something you could manage very well in an organization.

During the late sixties/early seventies of last century, Frank E. Bird Jr. renamed the domino's to suggest the relation between the unwanted event and its consequences on the right and the management system on the left via direct- and basic causes. It was Mr. Bird who showed the way by making the sequence manageable and controllable.

While some people may refer to the basic causes as "root" causes but the model suggests that the real root causes are to be found in the management system and its application. I agree with that but also think that the real root causes are even further to the left and beyond the management system.

The model above is a simplified reflection of the real life situation but powerful for communication purposes: it relates the management system to the event and the results thereof, either good or bad, depending on the quality of each link in the system. It indicates three cause levels:

- Direct causes
- Basic causes
- Management system

This model – relating the management system to success and/or failure - is widely accepted in business including such areas as safety, quality, and environment. This broad acceptance was expected: if you want to get somewhere you need a plan and carry it out; true in business and in all other aspects of life. If you do not build your plan or "management system" properly it may have inherent defects that will lead to unwanted events keeping you from reaching your objective. This is why you want these unwanted events and their consequences identified so you can learn from them to eliminate or reduce future (similar) occurrences.

The 3 dimensional cause-consequence model in picture 1.16 is an extension that I made to show the complexity that cannot be seen easily in the 2 dimensional model above. The 3-D model may appeal more to professional people.

In principle both models are the same. Both also seem to indicate that the unwanted event is caused by a direct cause – such as an act of a person – directly preceding the event. However, while direct causes may have triggered the event, it should be remembered that there are other causes created by other people. Those people can be found more "upstream" in the organization and further away from the event; they may have had their share in creating the causes leading to loss.

The text on the dominoes in picture 1.16 is a little different from the 2-D model but, without any further explanation, I think you get the idea about the complexity that unwanted event causation models may have. I included the "barrier concept" between the event and the initial loss. I also realized that the final loss depends on the actions after the event occurs and added the emergency services as well as the Post Event or Post Emergency Plan (PEP) intended to get the operation back to normal as soon as possible. Please note that I only have one management system at the far left. Obviously there could be more than one - not really preferable but often practice following various certification processes and legislative requirements.

Many people may have their role in relation to unwanted events. Similarly, those people also play their part in obtaining success; they share the results either good or bad.

The principle of shared results

The outcome of an organization is the combined work of many people at different levels and at different times. They all share responsibility for the company's success or failure.

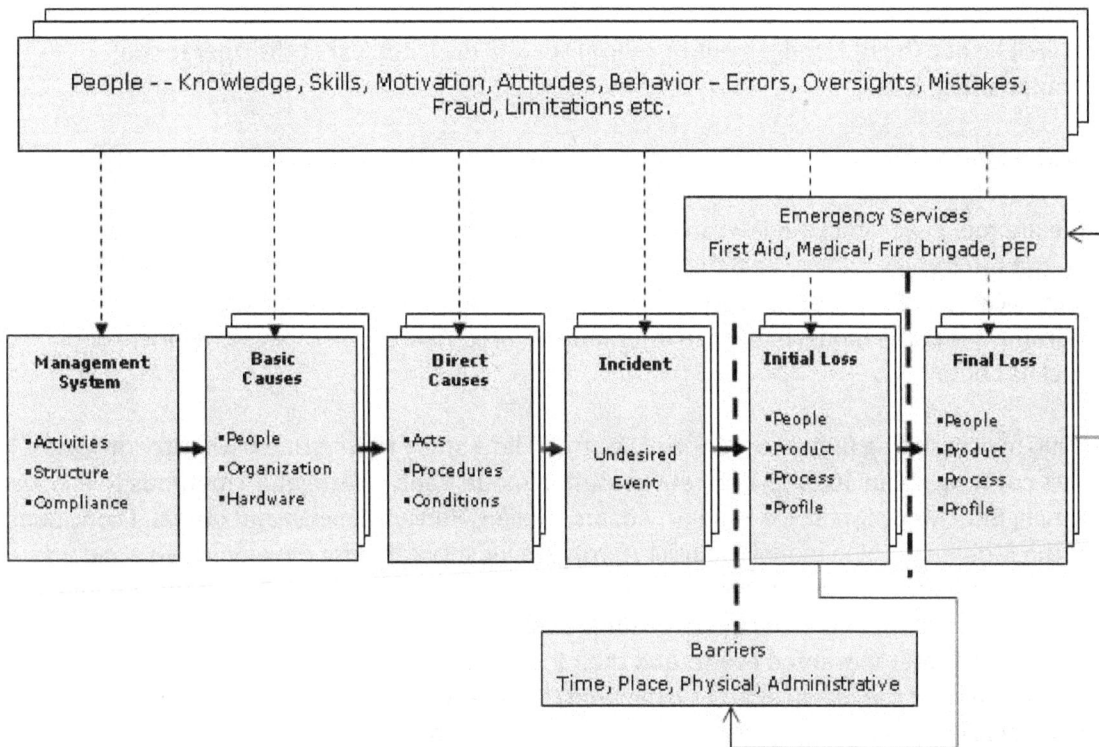

Picture 1.16 – The process from management system to success or failure

Loss Control - a matter of Top-Down AND Bottom-up

Although the "management system" will be initiated by (top) management, it should be clear that various organizational levels and functions have to work together to make the management system a success. This involves all management levels, staff and operational personnel.

Top-Down and Bottom-Up and remember the "Principle of Point of Control":

> **The principle of point of control**
>
> The greatest potential for control tends to exist at the point where the action takes place

The "action level" depends on what the action is assumed to produce. It could the design or training department. The level where products or services are being purchased or people are being hired. The level at which contracts are made or where marketing efforts are being put together. Or the maintenance department. Basically any level or department where activities may produce loss - or success. And of course it could also be the level at which the (end) product is being made or where services are provided. So keep that in mind: the "point of control" could very well be at a (high) management or specialist staff level, not just at the operational (manufacturing) level.

Causation model study

There are more causation models ranging from simple to complex. If too simple, you can do little with it; if too complex it may be difficult to explain. What is important is that the model has communication value: to explain the model to management, employees and others. Also important is that the model has broad international acceptance. The 5-phase Heinrich/Bird model has both.

In 1990 my consulting firm – Loss Control Centre – did a study for the Dutch Ministry of Social Affairs covering about 10 to 15 different causation models and investigation methods to include: Heinrich, Bird, Mort, Swain, De Reamer, Adams, Kjellen, Hudson/Reason and others. I concluded that the 5-phase domino model (Heinrich/Bird) was most suitable for developing an accident investigation guide for more general use and application in industry. The Bird model relating the management system to the unwanted event provides sufficient opportunities for controlling accidents and other unwanted events and their losses. It is my preferred model to communicate the importance of the management system and the roles of both management and operational personnel in controlling loss. The study produced the Dutch government publication S137. You will, however, not find my name connected with it as I could not agree with the 4-phase model that is suggested in the publication and in which management system and basic causes are combined into one phase.

While management system and basic causes are closely related, they represent different organizational levels. It is the management system - and its related procedures - that may produce conditions that are then "build-in" and considered as basic causes producing unwanted events later on. So to work with the model, I think it is better to separate management system and basic causes. I think the 4-phase model came from a compromise between a 3-phase model that was favored by the government officials involved in the project and the 5-phase Bird model that I knew since the early seventies.

In 1991 I got a request from another contact within the Ministry to write an article based on the 3-phase HEB model that also received some interest (HEB is a Dutch abbreviation that would translate into IEC meaning: Identification – Evaluation – Control). I did write the article - which was published in a health and safety handbook in The Netherlands – extending the simple 3-phase model into the problem solving/risk management process that we discussed earlier.

So, be careful: a simple model may look attractive but may not do the job and it needs to be expanded so it can be sufficiently understood and act as a basis from which to work.

Unwanted Event Consequences

Unwanted event consequences could be many and multiple and, depending on the character of the event and the circumstances that are present during and after the event, may include:

- Property damage - product, buildings, installation
- Environmental damage
- Personal injury – fatalities, lost time
- Loss of information - knowledge, expertise
- Damage to company image
- Liability claims - product, contractual, other
- Delivery problems
- Loss or disappearing of goods
- Loss of customers
- Loss of market
- Loss of work days
- Personnel turnover
- Production delays
- Quality problems
- Waste

Peter Drucker

The first duty of management is to survive and the guiding principle of business economics is not the maximization of profit – it is the avoidance of loss

---

Peter F. Drucker (1909 –2005) - management consultant, educator, and author

Unwanted event consequences are not limited to the more visible losses such as injuries and property damage. Unwanted events may occur during the execution of work and decision-making at all levels in the organization and within every discipline. Not properly carrying out work may mean that one person cuts off his thumb; another person may close an unfavorable contract while the third takes unnecessary risks when marketing an insufficiently tested product; others may design an unsafe product or purchase unsafe materials, tools or equipment.

Risk identification should be the first step in preventing unwanted event consequences. What can go wrong? What if?

Management System	Basic Causes	Direct Causes	Event Facts/Contact	Results Losses

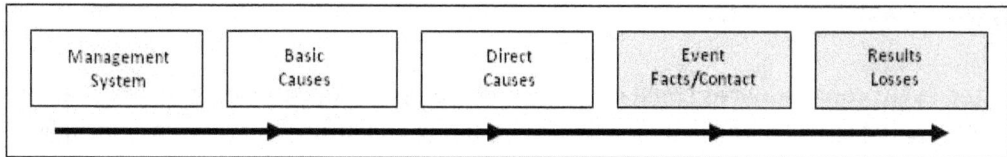

The costs of accidents and other unwanted events can have an important influence on business results, ranging from reducing financial results to termination of activity.

Although exact figures are often missing as most companies do not register those – often unnecessary and preventable – costs, there are indications that these costs could reach 5 to 10% of the gross national product. Or 20% or more of turnover of individual companies. In the construction chain in The Netherlands, these "failure costs" have increased from 6% of gross turnover in 2001 to 12% in 2012 and may even be as high as between 15 to 20%. (Source: http://www.usp-mc.nl)

1.6.2 Different losses – common causes

In our day to day work we see the results of unwanted events as errors, mistakes, damage, injuries, complaints, liability claims, etc. All different losses, yes. But look at the basic causes and they may not be so different anymore. Unwanted events are caused! By people! Because they do not know how to do their work properly, they cannot do it the way they should do it, they grew into the habit to do it differently, they are not motivated, they are encouraged to cut corners, they do not have the right tools or the proper equipment, etc.

"If you want to make an omelet, you got to break some eggs" is a well known saying but it is also not acceptable as a reason that things go wrong and consider them as "business as usual".

Look at the matrix in picture 1.17 and check the boxes if you think that aspects on the left may be contributing to losses at the top and you may conclude that most or all losses we see come from one or more of these causes. Likewise you may conclude that one single cause could lead to more than one consequence.

Most of these causes mentioned on the left side of the matrix should be elements of a management system to reach objectives and control unwanted events.

	Product loss	Quality problems	Property damage	Waste	Liability claims	Occupational illness	Personal injury	Environmental damage	Personnel turnover	Loss of customer	Loss of market share	Damage to company image	Loss of information	Decrease shareholder value
Training/instruction														
Design of installations, workplace														
Purchasing of goods, services														
Hiring and placement of personnel														
Management / supervision														
Inspections														
Learning from unwanted events														
Emergency preparedness														
Post emergency plan														
Change management														
Work procedures/instructions														
Communications														
Task observation														
Risk/problem identification														
Abnormal situation management														

Picture 1.17 – The cause – consequence matrix

There are two management principles that apply in relation to the above:

1. The principle of multiple causes: "Accidents and other loss producing events are seldom, if ever, the result of a single cause"
2. The principle of multiple consequences: "More often than not will a single cause result in multiple consequences"

The message contained in the above principles is that you can gain tremendously if your unwanted event cause analysis goes deep enough - into the basic causes and into the management system. Use a risk classification system to select the events that are serious enough to get serious attention. Broaden your scope to get the multiple benefits from an in-depth single event cause analysis. Consequences of unwanted events are often consequences of failures of management system and the resulting basic and direct causes and can be prevented or reduced.

1.6.2.1 Accident Triangle

There are many accident triangles or -pyramids. If you search the Internet you will find them with different descriptions and different numbers. One of the most extensive was the accident ratio study carried out in 1969 under the guidance of Frank E. Bird, Jr., Director of Engineering Services for the Insurance Company of North America (INA). The study included the analysis of over 1.750.000 accidents that were reported by close to 300 companies representing over 20 different industry groups and employing close to 2 million employees working more than 3 billion hours during the exposure period analyzed. The result is shown below as the "accident triangle". Other similar studies are mentioned in the book "Safety and the Bottom Line" (Bird, Davies, 1996, chapter 8 pages 277 – 287).

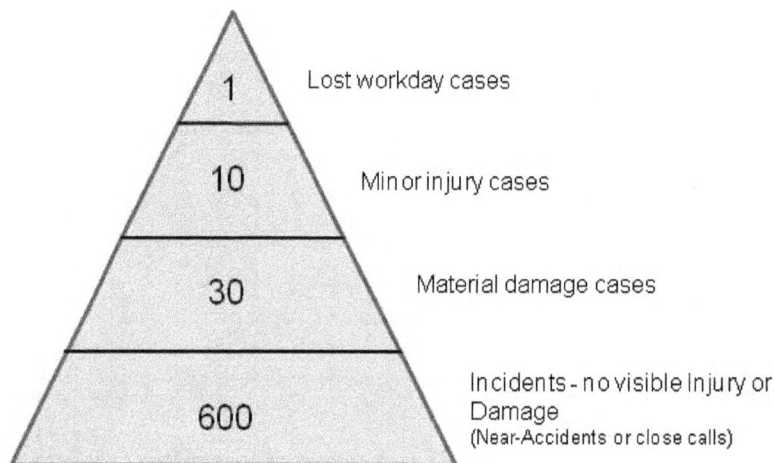

Picture 1.18 – Bird (INA – 1969) Accident ratio study results

Accident triangles or -pyramids tell us this: there are many more unwanted events than there are lost time injuries which are traditionally the focus of industrial safety.

The bottom of the triangle is formed by "incidents", the no-loss unwanted events or near-misses following "substandard acts or conditions"; substandard meaning that they are not in line with proper work methods, instructions or procedures. Possibly because these methods and procedures are not correct, outdated or not available.

Please bear in mind that the consequences of an unwanted event may range from no (visible) loss (a "near miss" or "close-call") to catastrophic depending on:

- The circumstances at the time of the event
- The effectiveness of barriers between the event and the initial loss
- The effectiveness of the emergency actions and Post Event Plan

"Near-miss" or "close-call" events are unwanted events that could have resulted in property damage, injury or other loss under different circumstances. They are a good learning source to improve the management system. Use risk classification to select the events that are worth an in-depth investigation and cause analysis.

1.6.2.2 Accident Cost Iceberg

Experience in North America and other countries has led to the assumption that the costs resulting from "accidents" could be 50 times the costs associated with injury alone (medical and compensation costs).

Louis A. Allen

Minimizing loss is as much improvement as maximization of profit

---

Louis A. Allen, management consultant and writer. Founder of Louis Allen Worldwide

In 1966 Frank E. Bird, Jr., when working for Lukens Steel wrote the book "Damage Control" in which the message was: "Hey guys there are a lot more accidents than injuries alone, they cost a bundle and we can learn from them to also prevent harm to people". Did his message come across? Hard to say.... in 1997, 30 years later, he wrote the book "The property Damage Accident – The Neglected Part of Safety" with the same message. Even today and in high hazardous industry, safety is measured by the number of reported lost time injuries per million hours. Note that this measurement is based on (reported) lost time injuries - that is only the top of the triangle. But there are many more unwanted events that result in loss. Why separate these events from (traditional) safety while they can be controlled using the same measures that should be part of the same management system?

The principle of dimensional value

The degree of management attention is directly related to the size of the problem

---

While there are more of these accident cost icebergs to be found through the Internet, they all point into the same direction: the cost of substandard work and conditions is much greater than those of injuries alone. It follows then that there are much greater cost reduction opportunities by having a broad look at unwanted events, including those we traditionally refer to as "accidents".

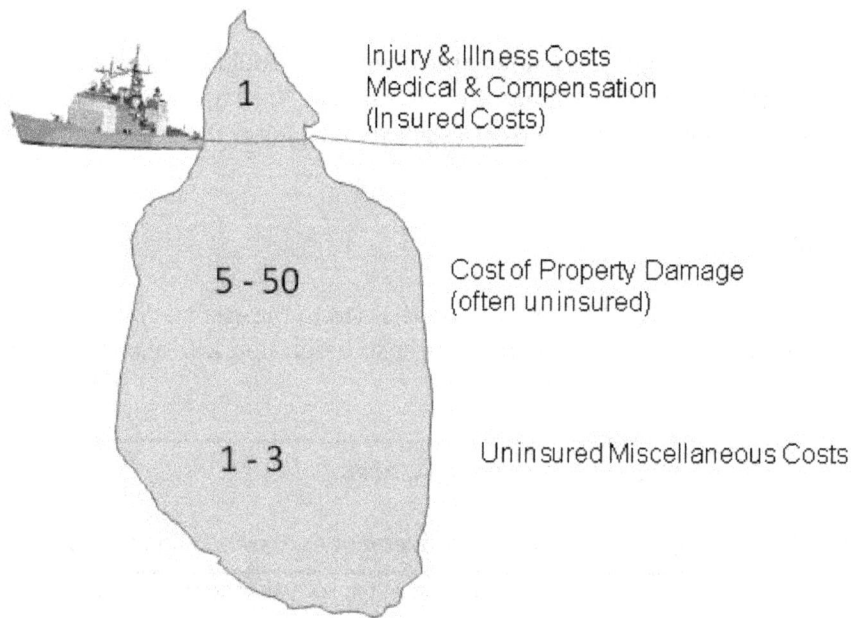

Picture 1.19 – Accident cost iceberg

Depending on your profit margins you may have to sell quite a lot to make up for the costs of unwanted events. The table below indicates this.

Yearly Incident Costs	Profit Margin				
	1%	2%	3%	4%	5%
1.000	100.000	50.000	33.000	25.000	20.000
5.000	500.000	250.000	167.000	125.000	100.000
10.000	1.000.000	500.000	333.000	250.000	200.000
25.000	2.500.000	1.250.000	833.000	625.000	500.000
50.000	5.000.000	2.500.000	1.667.000	1.250.000	1.000.000
100.000	10.000.000	5.000.000	3.333.000	2.500.000	2.000.000
150.000	15.000.000	7.500.000	5.000.000	3.750.000	3.000.000
200.000	20.000.000	10.000.000	6.666.000	5.000.000	4.000.000

Picture 1.20 – Required additional sales to make up for offset annual costs of unwanted events

If annual cost from unwanted events – any type - totals $ 10.000 and your profit margin is 4 %, your sales people have to bring in $ 250.000 in addition to what they are doing already. Realizing this, you will understand the quote below from Peter Drucker.

> **Peter Drucker**
>
> In case of keen competition and low profit margins, learning from accidents can contribute more to profits than an organization's best salesperson

Peter F. Drucker (1909 –2005) - management consultant, educator, and author

Louis A. Allen gave the same message: "Minimizing loss is as much improvement as maximization of profit". Both gentlemen were not safety professionals and both quotes are in line with Bird's 1966 Damage Control message.

An effective (safety) management system can help you to bring down the unnecessary cost of business resulting from unwanted events. The 17-step process may be your guide to set up the management system that will do this for you.

> **"SAFETY"**
>
> If you want to improve your safety performance with less effort: LIMIT the definition of what an accident is – you may even get away with it.
>
> If you want your efforts to be more effective and learn from what goes wrong: EXTEND the definition and broaden the scope of your safety efforts.
>
> Which one shall it be?

1.6.3   The unwanted event leading to Loss

The event in the cause - consequence sequence could be anything, including:

- Fire, explosion
- Flooding, landslides, windstorm, earthquake
- Theft, mysterious disappearance
- Loss of customer or market
- Not being able to enter new markets (product, geographical)
- Accidents leading to loss: human, property, environment, business
- Unplanned production interruption
- Riot, civil commotion
- Loss of key personnel
- Loss of information
- Industrial espionage

- Loss of suppliers
- Loss of resources, energy, water
- Quality problems
- Inefficiency, waste

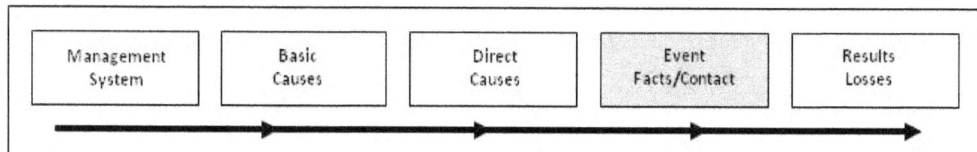

Management System	Basic Causes	Direct Causes	Event Facts/Contact	Results Losses

In relation to injury, environmental and material damage one of the concepts is the energy trace/barrier concept. The concept assumes a contact and energy exchange between a source of energy and a body or object at the time of the event. If the energy exchange is above the threshold limit value of body or object and no adequate barriers are present then the result will be (visible) harm (injury or damage) and, of course, their "indirect" or consequential losses. If the energy exchange is below the threshold value or when adequate barriers are present there may not be any (visible) loss. However, the event may still have to be taken seriously; under the different circumstances the event results could be quite different.

Within the safety area, the types of contact considered include:

- Struck against (running or bumping into)
- Struck by (hit by moving object)
- Fall to lower level
- Fall on same level
- Caught in (pinch or nip points)
- Caught on (snagged, hung)
- Caught between or under (crushed or amputated)
- Contact with (electricity, heat, cold, radiation, caustics, toxic, noise)
- Overstress, overexertion, overload

Barriers preventing the event from producing actual loss include:

- Physical barriers, walls, shields
- Place related barriers, separating energy source and body or object in place
- Time related barriers, separating energy source and body or object in time
- Administrative barriers, procedures, work instructions *)
- (Personal) protective equipment

*) Many, non-safety related, events can only be controlled by administrative barriers. Those include decision-making as well as processes such as design, purchasing, training and maintenance. This is why procedures, work instructions and rules require serious attention. In fact this may require a procedure to make procedures – see appendix D, page 238 for headings to be included in such procedure.

1.6.3.1 Reporting the unwanted event

The unwanted event can produce visible loss or not and the loss could range from minimal to catastrophic. To learn from no-loss events or minor losses, use risk classification and establish if the loss could be significantly worse under different circumstances. These HIPO (High Potential) events need serious attention.

Minor or no-loss events may not get reported for various reasons. But they should, as their results could have been very different if the circumstances during event occurrence would have been different. The unwanted event or accident investigation protocol should indicate what shall be reported, investigated etc. to come up with remedial actions so the same or similar would not happen again in the future. (See an unwanted event protocol example in appendix J on page 331.)

PLEASE ….

When reading the next few pages on direct causes, basic causes and the management system or "root" causes, consider that the cause-consequence model is a simplification of real life. If you look closer and think harder the lines between the phases of the model may become vague and may even disappear.

Just keep in mind that the main message of the model is that it is the quality of the management system on the left that will determine what will come out at the other end of the model.

1.6.4   Direct Causes – preceding unwanted events

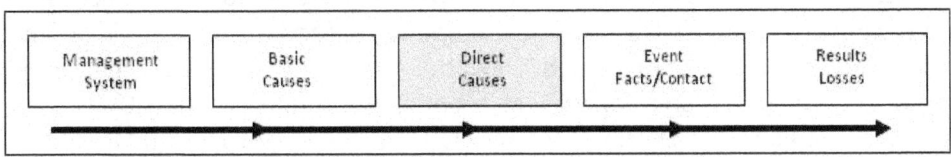

Management System	Basic Causes	Direct Causes	Event Facts/Contact	Results Losses

The above picture indicates that the events that lead to the consequences that we see are triggered by "direct causes". We divide the direct causes in: (i) causes that are related to a person – what people do and how, the "acts" and, (ii) causes related to the (work) environment including equipment and installations - the "conditions".

Direct causes of accidents, incidents and other unwanted events are therefore divided in two categories:

- Substandard acts
- Substandard conditions

We use the term "substandard" to indicate that there must be a right or "standard" way of doing things -the acts - and right or standard situations or environments – the conditions. "Standard" meaning safe, good, without undue risks. Of course the unwanted event could also be the result of a combination of acts and conditions implying that tasks and conditions need to be in balance with each other and with the capabilities of the people that do the work.

Below, I give some examples of substandard acts and conditions. While these are safety related, the issues as such – substandard acts/substandard conditions - are generic and can also be used considering the cause-consequence sequence in other business areas.

Sub-standard acts and conditions are in the "management gap"; between what and how "it" is (done) and what and how it should be (done).

> **One of the main aspects of the management function is to control loss**
>
> To close the gap between "practice" and "theory"
>
> Between "how it is (done)" and "how it should be (done)"

The simple 2 D model above seems to indicate that we are mainly concerned with the acts of people carrying out work directly prior to the unwanted event. But that is because the model is a simplification of real life and you should realize that the actual situation is more complex. Sometimes there is only a thin line between direct causes and basic causes. Another substandard act could have been by a person at a different level in the organization, further away from the unwanted event and at a different time; an act contributing to the substandard act carried out prior to the event. For example: lack of adequate training to carry out work could be the cause of a substandard act by the person on the job. Could the "underlying" act have been committed by the supervisor or human resource department not providing proper training? Or by higher management not requiring proper training through the management system? Or did the purchasing department buy the cheaper product to create a substandard condition? Or was a substandard condition created by the person designing the work environment or installation?

Substandard acts may exist because (i) there is no "standard way" of doing things, (ii) there is no initial training on how to carry out tasks, (iii) there are no regular observations or discussions to see if the work can still be done according to the standard procedure, (iv) the standard way to do the work is not being updated, (v) substandard work practices are being tolerated by supervision and management, (vi) carrying out work as it should be done is considered "for sissies".

Substandard conditions or situations may exist because: (i) they are designed that way, (ii) there is no proper management of change program, (iii) there is no proper inspection program to find substandard conditions, (iv) they are not corrected when found, (v) there is no housekeeping program, (vi) substandard conditions are being tolerated by supervision and management, (vii) they are seen as "part of the normal work environment".

Substandard acts and conditions are closely related. A substandard condition or situation may be created through a substandard act of a person, operational, managerial or staff. Once the substandard condition is there, the act of another person may be looked upon as substandard while in fact it may have been the condition contributing most to the unwanted event.

Direct causes of unwanted events can often be seen at the actual work site and may be found during execution of procedures such as work permits or Last Minute Risk Assessment (LMRA). They can be seen during formal inspections/observations and, preferably, should be noted and acted upon during day-today operations. Since direct causes relate to acts and conditions that may be there only momentarily, they should also be considered during incident or accident imaging exercises asking the "what if" questions.

Substandard acts and conditions can be found during investigation of unwanted events leading to remedial actions which may include revision of work procedures or changing the work environment.

Substandard Acts – triggers to unwanted events

Substandard acts may lead to unwanted events. They could be performed by various people at various levels in the organization, close to the unwanted event or further upstream. By operational personnel, by management or staff specialists and related to hiring/placement of people, training etc.

Substandard acts may be present from the start of an undertaking or develop over time due to lack of proper work- or task procedures, training, periodic task observation/discussion or simply because management and supervision allow such acts to exist.

(Safety related) substandard acts, as part of direct causes immediately preceding the unwanted event, include:

- Operating without authority

- Failure to warn
- Failure to secure or to make safe
- Operating at improper speed
- Rendering safety devices inoperative
- Using defective equipment
- Improper use of otherwise safe equipment
- Servicing equipment in operation
- Not following proper work instructions or rules
- Not using or improper use of protective equipment
- Not using proper equipment
- Improper loading or stacking
- Improper placement
- Improper lifting
- Taking up improper position for task
- Games/horseplay

Substandard Conditions - hazards in the business environment

Substandard conditions may lead to accidents or other unwanted events. These substandard conditions could be created by various people at various levels in the organization, close to the unwanted event or further upstream. By operational personnel, management or staff specialists and related to such areas as design and modification, purchasing, inspections and maintenance.

Substandard conditions may be present from the start of an undertaking or develop over time due to lack of proper modification procedures, inspection and maintenance or simply because management and supervision allow such conditions to exist.

(Safety related) substandard conditions, as part of direct causes immediately preceding the unwanted event, include:

- No or improper guards or barriers
- No or inadequate personal protection
- Defective tools, equipment or materials
- Proper tools not available
- Congestion/restricted action
- Lack of adequate housekeeping
- Inadequate warning systems
- Fire or explosion hazards
- Excessive noise
- Inadequate ventilation
- Substandard lighting

- Inadequate design of workplace
- Exposure to chemicals
- Exposure to radiation
- Hazardous atmospheric conditions: fumes, dusts, vapors

<u>Substandard acts leading to substandard conditions</u>

Direct causes could be temporarily, like someone misplacing a drum or pallet; a substandard act leading to a substandard condition. Assuming appropriate actions taken, such direct causes would be there for only a short period of time. However, if no actions are taken, for whatever reason, those direct causes may become more or less permanent.

There are also other types of direct causes having a more permanent character and they may be more difficult to correct. Those are the acts and conditions that are there by design, because they are purchased or hired and because of lack of supervision and management, lack of training etc. That will bring us to the basic causes.

A well-known American safety professional once asked me to write an article regarding "accident prone people". I thought about this and concluded that a substandard act is normally labeled "substandard" in relation to the environment in which the act is carried out; the way installations and work areas are designed, tools are purchased, work procedures are developed, etc. My conclusion then was that there are really no accident prone people but, given the limitations that we all have, there are accident prone environments, the extent of which depending on the people selected to do the work. This ties in with the thinking that, if you wish to reduce losses, the environment should be adapted to the people, not the other way around. Can that always be done? Probably not, but you can come a long way. Anyway, I never wrote the article.

Mind you there are risk takers and we all are; one more than the other and when we take more risks we may have more accidents but that does not mean that we are accident prone. Life without risk may be pretty dull and as the saying goes: "A little risk is a joy in life". But then there is also this: "Don't risk a lot for a little".

1.6.5 Basic Causes – the more permanent sources of unwanted events

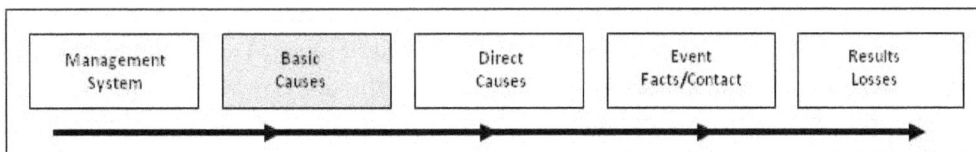

Management System	Basic Causes	Direct Causes	Event Facts/Contact	Results Losses

Basic causes are sometimes also called "root causes". As such they are the "source", so to speak, from which the direct causes and unwanted events evolve. Basic causes are also called the "underlying causes".

In my opinion, however, the real "root causes" should be found in the management system. The reasoning behind this is that basic or underlying causes are caused when the management system fails to produce the proper results. This may be due to insufficient content of the system (activity areas and activities) or inadequate structure of system elements to make sure that necessary activities are being implemented, evaluated and improved when necessary.

Please remember that all levels of the organization should play their role in the performance of the management system and the subsequent phases of the cause-consequence process or sequence. Management, supervision, staff specialists and operational personnel all share responsibility for the functioning of the total sequence, its success or its failure. Remember the principle of shared responsibility. Final success or failure is separated only by the quality of the plan or management system to make sure that the future will be different from the past and different from the present.

Similar to direct causes, here too we recognize two main categories: (1) personal factors, related to a person, and (2) job factors, related to the organization, work conditions and processes.

Basic causes of undesired events are divided in two main categories:

- Substandard personal factors
- Substandard organizational or job factors

Basic causes form the breeding ground from which the direct causes can develop that may result in unwanted events with consequences such as: injury, material damage, quality problems, liability claims and other losses.

Basic causes are more directly related to the management system and to the quality of the implementation of the activities contained therein. Basic causes can be found through activities such as design reviews, risk identification, inspections, (task) observations and accident imaging.

Substandard Personal Factors - personal issues related to unwanted events

Personal factors are related to people committing a substandard act. That could be the act immediately preceding the unwanted event or an act by someone contributing to the substandard acts of others or to substandard conditions considered under direct causes. Acts by people further away from the unwanted event and its consequences, who may have been responsible for such areas as design of product and work procedures, installations or work environment; maintenance; purchasing; training; inspections, etcetera. And, of course, people in management or supervisory positions responsible for decision making and supervision of the work being done. The results of the work done by these people may also be seen under "job factors", their skills and motivation play important roles when creating the environment from which unwanted events may develop - or not.

Substandard personal factors that may lead to basic as well as direct causes include:

- Inadequate mental or physical capability
- Stress – mental or physical
- Lack of knowledge
- Lack of skill/experience
- Improper motivation
- Abuse or misuse

The substandard personal factors listed above may apply to people at all levels in the organization and in all functions at various phases of the causation model. These personal factors may be temporally or permanent and may be reasons for existence of substandard job factors as mentioned below.

Substandard Job Factors - organizational threats to loss

Job factors are related to "the organization". Job factors often have to do with people further away from the unwanted event. People responsible for design of product, installations or work environment; maintenance; purchasing; training; and inspections. The results of their work depend on their skills and motivation – the personal factors - and play an important role in creating the environment from which unwanted events may develop at a later stage and involving other people.

Closer to the unwanted event is the role of managers and supervisors. Their attitude, behavior and knowledge play an important role where it concerns the acceptance of substandard acts and conditions at the point of control.

Substandard job factors that may lead to basic as well as direct causes include:

- Inadequate leadership/supervision
- Inadequate engineering, design of workplace/facility
- Inadequate design of work procedures/-instructions
- Inadequate purchasing
- Inadequate maintenance/excessive wear and tear
- Improper tools and equipment

These basic causes - organizational or job factors - often occur because of unclear or improper criteria concerning the way work that needs to be done. They may occur due to not complying with management system criteria or activities or because of gaps in the system, allowing substandard practices to develop and remain.

Substandard organizational or job factors may very well develop from the substandard personal factors mentioned above.

1.6.6   Root Causes – the management system, source of good and bad

While some consider the basic causes as the "root causes" of unwanted events, you need to consider that these basic causes are created. They are there because controls that should have prevented their development were: (i) either not there, or (ii) not adequate, or (iii) not properly implemented. Those controls precede the creation of basic causes and are part of the management system directed at: (i) reaching objectives and, (ii) preventing and controlling unwanted event that may be in the way of reaching those objectives.

These controls may also come under the umbrella of Abnormal Situation Management (AMS) and include: (i) early recognition of deviations that may lead to unwanted events and, (ii) taking action to prevent those events from happening.

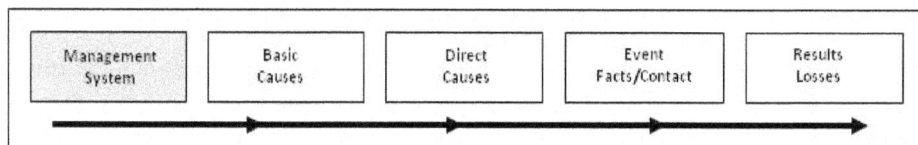

Unwanted events should be seen as results of a management system that is not working as it should. Causes of unwanted events can be prevented and/or controlled provided that:

1. The management system contains activity areas or elements, relevant to reach objectives and control causes that could lead to unwanted events, including: design, training, maintenance and inspection, management of change, abnormal situation management, emergency preparedness
2. The content of those elements is adequate in terms of specific element activities to also prevent and control unwanted events and their consequences
3. The elements are structured to make sure that their activities are properly carried out to deliver the wanted results: reach objectives while, at the same time, prevent and control causes that may lead to unwanted events and their consequences

Management system shortcomings or failures can be found through regularly carrying out audits to make sure that element activities are being carried out as intended and element and overall management system objectives are being obtained. These shortcomings also come to light through unwanted events and the losses that could be one of the end products of the (failing) management system.

Building the management system to include the necessary content and structure is part of chapter II "Making the Management System".

PLEASE remember that management systems and related basic and direct causes not only produce unwanted events and losses. They also create opportunities for success!

The two main goals of a management system are:
(i) reach objectives and (ii) control loss

To close the gap between
"what is (done)" and "what should be (done)"

Mishaps, errors, accidents etc. occur in that gap and are barriers to success

---

For practical reasons, I consider the management system and its elements as the "root causes". However, the management system itself is also made by people so we have to look beyond the system to find the real root causes and we may even go beyond that asking why people are the way they are and do what they do. The real root causes have to do with their skills, motivation, intentions, their social environment, vision, etc. This is why I listed these aspects in the box extending the entire cause-consequence sequence, as shown in picture 1.21 below. These aspects are very similar to the personal factors mentioned earlier under basic causes.

Please remember that management systems are often made as part of an effort to obtain a certificate required for commercial or legislative reasons. Because such certificate may be considered mandatory for the existence of the organization, the attitude may be to get it as quickly as possible, with a minimum of effort and the least expense. If done that way the management system may be directed at the minimum level at which the certificate can be issued by a certification institute. In fact it may even be below that minimum level because certification institutes are competing with each other in a commercial market that, by its nature, is limited.

Certification has its limits - Leadership doesn't

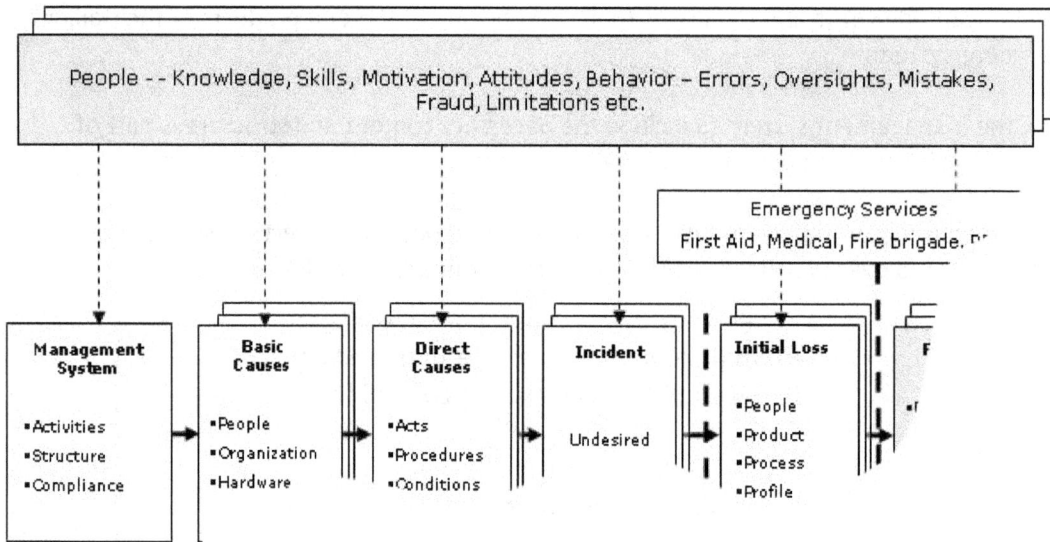

Picture 1.21 – People aspects are the true root causes of unwanted events and loss

A certification process leads to a certificate and produce a minimum level management system which, in practice, may also be the maximum level of performance. A management system or plan directed at improvement needs leadership and leadership for improvement does not know such minimum level.

Root causes of failure are also the root causes of success

CHAPTER II   MAKING THE MANAGEMENT SYSTEM, THE PLAN

Making a management system or plan that works is really the essence of this book. Knowing how to make the plan to direct an organization towards desired objectives is essential for all people and in particular for those in management positions. From organization leaders or top managers to direct supervisors and everything in between or around those; from the top down and including point of control level personnel.

In this chapter the following subjects will be dealt with:

- Platform model for organizational change – six aspects of which four essential
- Process to build the plan or management system – 17 steps towards success
- Contents of the management system – elements to obtain system objectives
- Structure of the system elements – to drive implementation towards success
- Rating method – a quantitative indication of the overall process and its 17 steps

The subjects will first be introduced and after that treated in some more detail. I did it that way as I think it may reinforce what I am trying to put across.

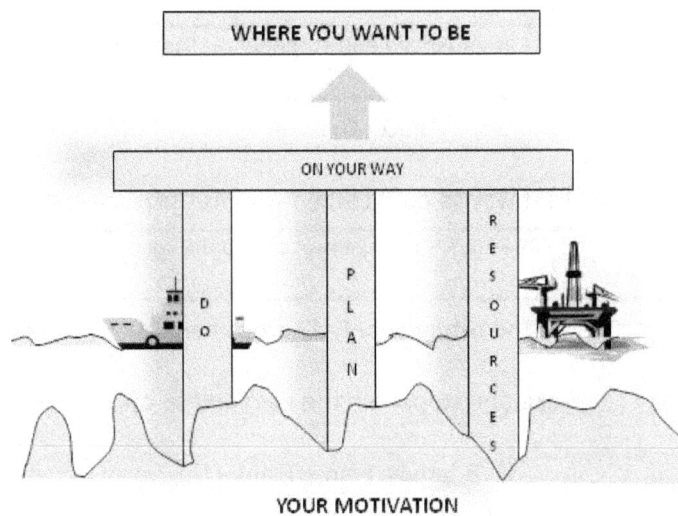

Picture 2.01 – Front view of generic platform model

Picture 2.01 above shows the platform model as it can be applied in business, non-business and private environments. The model includes the necessary aspects for success, for making your future: (i) the objective, where you wish to be, (ii) the plan to get there,
(iii) the knowledge and other resources necessary to execute the plan, (iv) doing what needs to be done, and (v) the motivation, leadership, persistence and endurance to get where you want to be.

Peter Drucker

What you have to do and the way you have to do it is incredibly simple.
Whether you are willing to do it, that's another matter.

Peter F. Drucker (1909 –2005) - management consultant, educator, and author

---

Jim Rohn

If you really want (to do) something, you will find a way.

If you don't, you will find an excuse.

E.J. Rohn (1930 –2009) was an American entrepreneur, author and motivational speaker

---

Peter Drucker

The best way to predict the future is to create it

Peter Drucker (1909 – 2005) – management consultant, educator and author

---

The future is only 17 steps away

Take one step, then the next and so on.

Or 3 jumps: Plan – Train – Do

It requires MOTIVATION and LEADERSHIP to do it

2.1   PLATFORM MODEL – plan & train & do towards success

A simple model to reflect the basic elements of an improvement or change process. I kept it simple because:

1. Communication value
2. Change is based on few simple issues

I also kept it simple because I think that most people – possibly all – would agree that the 4 to 6 basic ingredients presented are fundamental to any improvement and success directed process, no matter what purpose and objective.

The principle emotional ownership (1)

People tend to be more willing to participate in planned change when they have an opportunity to participate and influence the process leading to change.

The six basic improvement ingredients of the platform model are:

- The objective of the plan or management system – where you want to go
- Leadership and motivation – the will to get there
- Making the PLAN - know what to do to get there
- TRAIN/instruct people – knowledge and resources to do what needs to be done
- DO what is in the plan – do it, do it and keep on doing on the way to success
- The performance level – where you are on your way to success

Six ingredients of which four are truly essential: Leadership – Plan – Train - Do.

Do you wonder: Where are the Deming's Check and Act? They are there but I made them an integral part of what is being done (DO) and they are also part of the structure that I suggest for all elements of your plan or management system. Doing something without checking that it is being done and that results are being obtained does not make much sense, does it? So that is why doing includes those activities. Making a plan without having an objective does not made sense either. That is why I say six aspects of which four essential.

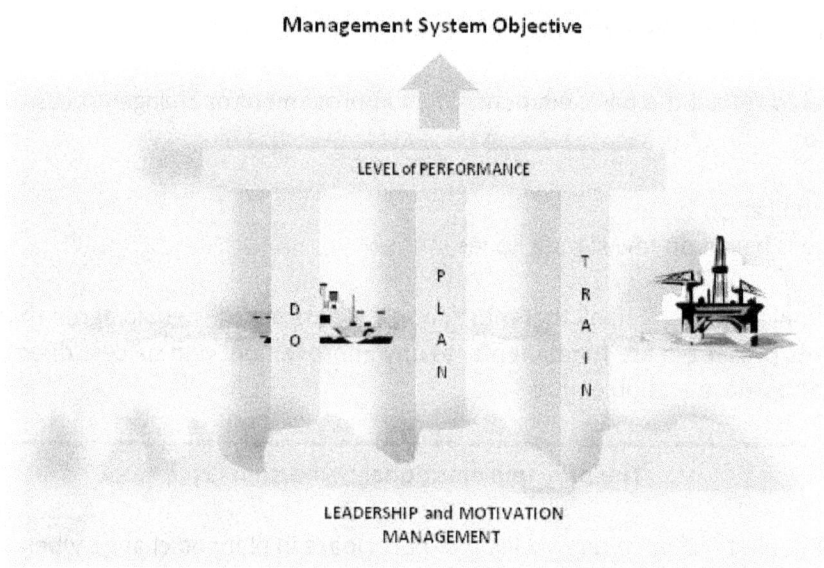

Picture 2.02 – Front view of the business platform model

These ingredients to bring success (in risk management/safety/loss control/quality etc.), can be visualized as a platform in which the temporary performance level rests on the three columns: Plan-Train-Do. Three columns carrying the level of performance to the desired objective while standing of the bedrock of "Leadership and Motivation" – four essentials.

Picture 2.03 – Platform model seen from above

The platform model forms the basis of the 17-step process for developing the management system – the plan - implementing, maintaining and improving it.

Balanced approach

The performance level rest on three columns: Plan, Train and Do. These columns need to be in balance with each other. If not, you can figure out what will happen to the performance level supported by these columns. It does not make sense to have a plan and asking people to carry out the work without making sure that people have the knowledge and resources to do it. Likewise training people how to do certain things and not asking them to do it, possibly because the plan does not ask that, does not make much sense either and may only work the wrong way. "Do" needs to follow "Train" needs to follow "Plan". And that needs to be monitored, evaluated and repeated to get the success that is wanted!

In my experience, training is often thought to be THE solution to (work related) problems and it is, but only after establishing what needs to be done, why, by whom, when, where and how. Training is not a magic wand or a "cure all". Training people and then sending them back into the organization where the knowledge gained is not to be put into practice has a counterproductive effect and may lead to demotivation. When done that way it is two steps back while it should have been one step forward.

Just a little sidestep here. Mentioning training as being considered the solution to work related problems reminds me to another case but this time related to "communication". This concerned a power station in The Netherlands that tried to improve (safety related) communication by running courses on transactional analysis (then costing about Fl. 90 000 – this was during the eighties of last century). However, this company only scored 9% in the ISRS element "Leadership and Administration" in a very limited audit exercise – one element only. Nine percent! Even without knowing any detail about ISRS you will understand that this was a very minimal score in a very important element related to the foundation of the platform model. I never was invited to do a proper ISRS audit there which would have cost about 15% of the amount spent to the transactional analysis training. But it would have been much more effective as it would have revealed what was missing to allow the communication that the company was looking for. It certainly helps communication when you know what to communicate about!

The platform model looks somewhat like the Deming circle. I developed the model during the eighties of last century when working as a safety management consultant. The first time I published about the model was in my book "Risk Management/Loss Control" that I wrote in 1989 and which was published in Dutch by Kluwer Bedrijfswetenschappen in The Netherlands. The platform model has the advantage that it shows two main items that I consider vital for success:

- Training/instruction of people to do the necessary work, to execute and improve the plan activities – making sure that people have the knowledge to do what needs to be done.
- Leadership and motivation providing the foundation on which the whole platform structure and the improvement process is based – making sure that necessary resources are there to reach objectives and success

---

The principle of emotional ownership (1)

People tend to be more willing to participate in planned change when they have (had) an opportunity to participate and influence the process leading to change

---

The Principle Emotional Ownership (2)

The more ownership people have in the way a present situation has developed, the more difficult it is to change

---

Performance level, supported by Plan - Train - Do

The platform model is a good starting point to raise the performance level – no matter what objectives - of your organization. The model contains the few critical items that should be included in your efforts when making your future, in business or otherwise.

Performance Measurement

Being able to quantify and measure performance is important as you want to know where you are and where you want to be.

What gets measured gets done

You have probably seen or heard the above expression. While this may be true, it also may not be right.

I like to think: "What gets measured gets the attention". If you measure the wrong things, the attention may go the wrong way.

```
┌─────────────────────────────────────────────────────────┐
│                What gets measured gets:                  │
│                                                           │
│                        Done?                              │
│                        Valued?                            │
│                        Managed?                           │
│                        Attention!                         │
└─────────────────────────────────────────────────────────┘
```

An example is the way that safety is traditionally measured: in terms of accident frequency rates. But look closer, it is in reported lost time injury rates. Remember the accident triangle (page 82) and you may conclude that the usual safety measurement is based only on the top of the triangle, on only a limited number of the unwanted events that occur. In fact, depending on where you are this measurement may not even include personal injuries with less than 3 workdays away from work. Because of this measurement, the attention goes to reported injuries that resulted in lost time and the focus of that may very well go to the person involved in the accident, most likely the victim. This is possibly why traditional accident investigation did not go much further than the direct cause: substandard act and "person did not follow rules". This could also be a reason why behavior based safety often concentrates on behavior observation related to operational work while the causes of that behavior may have to be found further upstream in the cause–consequence model, further to the left. Substandard behavior is an unwanted event and should be treated as such. Measuring safety in terms of lost time accidents does not tell much or anything about the safety performance (input) level, the efforts to prevent unwanted events including substandard behavior. It is an after the fact, end of pipe, (output) measurement that relates only to a small part of the unwanted events that occur.

In line with the above: people will not fall from the roof because they do not wear fall protection and if you reward them for not having an accident indicating: "you did a good job so I give you this as a token of my appreciation", you may actually stimulate unsafe (= substandard) behavior (not wearing fall protection).

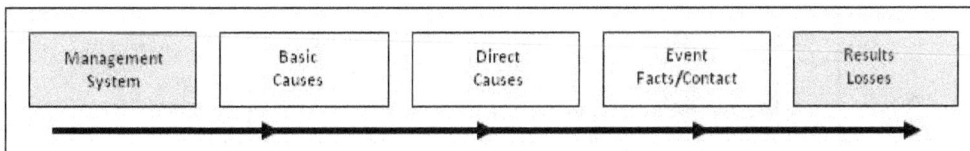

To properly manage the control of risks or unwanted events you should be measuring input as well as output. If you do this wisely, you can get input (= management system activity) balanced with results, preventing a "management overkill".

Measuring performance criteria may not always be possible in an absolute, objective, way. However, measuring in subjective terms may come close to "objective" if the criteria are agreed upon by many people having knowledge about the subject. The rating system which I made in relation to the 17-step process (chapter 2.7, page 180 is an example providing a subjective numeric value (score). I have to add that this was done only by me so still far from being "objective".

Below I mention some indicators allowing performance level measurement concerning risk control, health, safety and environment. I have not tried to be explicit and I am sure that you will be able to come up with a number of other indicators that are not on my list.

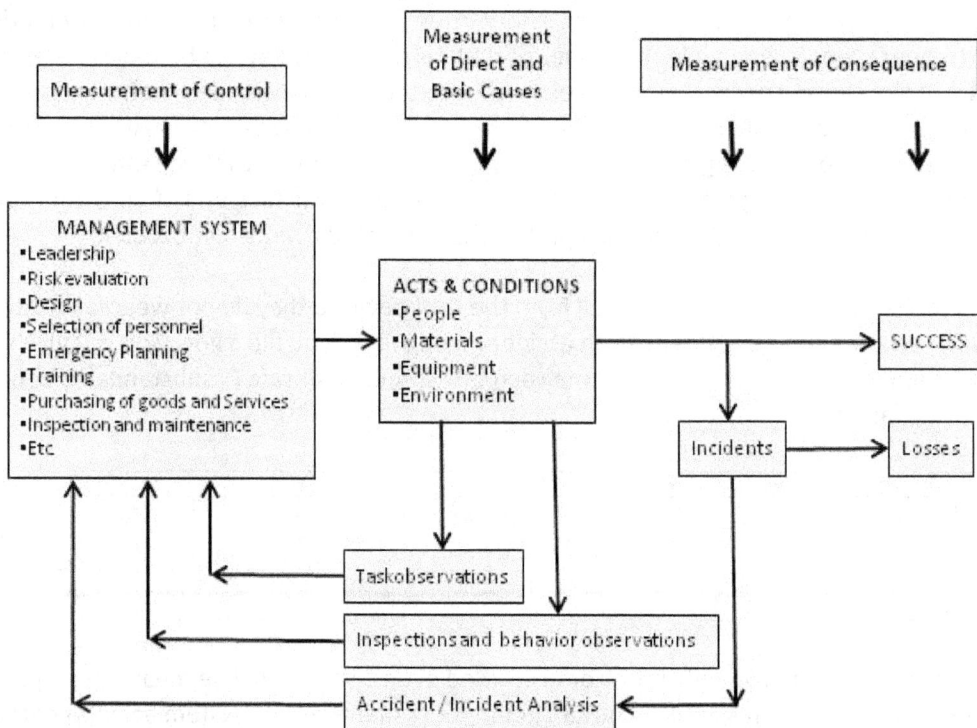

Picture 2.04 – Opportunities to measure efforts and results

I have tried to arrange these indicators in three categories:

- Measurement of control (input)
- Measurement of direct and basic causes
- Measurement of consequences (output)

Measurement of Control such as:

- Management system audits
- Employee opinion survey results
- Risk classification results (potential for losses)

Measurement of direct and basic causes such as:

- Inspection reports – number of substandard conditions and the (actual/potential) size of consequences if left untreated
- Behavior observation reports - number of substandard acts/behavior and (actual/potential) size of consequences if left untreated

Measurement of (actual/potential) consequences such as:

- Various injury rates (frequency/severity)
- Material damage rates
- Maintenance reports (abnormal/normal)
- Insurance claims
- Absenteeism rates
- Customer complaints
- Environmental incident rates

Lord Kelvin

When you cannot measure, your knowledge is meager and unsatisfactory

---

William Thomson, 1st Baron Kelvin (1824 – 1907) British mathematical physicist and engineer.

Performance measurement can and should be done at several places in the cause-consequence sequence, not only at the end. If you manage performance on end of pipe criteria alone, you may expect a very unpleasant surprise which could mean fatalities, catastrophe and termination of business. Besides that, managing your organization only, or mainly, based on end results seems to me like driving a car with the occasional look in the rear-view mirror; you know what is behind you but not what may be waiting for you ahead.

HWE MU DUA - the measuring stick, symbol of examination and quality control

---

Dr. H. James Harrington

Measurement is the first step that leads to control and eventually to improvement.

If you can't measure something, you can't understand it. If you can't understand it, you can't control it. If you can't control it, you can't improve it

---

H. J. Harrington (1929), American author, engineer, entrepreneur and consultant

2.1.1 Plan - the Management System towards success

Should you decide to go somewhere, you probably want to make a plan unless it does not matter where you end up. In that case it is not "going somewhere" but "going anywhere" and you may not need a plan for that; only maybe an "escape plan" if you end up where you don't want to be. But we will not consider this and assume that you want to go to where you want to be. For that you need a plan, a well-defined plan!

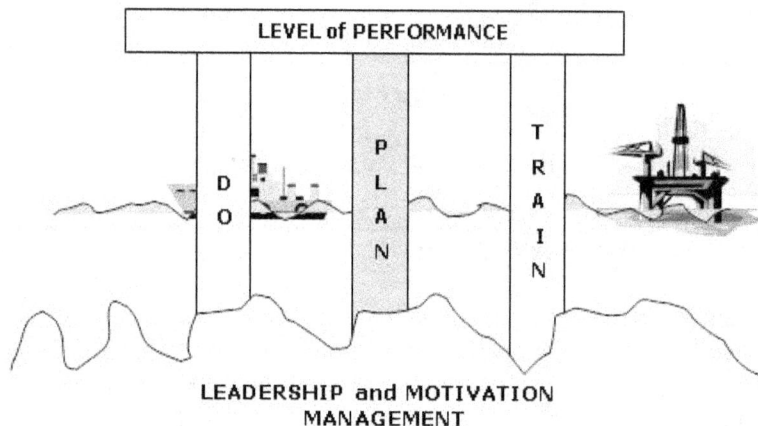

Picture 2.05 – Making your plan, the first step to your new future

When making the plan that will bring you to where you want to be, it may help to know where you are before you start. But more important, you must know where you want to go, even if you do not yet have the specific objective(s) in sight. A broad objective may be good enough at the start and may become more specific while you are on your way. A broad objective could be "to have less accidents" while a more specific objective later on may be not to have unwanted events over and above a certain (risk) level. Now, be aware, these are output, "end-of-pipe", objectives. While you want to measure those performance levels, you better should also have performance input levels. These would tie in with audit systems allowing scoring or "rating" of activities – see a safety related example in appendix H on page 298.

Making a plan in an organization where you are with other people needs the support an involvement of all people affected by the plan and its objectives. You need a process to make such a plan, a process that starts at the top of the organization and goes all the way down. The process that I developed for making, executing and improving a plan includes 17 steps.

For proper understanding of the next few pages, here are those 17 steps of the improvement process that will later be discussed in more detail:

1. Top manager leadership – top manager leading the improvement process
2. Management team leadership – senior management team leadership for process
3. Management improvement team – coordination of process by management team
4. Internal expertise - expertise available to guide the process
5. Project communicated - communication of process to all concerned
6. Opinion surveys – finding out what people think and feel about process objective
7. Base-line assessment – assessing present activities related to process objective
8. Selection of elements/activity areas - selection of critical elements for success
9. Introduction training – information to all levels and all people
10. Element coordination – teams to develop and coordinate elements and their activities
11. Element coordination team training – training/instruction of element team members
12. Element development – making of the plan or management system
13. Element implementation training – providing people with skills and knowledge to carry out plan activities
14. Management briefing – coaching, guidance and support provided by managers and supervisors
15. Carry out element activities – execution of element activities and periodic assessment of activity implementation and their results
16. Review by the management improvement team – elements and overall management system results including action plans as needed for further improvement
17. Extend project, repeat process – to reach element and system objectives, maintain and improve the level of performance

When discussing plans, it is not uncommon to consider two types of plans:

- Standing plans
- Single-use plans

While these plans may be considered somewhat different, they are also very much alike and the same principles apply to both. I also think that the platform principles and all, or most, other principles and tools contained in this book - including the 17-step process - apply to business as well as to our private lives. To any plan you may have and any situation in which you want to move away from where you are to another future.

Standing Plan

These are plans that will be there for a long time, if not "forever". Most likely, they will be there for the duration of an undertaking or company.

Standing plans will be adapted over time depending on results obtained and following changes in the industrial/technical, social and political environment. Standing plans will normally affect a whole organization or a major part of it.

A standing plan often includes "programs", policies and procedures to ensure that the internal operations of a given business are running smoothly. Examples of standing plans include policies for employee interaction, procedures for reporting internal issues in the company and regulations in terms of what is allowable and what is prohibited in the business. Safety, quality, HACCP and other management systems are well-known standing plans.

Budget and objectives of a standing plan may not always be well defined as it is often difficult to draw a line between a specific standing plan and other areas of business. Targets and budgets may be adjusted from year to year depending on the results of the standing plan and its elements while the plan is becoming part of "the way we do things around here" and part of the culture.

> **Standing Plan = Management System**

Within the context of this book, I consider the standing plan the same as the management system that will bring a company from A to B and beyond, from today's situation to a better tomorrow. If you want, you could also see the management system as a set of standing (sub-) plans or "work processes" which I call "management activity areas" or "elements", to include areas such as:

- Inspections
- Risk assessment

- Purchasing
- Design
- Accident investigation
- Emergency preparedness
- Training

When discussing issues in this book, I may use the term "management system" as well as "standing plan" both referring to a combination of management activity areas to reach a certain objective.

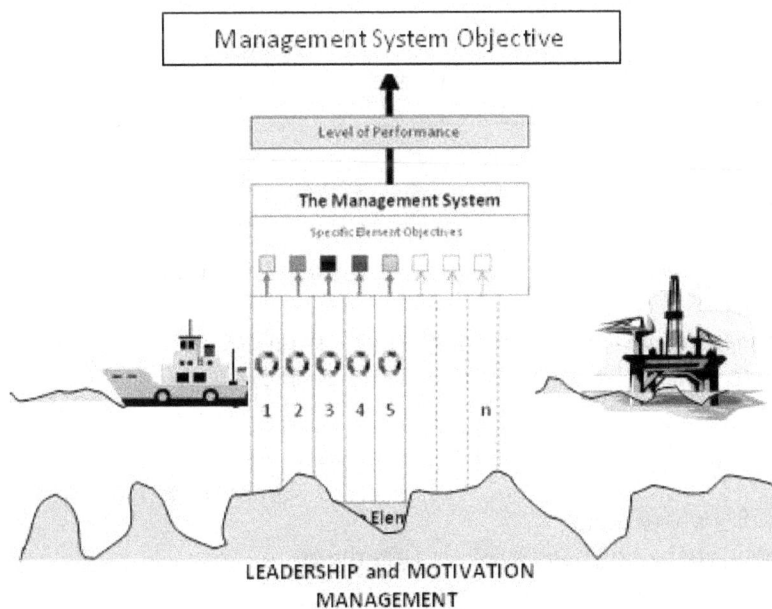

Picture 2.06 – Combination of platform model and management system

Single Use Plan

These are plans including an identified set of specific activities directed at coping with a specific issue, solving a particular problem or reaching a well defined goal or target within a pre-determined (limited) time period.

These plans, which may also be labeled "projects", have a start date and an end date and well-defined objectives and budget.

Single-use plans are essentially one-time and may run from a few days to several months or even years. Although individually these plans may be one-time only, their structure would normally be rather a generic. In principle, that structure will be very similar to the structure that I suggest for management system elements. That structure will be discussed further in chapter 2.6, page 163.

Single-use plans may only affect a small group of people or a department but in some cases may also include an entire organization or department.

Single-use plans, intended to provide solutions to identified problems or reach certain objectives, may produce issues that should be considered for insertion into the management system or its elements. To maintain performance at a desired level or prevent re-occurrence of the same or similar problems in the future. This way, projects feed and improve the management system.

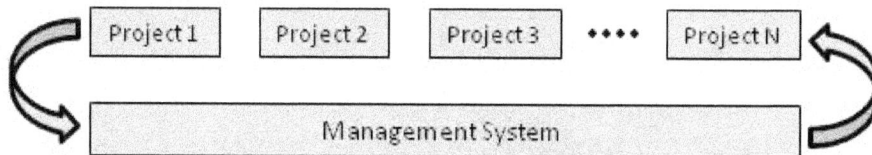

Picture 2.07 – From project to management system and vice versa

While single-use plans may add to the management system, the management system may also generate single-use plans or "projects" to cope with specific issues.

Any PLAN should include:

1. OBJECTIVE – where to go
2. WHAT needs to be done and WHY – to get there
3. WHEN the work needs to be done
4. WHO shall do it
5. HOW the work needs to be done
6. TRAINING of the people who will do the work
7. Periodic ASSESSMENT of work done and results obtained
8. REVIEW and IMPROVEMENT

In other parts of life

In other parts of life your plan would normally be a "single-use" plan as your plan would probably not be there for the rest of your life. Your single-use plan could be there for several weeks or months but also for several years and longer. It does not really matter - standing plans and single-use plans are basically the same; the main difference is the time factor.

2.1.2 Train - for motivation, knowledge and skills

In this section I consider: (i) the training prior to the development of the plan and (ii) training prior to implementation of the plan activities.

Training/instruction prior to plan development:

This training/instruction/communication involves the more general (introductory) information that comes prior to the development of the plan including such groups as:

- Top management (steps 1 and 2 of the 17-step process)
- Management improvement team members (step 3)
- In-house expertise (step 4)
- Senior and middle level managers, supervisors, staff and operational personnel (step 9)
- Members of element coordination teams (step 11)

The above mentioned training is very important to the improvement process; to provide the necessary motivation, put noses into the same direction and to communicate leadership.

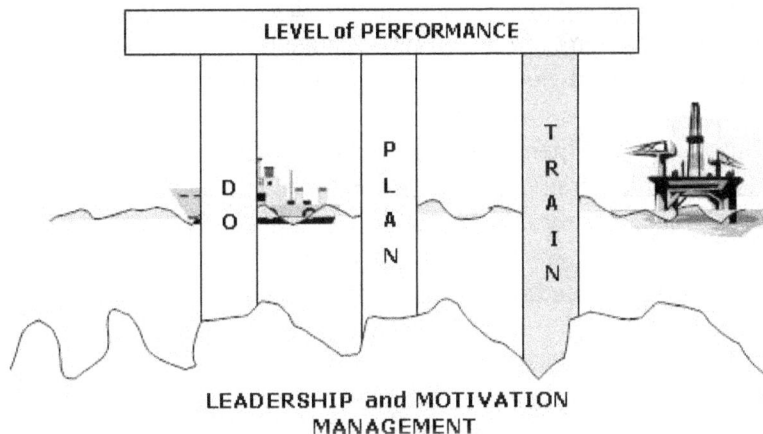

Picture 2.08 – After the plan, train people to do what is in the plan

Training/instruction prior to execution of plan activities:

This is the training provided in steps 13 and 14 of the process following plan development in step 12. This is the training in relation to the execution of the plan, more particularly in relation to the execution of the element activities. This training precedes the last aspect of the platform model: DO. Step 15 of the 17-step process.

The plan or management system - indicating what needs to be done, why, when by whom and how - provides the basis for training of people including:

- Training of people who need to know the HOW of the work involved when implementing element activities (step 13, "Implementation training", of the 17-step process). For example: how to investigate incidents; how to carry out inspections; how to deal with customer complaints; how to use the management of change procedure; how to design products, work environment, installations, work procedures; how to select personnel and train them, etc. This training depends on the subject of the management activity area or element of the management system. This training will vary per element and may range from minimal or extensive depending on the knowledge/skill levels of people involved. Training should be based on the "how to" procedures or guidelines related to the element specific activities. Depending on their complexity, these "how to" documents should be referenced in the management system elements – as part of the system manual - and further detailed in separate documents.
- Training of people who need to manage, supervise, coach and guide the activities to be done by others. This training includes the critical aspects of activities that a supervisor or manager needs to know to evaluate and stimulate the activities that are to be carried out in his/her unit or department (step 14, "Management briefing", of the 17-step process).
- Training of people who need to periodically evaluate the management system activities carried out in order to establish whether these activities are done as planned and desired results - per element - are being obtained (step 15, "Do", of the 17-step process). This training is best combined with the implementation training mentioned above.

The latter two training activities mentioned above should preferably be provided prior to implementation (step 15). This training could be combined and an extension of the instruction of element coordination team members in step 11.

The training mentioned above needs to consider the reason for change, element objectives, the activities to be carried out, tools/forms to be used etc.

2.1.3 DO - execute the plan towards results

The ultimate purpose of the plan is to implement, carry out, execute, or DO, the activities that are described in the plan or management system elements, after proper training has been provided to all concerned:

- Those who have to do the work and who have to know the why, what when and how
- Those who have to guide, supervise, coach and stimulate the work to be done
- Those who have to periodically evaluate that the work is done and what the results are

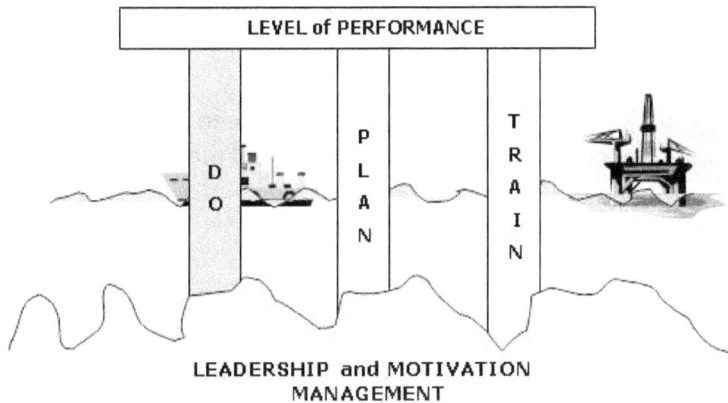

LEVEL of PERFORMANCE

LEADERSHIP and MOTIVATION
MANAGEMENT

Picture 2.09 – Do follows train follows plan

DO contains the execution of PLAN activities including periodic assessment of what is being done and of results being obtained; in line with the Deming Check and Act steps:

1. Periodic assessment of the work done (CHECK)

    This assessment could be done by people within the unit or department where the activities should be carried out or by people from other departments, staff personnel and even by external people.

    This assessment should include all activities contained in the management system elements.

    Preferably people should be allowed to evaluate their own activities as part of self-management and employee empowerment. Where needed this evaluation can or should be supplemented by others more distant from the actual work and with less vested interest. Self-management is part of empowerment and made possible through a management system providing activity details in line with personnel qualifications.

The principle of self-regulation
Self-regulation is usually the most effective way of management.

    The above principle is in line with the "point of control" principle: the greatest potential for control is where the action takes place."

    Don't get me wrong here. Self-regulation is not a free ticket. It has to take place within a well-defined management system, the detail of which will depend on the margins for acceptable performance in relation with the skill and responsibility level of the people concerned.

This assessment is about what and how work has been done in comparison with what and how it should have been done. Remember the "management gap".

2.   Periodic evaluation of results obtained (CHECK)

In principle the same as mentioned under the point 1 above. Now the objective is to evaluate what results have been obtained from the activities carried out in comparison with the targets/objectives set for each individual management system element

Following the periodic assessment and depending on the results thereof action plans may need to be developed.

If the work is not carried out as intended by the plan:

3.   Find out why not and take action to correct deviations between how the work is described in the element and how it is actually being carried out (ACT).

If work is done properly but element results are less than expected:

4.   Improve and/or add activities to existing management system elements if the objectives of the elements have not been obtained (ACT)

If element objectives are obtained but the overall system objectives are not:

5.   Add elements to the management system and/or alter or augment the objectives of existing elements as applicable (ACT)

The periodic assessments/evaluations (points 1 and 2 above) are part of the structure that I recommend for each of the elements of the management system.

"DO" is step 15 of the 17-step process and includes points 1 – 3 above while step 16 of that process includes the reviews considering points 4 and 5 above.

The process to reach objectives is visualized in the picture below where I used my Topves logo combining of the platform model (Plan – Train – Do) with the continuing improvement cycle that is provided by the element structure detailed in chapter 2.6 on page 163. Purpose of the process represented by my logo is to upgrade the level of performance towards the desired objective. That objective may change over time in line with the idea of continuous improvement in a world that will never be the same.

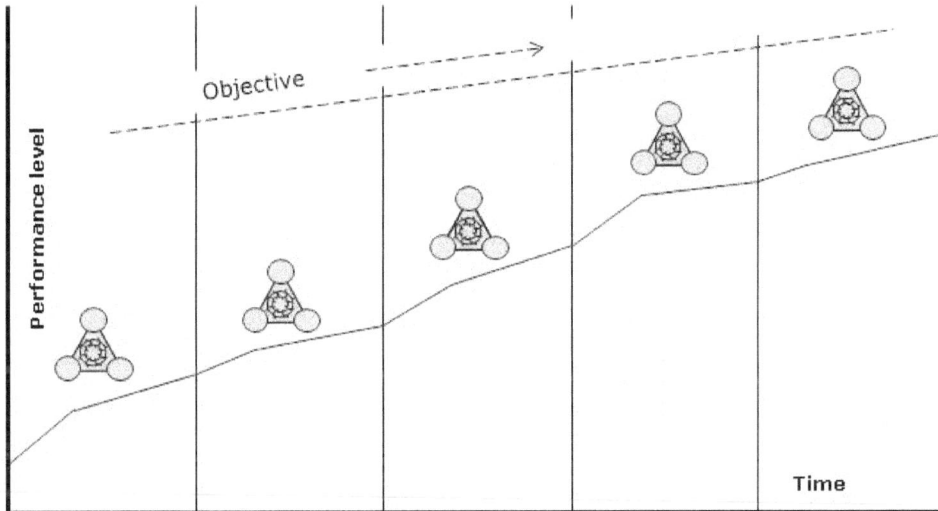

Picture 2.10 – Repeating platform model essentials towards success

2.1.4   LEADERSHIP and MOTIVATION - foundation for success

Leadership and motivation go hand in hand. Leadership will be provided if the proper level of motivation is there.

The principle of economic priorities

A manager will usually give priority response to items possessing the potential for the greatest proportion of results from the least investment of available resources

---

You cannot lead if you are not motivated to lead. Of course, you also have to know how to put leadership into action; it is more than having charisma or standing on a toolbox or addressing the shareholders meeting. You will have to know the process to incorporate leadership into the organization, at all levels.

In principle, this motivation to lead needs to be first at the top of the organization to assure leadership at that level. To get the proper leadership at lower levels, motivation to lead also needs to be established there, even though some of the motivation may come from "because the boss wants it". Nothing wrong with that, by the way, as long as the proper arguments are being used and desired results are being obtained.

Motivation to provide leadership normally will come from various directions: from within yourselves, from your friends and family members; from within your organization - bosses, peers, colleagues, your (management) profession; from external parties such as the neighborhood, clients, legislation, pressure groups, etc.

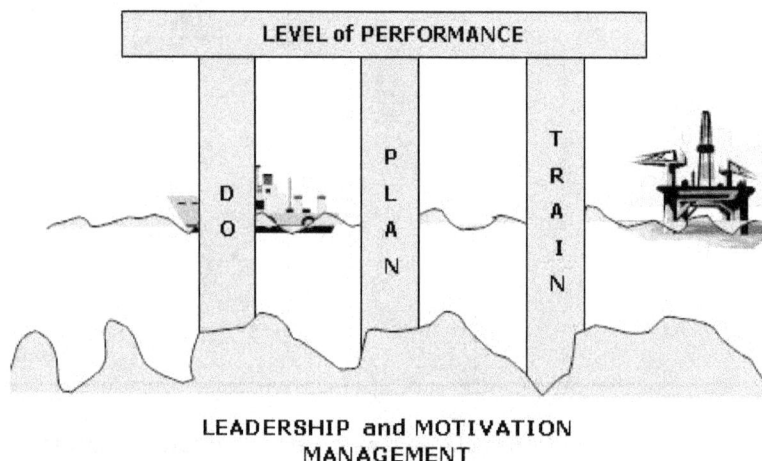

LEADERSHIP and MOTIVATION
MANAGEMENT

Picture 2.11 – Leadership, the foundation on which to build success

Leadership – what is that?

Some "definitions" found on the Internet:

- Peter Drucker: "The only definition of a leader is someone who has followers"
- Warren Bennis: "Leadership is the capacity to translate vision into reality"
- Bill Gates: "As we look ahead into the next century, leaders will be those who empower others"
- John Maxwell: "Leadership is influence – nothing more, nothing less"
- Kevin Kruse: "Leadership is a process of social influence which maximizes the efforts of others, towards the achievement of a goal"

Go to page 28 and read again what Mr. Kets de Vries said about good leaders: "(Good) leaders almost always have the four H's: hope, humility, humanity and humor. They are able to give people hope of improvement, and to this end turn to humility, humanity and humor."

I took the liberty to add one word to that: "care"; care for stakeholders and first on the stakeholders list should be care for the people of the organization or company. People that will produce the success of the company or organization; people with care for the product or service and care for customers that ultimately determine the success of the company. By the way, "care" is not a one-way street in my world; it has to be from the top down and from the bottom up! Leadership includes the obligation to care. Also look at pages 16 to 20 where I also referred to this leadership issue.

As I said earlier, leadership does not necessary mean climbing on a crate or tool box to provide a pep-talk. That may happen from time to time but what I really mean is the leadership that provides direction based on setting objectives in combination with well-founded plan or "management system" to reach those objectives.

Leadership is putting vision into reality, directing the organization and leading people towards desired goals/objectives. Leadership is setting objectives and reaching those together with those who will do the work; a leader cannot do it alone!

What is more important than having a good definition of "leadership" is knowing the process to involve others to reach objectives and make the future. That, I think, is the essence of good leadership and the 17-step process will help to put leadership into practice and into action. At least, I think so and I hope that it will help you to go where you want to be, where your company wants to be, or your client in case you are a consultant.

Leadership needs:

- An objective – to be shared by all
- A process - involving all - to make the plan or management system answering the question: "What do we have to do to reach objectives?"

The principle of leadership force

The greater the divergence of the individual objectives of the members of the group, the greater the leadership force required to ensure cohesive action.

Louis A. Allen, management consultant and writer. Founder of Louis Allen Worldwide

The above principle implies that, when starting with the improvement process, you should preferably include those elements in the first action plan that will produce visible results on a short time and effecting as few people as possible. Early success may help to reduce any resistance to change that may be present.

Mind you, I am a chemical and industrial engineer by education; I am not an expert on motivation but, like we all do, I got some experience by getting older and keeping at least somewhat in touch with the environment in which I am living. So, don't expect all the right answers here, just some points that you may want to consider when looking to get the proper motivation for leadership in action. Of course, there are plenty of books on motivation, written by greater spirits than I.

Some points that may motivate management people to accept their leadership role:

1. Personal attitude - how the manager as a person feels and wants to be seen in relation to taking care of "his/her" organization/department/people
2. Management profession - how the manager wants to be compared with colleagues, the management profession
3. Expectations/requirements of stakeholders including authorities, customers, neighbors, employees and shareholders - what others demand or expect
4. Company profile/image - how the company wants to be recognized in the world and their market
5. Actual loss level - what is being lost in comparison to business results, human suffering
6. Potential loss or risk level - what can go wrong: direct damage, business losses, human suffering

---

The principle of economic association

A manager will usually pay more attention to statistical or general information when expressed or associated with cost terminology

---

I like to think that people who are leaders come with a high degree of self-motivation which will be rewarded by the results that "their" organization and "their" people are able to get. And by the motivation they manage to install within others in their organization, unit or department. The 17-step process to build a management system can contribute to this. I say CAN contribute on purpose - the 17-step process is a tool and the outcome will depend on the input all involved.

The principle of self motivation

Self-motivation is the strongest type of motivation.

Self-motivation is a state of mind to achieve goals and dreams, able to produce a driving force to promote them and maintain a positive mental outlook. Self motivation includes regularly taking a step back to look at what you have done, and how, to reach objectives. Step back and use that for opportunities to do different and better.

Top management leadership also becomes clear through the periodic review of elements and the total management system results (step 16 of the 17-step process) and the resulting plans for further improvement. These reviews should be based in internal assessments (part of step 15) and consider external changes - technical, political and social - which may require adaptation of the management system.

Peter Drucker (1909 – 2005) – management consultant, educator and author

Depending on the management improvement team review in step 16, step 17 may include adding new elements and activities as well as repeating existing activities to reach and maintain the success that you are looking for. Step 17 may include most or all points of the 17-step process (in case of adding new elements) or a selection of those (when repeating and adding existing elements activities).

Some Louis A. Allen principles on motivation:

- The principle of meaningful goals: Motivation to accomplish results tends to increase when people have meaningful goals toward which to work.
- The principle of delegated authority: Motivation to accomplish results tends to increase as people are given authority to make decisions affecting those results.
- The principle of reciprocated interest: People tend to be motivated to accomplish results you want, to the extent you show interest in the results they want to achieve.
- Principle of communication: Motivation to accomplish results tends to increase as people are informed about matters affecting those results.
- The principle of recognition: Motivation to accomplish results tends to increase as people are given recognition for their contribution to those results.

2.1.5   17-Steps to make your plan – a bird's eye view

The Platform model with its four essentials (Leadership – Plan – Train and Do) forms the basis for process consisting of 17 steps.

If you are a consultant, the 17-step process could form the basis on which to make the agreement with your client, provided your client wants to use your services to really improve his or her organization. It does not matter whether you are an internal consultant or external. And it does not matter whether it concerns safety or quality or environmental issues or a combination of those into a more integrated approach.

> I am not talking here about certification which may not mean real improvement. In fact, certification may give a false feeling and impression of being good or better; to the company getting the certificate as well as to those who use the certificate in their decision making process. In principle, I consider certification more a barrier to improvement than a contribution.

But even if your client or manager does not want to go "all the way", knowledge of the 17-step process may help. You may, for example, suggest to first carry out an assessment of the situation (steps 6 or 7 or both) or have a management session including the use of the maturity profile that is shown in appendix B, on page 224 - to start a discussion and get opinions of the people who can influence change.

Change and the process of 17 steps

The 17-step process is all about change so notice the four management principles below.

- The principle of resistance to change: The greater the departure of any planned change from the accepted ways of the past, the greater the potential resistance by the people involved
- The principle of emotional ownership (2): The more ownership people have in the way a present situation has developed, the more difficult it is to change.
- The principle of participation: Motivation to accomplish results tends to increase as people are given opportunity to participate in matters affecting those results.
- The principle of emotional ownership (1): People tend to be more willing to participate in planned change when they have an opportunity to participate and influence the process leading to change.

Below is a brief description of the process that I developed when consulting clients on their way to success. During the eighties of last century I realized that my clients had to make their own success while my role was to help them to go through the process they had to follow. First the process consisted of 11 steps, then 13 and in 1994 the process had grown to 16 steps. More recently I added Step 17.

While the client has to do it, the consultant has to be able to let the client know which steps to take and, preferably, they both should agree to follow the 17-step guide - or similar - as the basis of their cooperation. That way the process becomes the "working agreement" between the organization and the consultant.

Application of the 17-step process allows you to further improve your services as a consultant based on client success. When doing this again and again, you are building your success database and will be able to tell new clients of the success that others had with your help. How much better do you want your marketing references to be?

Please note that the 17-step process is a guide. When using this with individual customers you may need to combine some steps, leave one or two out or add some and may choose to follow a slightly different sequence. Make the 17-step process your own process but be careful not to leave out what is essential.

The 17-step process is explained in further detail in the chapter 2.4 (page 143), in chapter 2.7 (page 180) and in appendix F (page 267).

The 17-step process is visualized in the diagram below where I have tried to put each step into one or more of the categories that we have also seen in the Platform model: Leadership - Plan - Train - Do.

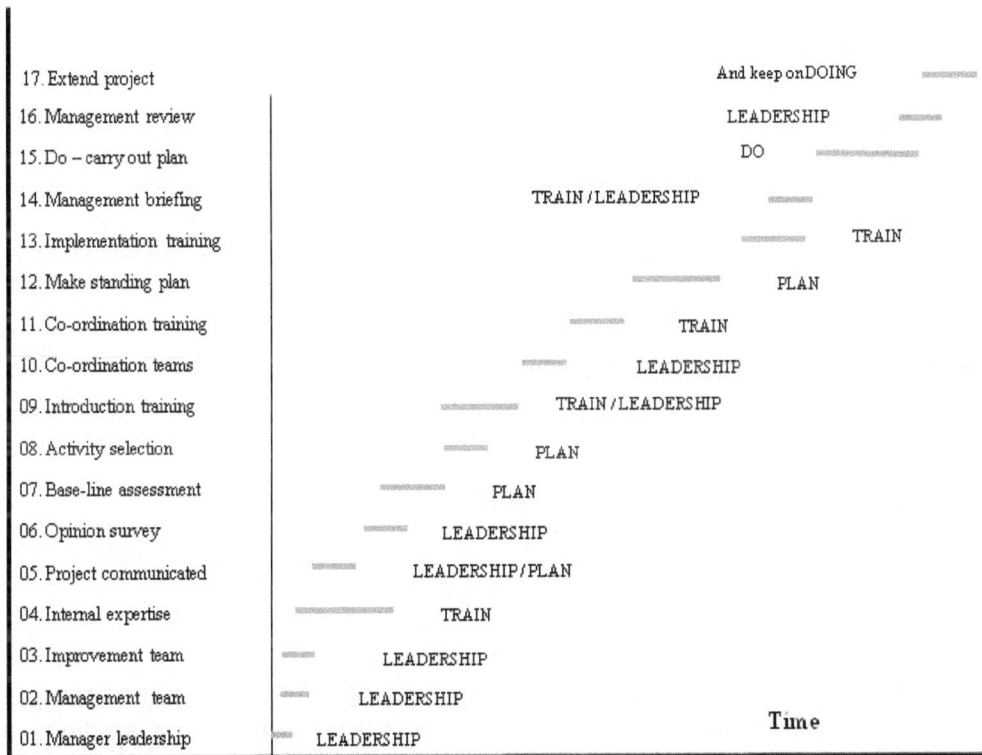

17. Extend project	And keep on DOING
16. Management review	LEADERSHIP
15. Do – carry out plan	DO
14. Management briefing	TRAIN / LEADERSHIP
13. Implementation training	TRAIN
12. Make standing plan	PLAN
11. Co-ordination training	TRAIN
10. Co-ordination teams	LEADERSHIP
09. Introduction training	TRAIN / LEADERSHIP
08. Activity selection	PLAN
07. Base-line assessment	PLAN
06. Opinion survey	LEADERSHIP
05. Project communicated	LEADERSHIP / PLAN
04. Internal expertise	TRAIN
03. Improvement team	LEADERSHIP
02. Management team	LEADERSHIP
01. Manager leadership	LEADERSHIP

Time

Picture 2.12 - Combining leadership and management in one improvement process

17 Steps of the process – overview

The process starts at the top of the organization and goes down while providing information and training and obtaining the cooperation of people at all levels to develop, implement and improve the management system.

1.   *Top Manager Leadership*

Leadership by the highest senior manager of the company, unit or department providing support, resources and ongoing attention to assure that objectives will be obtained as intended.

2.   *Management Team Leadership*

Information/training of higher management to put noses into the same direction and to obtain the leadership, cooperation and endorsement at the highest management level. Include worker representation as appropriate.

3.   *Management Improvement Team*

High level management team plus relevant staff and worker representation. This team will have the overall responsibility to see that the management system is properly developed, implemented and improved.

4.   *Internal Expertise*

Expertise available depending on the objective of the management system and its elements. To include adequate knowledge concerning process, content and structure of the management system to be developed. This expertise may include external assistance as needed.

5.   *Project Communicated*

Communication of the improvement project to include reasons why, the objectives to be obtained and the process how to do that. Include process steps on a time-path. In principle, this communication should be in writing and to all in the organization. The "risk" here is that people can, and will, hold you accountable and judge you on what you are actually doing. At the same time, such communication is leadership in action – stand up and be counted! Be sure to live up to your promise.

6.   *Opinion Surveys*

Opinion surveys at all levels to obtain a good impression about how the management system subject is being viewed and experienced by people throughout the organization. Include higher and middle management, supervision and operational personnel. See example of a (safety related) opinion survey for the higher management level in appendix C on page 228.

7.   *Base-line Assessment*

Use of a good reference (audit system), commercially available or otherwise, to obtain a zero-base impression of the present activity level. This assessment may serve as a basis for the plan to be developed and help to determine the possible gap between "what is" and "what should be".

8.   *Selection of Elements/Activity Areas*

The selection of the first subjects (activity areas or "elements") to be part of the plan or management system. Selection to be based on need, resources and anticipated (visual) results to be obtained within a limited time period.

9.   *Introduction Training*

Providing information to all relevant managerial, staff and operational personnel to convey the philosophy, concepts and models on which the management system and its development shall be based. To include concepts related to process, content and structure of the system. This communication should preferably include the results of steps 6, 7 and 8.

10.   *Element Coordination Teams*

Setting up coordination for element development, implementation and improvement. Persons included should preferably be representatives of relevant levels in the organization, managerial as well as operational and be knowledgeable about the element subject. Element coordination (teams) should provide the "what, by whom, when and how" of the specific activities in order to reach the element objective(s).

11.   *Element Coordination Team Training*

Training/instruction of people selected to develop, maintain and improve elements of the management system. This communication to include all aspects of the element, content as well structural aspects and of course: the role of element coordination.

12.   *Element Development – PLAN*

Include specific activities to be carried out for the selected elements (step 8); who shall do what, when and how. How to carry out activities should be described in documents including the tools, forms etc. to be used. Depending on the necessary detail, those documents should be separate from the management system core document, the system manual. Final approval of the element and its activities should be by the management improvement team (step 3).

13.   *Element Implementation Training - TRAIN*

Training of people who need to do the work to be carried out as indicated by the plan (step 12). Also include the training/instruction to carry out periodic assessments of work done and results thereof.

14. *Management Briefing*

Managers/supervisors throughout the organization need to know the critical issues concerning the work that needs to be done so they can stimulate, coach and guide the process and motivate the people who are doing the actual work. Just asking "How are things going?" will not do it; they have to be more specific.

15. *Carry out Element Activities - DO*

Carry out the activities according to plan (step 12) by knowledgeable people (step 13), coached and supported by managers/supervisors (step 14). During implementation of activities, periodic evaluation should take place of activities and of results achieved in comparison with objectives set.

16. *Review by the Management Improvement Team*

Review of element and overall management system results and, as necessary, set up properly resourced action plans for further expansion and improvement in step 17. Consider (external) developments – technical, social, political, environmental - requiring adaptation to the management system.

17. *Extend Project, Repeat process*

Alter or add element activities and/or add system elements following results and decision-making in steps 15 and 16.

The 17 steps in other parts of life

1. The leader. This is you, where do you want to go? Are you motivated? Do you really want to reach the objectives? Spent effort, time and other resources to get where you want to be?
2. Get support and endorsement of those that should be involved. Tell them what you want. Get them onboard. Do they share your desires? Are they motivated too? Do they see why?
3. The team: together on your way to where you all to be. Do they agree? Are they willing to give their support? Are they willing to make a serious effort? Ready to make a sacrifice?
4. Resources. Is knowledge available to help you? Does your team have the knowledge and resources to do what will get you where you want to be. Do you need help from outside?
5. Everyone on your team well informed and in agreement?
6. What do your team members think and feel about the present situation?
7. What are you doing now that has to do with where you want to go?
8. You may not be able to do all you need to do at the same time. What do you have to do first to get things moving? Early success is important for your motivation and that of your team.
9. Tell what is going to be and how. To put the noses into the same direction.
10. You and your team to make the plan in more detail, based on what you selected in step 8. Depending on the size of your team, divide tasks to involve everyone.
11. Does everyone know how to make the plan, what should be done and how, when and by whom?
12. Make the plan. Make a mind-map, start with the objective in the middle and surround that with "sub-plans" - each with their own activities and objective – necessary to get to the center, overall, objective. Fill the sub-plans with what needs to be done.
13. Make sure that your team members know what their tasks are. Can they do what they need to do? Do they know how and do they have the means to do it?
14. Do you and "sub-plan leaders" know how to coach and guide others? You and maybe one or two team members to help others to do their work and stay motivated.
15. Do what is in the plan. Is everyone doing what he or she is supposed to do? What are the results of what they are doing? Does that bring you closer to where you want to be?
16. Periodic assessment - discuss what has been done and the results of that. Are you getting closer to where you want to be? Do you need to do things differently? Need to do other things?
17. Adapt you plan, do different, do more, add as necessary. And keep on doing.

Since you may be with a small group – family or small business - it will probably be possible to combine steps. Basically any combination that you see fit, including this one:

- Steps 1 and 4
- Steps 2, 3, 5 and 9.
- Steps 6, 7 and 8
- Steps 10, 11, and 12
- Steps 13 and 14
- Steps 16 and 17

To obtain and continue the success of your management system you need more than a onetime action plan. The process needs to be repeated as appropriate while extending the management system in step 17 as needed. This continuing process is visualized in the picture below where I used my logo as a combination of the platform model and the structure I suggest for plan elements (chapter 2.6 on page 163) visualized as the wheel of improvement.

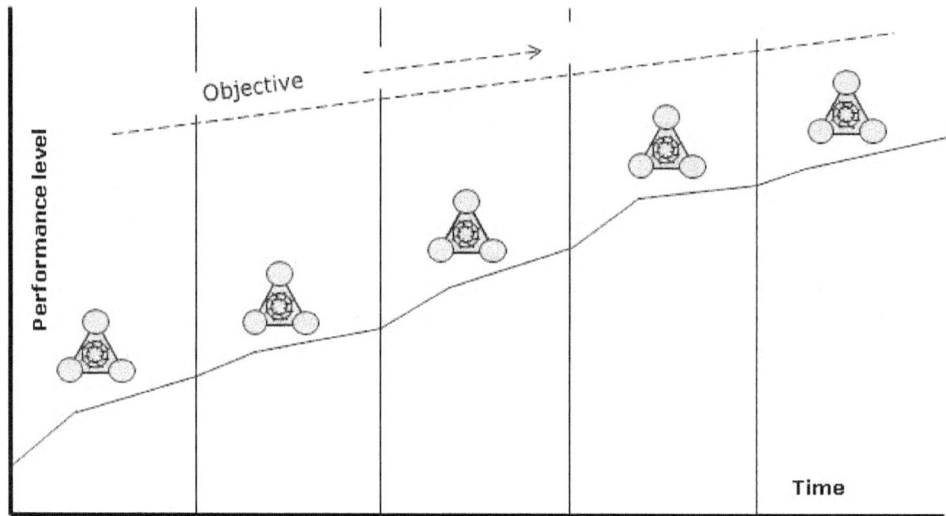

Picture 2.13 – Step for step, plan for plan, en route to your objective

In a way, the text in the box below sends the same message as the picture above. Improvement always builds on past experience. So with each plan you will make a better future and a better (future) past. Repeating that will make you better and better without reaching the ever moving objective as the world around us will never be as it was.

MAKING THE FUTURE – BUILD ON THE PAST

Build on the past to make a better future; repeatedly doing this will lead you to better pasts and to better futures further away.

Why wait?

The 17-step process is a guide to management success. Successful application requires leadership from the top down while channeling leadership action. The 17-step process will be further detailed in chapter 2.4 on page 143.

2.1.6   Rating the 17-step process

I transferred the 17-step process into a rating tool. Not a scientific instrument but an attempt to put a numbers on process and process steps for communication and to identify possible areas for improvement.

Lord Kelvin
Anything that exists, exists in a certain quantity and can be measured

William Thomson, 1st Baron Kelvin (1824 – 1907) British mathematical physicist and engineer.

If you are a consultant in communication with your management or client, it may help to put (relative) numbers on the process that should be theirs. Or, even better, let them put numbers on their own process with your help. For example as part of a management training session. The rating tool helps to put a number on the total process and each individual step to show potentially weak and strong areas.

The 17-step rating method is further explained in chapter 2.7 on page 180 and in appendix F on page 267.

2.2   IMPROVEMENT & MANAGEMENT SUCCESS

For success you need a plan containing what to do and how to reach your objective. Obtaining success depends on the success of your plan. True in private life and in business. In business we may call that plan the "management system". The success of a plan or management system depends largely on the following items:

1. The need to change felt by management and make a plan to reach objectives
2. The process along which the plan or management system will be developed
3. The contents of the management system in terms of activity areas or "elements", each with their own objective
4. The activities contained in the elements to reach specific element objectives
5. The structure of the elements – representing the "improvement loop"
6. The initial success when implementing the system
7. Keep on doing - persist in doing the right things the right way

The first item on the list above may be the most important one. It relates directly to "Leadership and Motivation", the foundation of the platform model.

> If you <u>really</u> want (to do) something, you will find a way.
>
> If you don't, you will find an excuse.

E.J. Rohn (1930 –2009) was an American entrepreneur, author and motivational speaker

And remember Peter Drucker: "The best way to predict the future is to create it."

In other parts of life

The success of your plan depends largely on the following items:

1. The need to make your future better than it is now – your objective, your motivation
2. Making your plan with all that should be involved - family, friends, colleagues
3. The main parts or elements of your plan – each with their own goal; your "mind map"
4. The activities to reach the goals of your plan elements
5. Regularly check the results of what you have done
6. The first successes of what you have been doing – "success breeds success"
7. Keep on doing – persist in doing what you need to do to arrive at where you want to be

---

In chapter 2.4 (page 143) I describe the 17-step process that I developed during my work as a (safety) management consultant. During that time, I worked with the ideas and tools that came from Frank E. Bird, Jr. one of the international (safety) management champions during the second half of last century. His concepts and ideas, including the ISRS (International Safety Rating System) live on today as you will find out searching the Internet for "Frank E. Bird, Jr." or "International Safety Rating System".

But, before describing the 17-step process in more detail, let us recap a little and put the Platform model and the 17-step process into perspective.

2.3.   IMPROVEMENT: CONCEPT AND PROCESS

The text below covers concept and process through which to obtain improvement. The principles are generic and can be applied to any improvement or change process,

2.3.1 The Concept

The concept is illustrated by the platform model.

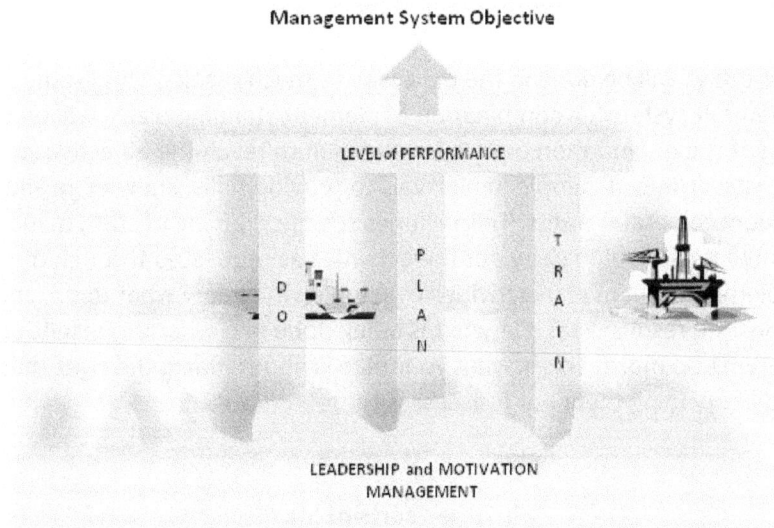

Picture 2.14 – Platform model, the concept for improvement

The five main aspects of the model form the basics to bring desired results. These aspects are:

1. The OBJECTIVE. I really don't see how you can make a plan without an objective so if I would consider the objective as an integral part of the plan that would bring the number of main aspects to four. However, I still want to put it as number one because it is the objective that would contribute largely to the needed leadership and motivation which I put as number two. The objective is what you want to have and remember Rohn: "If you really want (to do) something, you will find a way. If you don't, you will find an excuse."

Peter Drucker

Management by objectives works if you first think through your objectives. Ninety percent of the time you haven't.

Peter F. Drucker (1909 –2005) - management consultant, educator, and author

2. (Management) LEADERSHIP and MOTIVATION, the driving force behind the improvement process and the foundation of the "platform" model. This leadership and motivation should be throughout the organization, from top to bottom. While this leadership is at the base of the model, it is also at the top of the process to improve.

Leadership by top-management is the "ignition source" starting the process to make the future and the fuel to keep it running to where you want to go.

The level of performance (LOP) – on your way to the objective - rests on the platform columns:

3. The making of the PLAN to include the activity areas or elements with their specific objectives and activities: what needs to be done, why, by whom, when and how so that the right things will be done in the right way to reach results. This "standing plan" or "management system", a combination of element standing plans, will be there for the duration of the organization or activity; the plan to reach the objective (point 1 above).

4. TRAIN/instruct/inform people at all levels to provide skills, knowledge and motivation to do the work to obtain results. This includes specific training of staff, management and operational personnel to carry out the activities as requested through the plan.

5. DO, implementation of plan activities by people who know what to do, and why to obtain desired results. Evaluate what is being done and what the results are. Not happy? Do different! Do more! This is what your plan is about: doing the right things in the right way and keep doing them until success is there!

In other parts of life

- The objective: Where do you want to go – what do you want?
- Your leadership: the need to change from where you are now – do you really want this?
- The plan: to reach your objective – make your future
- Train: knowledge and resources: to do what you need to do
- Do: carry out what is necessary - check what you did and what results are and do not give up

---

PLAN – work to become better

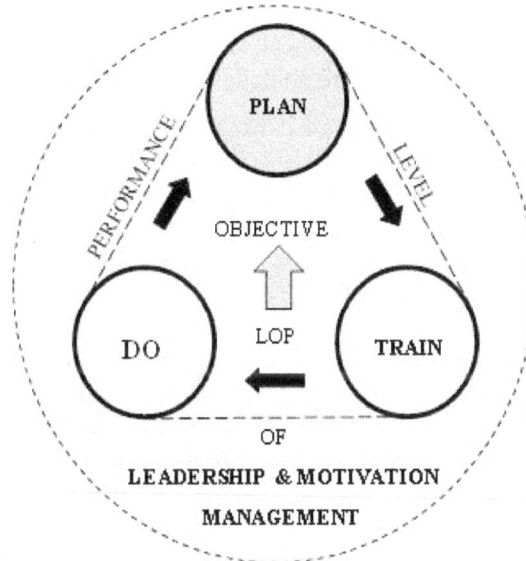

Picture 2.15 – The plan: to raise performance towards the objective

To reach results, management activity areas or "elements" of the management system need to be identified depending on the objectives of your plan. Selection of activity areas and the nature and quality of the activities in each of those determine the failure or success of your plan. To reach desired performance and the overall objective of your plan or management system, minimum activity criteria must be established for elements such as:

- Leadership and administration
- Management training
- Hiring and placement
- Risk/problem identification
- Engineering and change management
- Materials and services management
- Management of change
- Task analysis and -procedures
- Rules and work permits
- Knowledge and skill training
- Task observations
- Inspections and maintenance
- Emergency preparedness
- Learning from what went wrong
- System evaluation

Activity areas are main subjects or parts of your plan to reach the overall plan objective. These subjects, activity areas or "elements" need to be further detailed into activities – what needs to be done, why, when, by whom and how - to reach specific element objectives. These element objectives together shall result in the overall objective of your plan or management system.

In other parts of life

Activity areas or "elements" are the main "things you need" to make your future. Visualize your mind-map with "my future" in de the middle. One of the main elements leading to your objective may be resources you need divided in: knowledge, skills, money, and time. Another element could be support of family members, friends. Going away from the center (your future) of your mind-map, these elements will then be further detailed in things you and others need to do. Once your mind-map is more or less complete, you can attach priorities to what you need to do and put that on a time path. So you can do first things first and move to other things later on. Based on results and experience you will always be able to adapt your plan, your mind-map, to increase your chances for success.

Consecutive action plans, including activity areas such as listed above, should build the management system. Parallel to these action plans a management system manual forming the top document of the management system – see pictures 0.04 on page 32 and 1.05 on page 54 - should be developed to include what should be done, why, by whom and when. For practical reasons the detail of "how to do" the activities should better be described in separate documents. That way you can alter the "how to" documents based on experience without the need to change the core management system manual.

Management system elements should contain a structure to reach desired results. Setting objectives and periodic evaluation of what is being done and results obtained are the key aspects of that structure. This way, reaching element objectives contributes to reaching the overall objective of your plan or management system.

You should realize that, depending on the size of the organization, an effective management system may not be build overnight; it could take months and may take years. The total management system would normally be executed through various consecutive plans – see picture 2.13 on page 126.

Please note that I am not referring here to making a management system to get a certificate. To obtain the certificate you may be able to follow a different process not requiring involvement of many of people. Given the situation you may even hire a consultant using a pre-designed template and get the certificate without really bringing much improvement to the organization.

The selection of system elements for the first plan is crucial. That plan should include elements that are most essential to reach the overall objective(s) of the management system. Results of those first elements should be obtained within a relatively short period of time, preferably within 18 months after step 5 of the 17-step process. The shorter the period to visible results the better as this will show people that things are working and that management is serious about change and improvement. Obtaining early results is also important to top-management to see that "their" plan works - success breeds success. Knowing what brought success and being able to repeat that process is vital. The elements of the first plan should be selected during step 8 of the 17-step process.

The making of the first "PLAN" relates in particular to steps 8 and 12 of the 17-step process.

Mind-map

Since I mentioned the mind-map several times, I thought to show you what it basically is as making a mind-map could help you to set up and visualize your plan or management system. So I made a simple one as shown in picture 2.16.

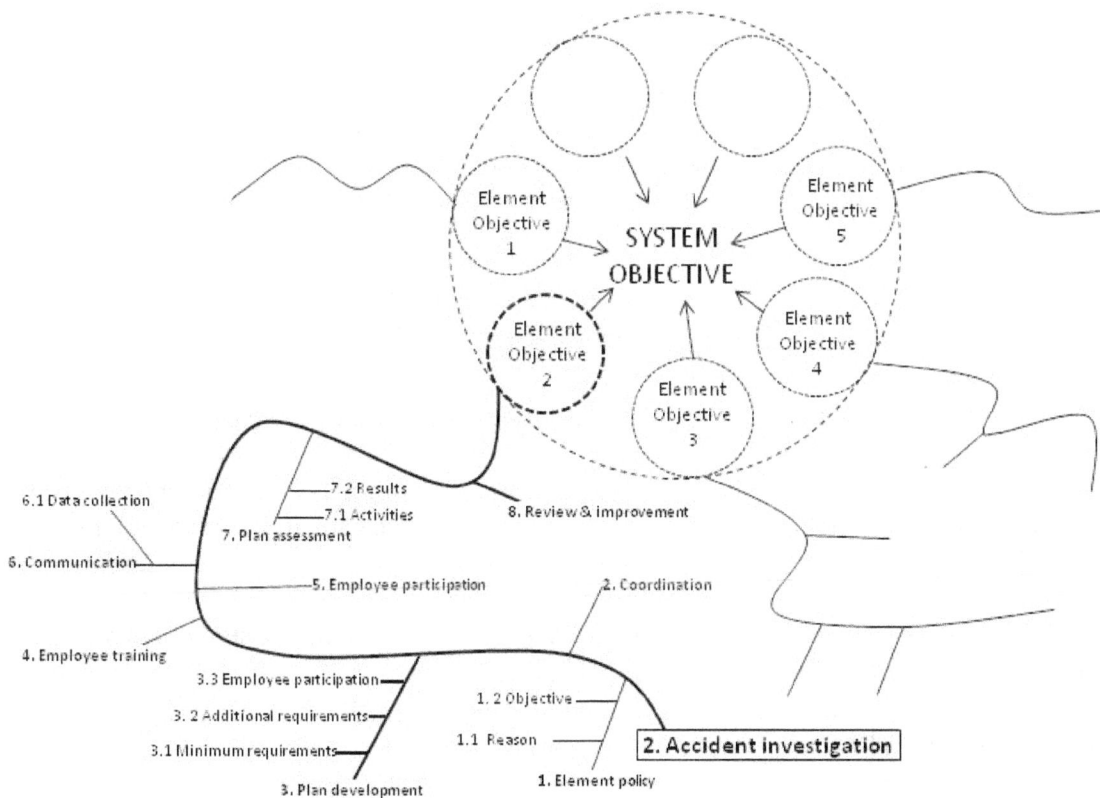

Picture 2.16 – Example of a simple mind-map

The mind-map shows accident investigation as the second element of a safety management system. Note the overall system objective in the middle of the large circle. Around that you see the specific element objectives contributing to the overall objective. I used numbers 1 to 8 from "element policy" to "review and improvement" to indicate the structure – see chapter 2.6, page 163, for further detail – making up the element. Following my reasoning that each element should basically have the same structure, all element routes to their objective will be very similar. The main difference will be in element step 3 - the (element) "plan development" which, in case of the accident investigation element example shown, will include activities that are relevant to the investigation of accidents, cause analysis and remedial actions.

TRAIN – Communicate & instruct

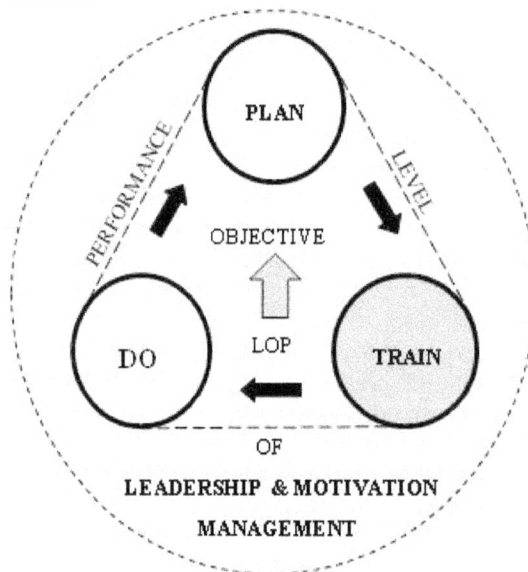

Picture 2.17 – Train & instruct: knowledge to do what is to be done

After establishing what needs to be done, why, by whom, when and how, people should receive adequate training/instruction for motivation, knowledge and skills to carry out the required work.

Knowledge and motivation are necessary for success and, as part of the 17-step process, should include:

Prior to making the plan:

- General introduction training to put all noses in the same direction: "This is where we want to go together and the way we will do it". This training should be provided top-down in the organization and include the cause-consequence and platform models and some definitions. Special attention should be given to the why of the anticipated change, how it will be accomplished and the need for cooperation of all levels of the organization. Very important is to convey the leadership, motivation and support by (top) management and this is why management should be visible and participate in those training sessions. The process of how the change will be accomplished should be part of this general training. This training is included in steps 2, 3 and 9 of the 17-step process.

- Training of people who play a role in the making of the plan. In particular for those who will act as (coordination team) leaders of management system elements. Those people will guide and coach others in a team effort to develop the element for which they are responsible. They should have a thorough knowledge of the specific element which they are to coordinate and the structure thereof. This "before making the plan" training could also include instruction of people who will carry out assessments of activities and results obtained during the implementation of the element. This coordination team training is in step 10 of the 17-step process.

After the plan elements have been approved by the management improvement team:

- Training of people to carry out the activities of the elements that are part of the plan. To include forms and tools to be used. It is this training that is the basis for execution of the element specific activities - DO what needs to be done. This training is in step 13 of the 17-step process.

  Related to this implementation training is the instruction of managers and supervisors in step 14 of the 17-step process. This "management briefing" is directed at knowing what the critical aspects are of the element activities that those managers/supervisors will support and coach in their area of responsibility.

See also section 2.1.2 on pages 111 and 112.

DO – Carry out the work that needs to be done

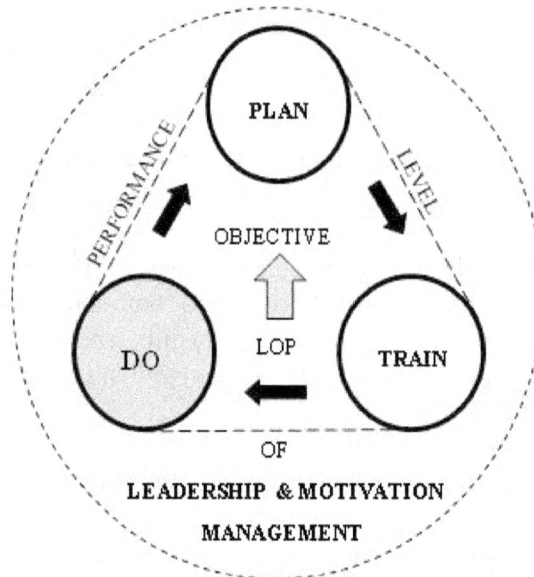

Picture 2.18 – Do: carry out activities on your way to success

Success can only be secured if the right activities are carried out the right way. This requires the necessary discipline to do the work and to continue doing it. Also required is discipline from top-management down to provide leadership in support of activities to be carried out as a mutual effort of all: managers, staff specialists, supervisors and operational personnel.

"DO" as part of the Platform model relates to steps 15 - 17 of the 17-step process.

See also section 2.1.3 on pages 112 – 114 in relation to the periodic assessments that should be part of the execution of element activities.

LEADERSDHIP and MOTIVATION

Motivation and leadership go hand in hand. Leadership will be provided if the proper level of motivation has been established and this needs to be first at the highest level in the organization. To get the proper leadership at lower levels, motivation needs to be established by involving management, supervision, staff specialists and operational personnel at all levels in the improvement process.

While "Leadership and Motivation" is the foundation of the platform model, and a main issue in all steps of the 17-step process, it is also a must to fuel the success engine, the structure of the system elements. Leadership and objective are closely related. If the objective is worthy enough, leadership will be provided and the personal believes of the person at the top of the organization is crucial. Without her or his personal believe in the objective it may not be worthwhile to even start the journey using the 17-step process as a guide.

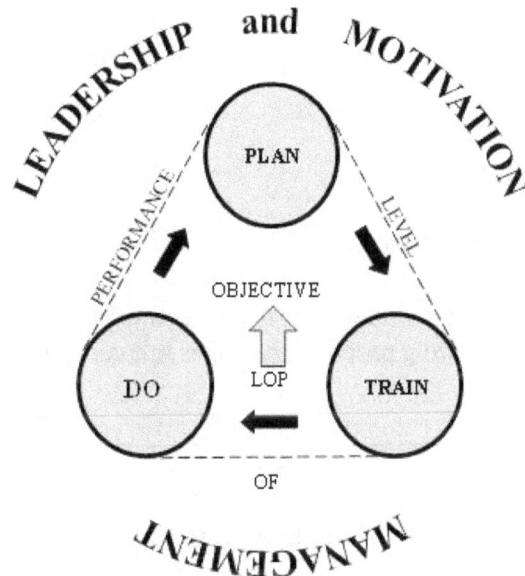

Picture 2.19 – Leadership and motivation: fueling the success process

Performance level - on the way to reaching the objective

Being able to indicate the performance level is important as you want to know where you are on your way to your objective.

Below some indicators are mentioned by which the performance level concerning risk control, health, safety and environment can be measured and evaluated. For the best results, you should use a combination of before the event (input) indicators and after the event (output) indicators.

Before the event (input) indicators could include:

- Management system audits
- Employee opinion survey results
- Risk analysis results (potential for losses)

Event indicators could include:

- Behavior observation reports
- Inspection reports

After the event (output) indicators could include:

- Various injury rates (frequency/severity)
- Material damage rates
- Maintenance reports (abnormal/normal)
- Insurance claims
- Absenteeism rates
- Customer complaints
- Environmental incident rates

Top-down AND Bottom-up for best results

Best and lasting results can only be obtained through a combination of top-down and bottom-up involvement and cooperation, during preparatory stages but certainly also when activities are being carried out and improved.

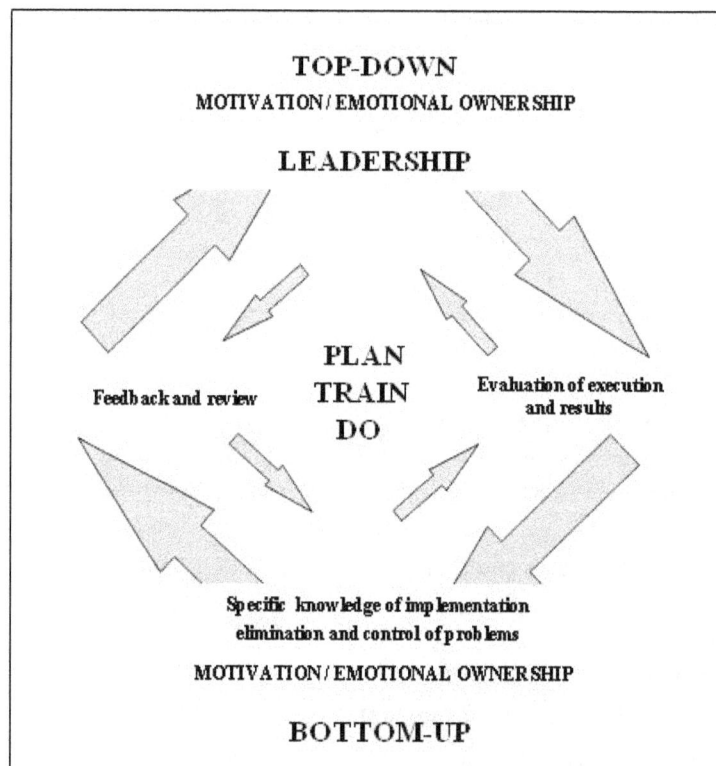

TOP-DOWN
MOTIVATION / EMOTIONAL OWNERSHIP

LEADERSHIP

Feedback and review

**PLAN
TRAIN
DO**

Evaluation of execution and results

Specific knowledge of implementation
elimination and control of problems

MOTIVATION / EMOTIONAL OWNERSHIP

BOTTOM-UP

Picture 2.20 – Top-down PLUS bottom-up for best and lasting results

Top-down support for the execution of the work to be done. By making important items truly important. By making necessary resources available – time, knowledge/skills and money. By implanting in the organization a system for (self-) management of what is to be done and results to be obtained. By providing feedback and commending people and workgroups whenever possible. By making sure that undesired situations or acts are being corrected based on their risk priorities. By asking about performance and progress at relevant meetings. By being pro-active rather than re-active. And above all: by example when possible and appropriate. By action, not just words!

Bottom-up approach involving people at lower levels of the organization in problem-solving within their area of operation. Using the expertise that is available in relation to the work to be done.

The principle of shared results

The outcome of an organization is the combined work of many people at different levels and at different times. They all share responsibility for the company's success or failure.

Involvement of (operational) employees and lower management levels may include:

- Design and modification of installations and workplace
- Identification of workplace hazards
- Identification of "critical" tasks, analysis of those and the establishment of task procedures or work practices and rules
- Purchasing tools, equipment, services, protective equipment
- Periodic review and improvement of existing procedures
- Conducting planned inspections in their own department and cross-departmental
- Investigating and analysis of unwanted events and follow-up of remedial actions
- Establishment of rules and regulations

BOA ME NA ME MMOA WO - symbol of cooperation and interdependence

Considering this bottom-up involvement, you should realize that this does not come by itself and, if it does, it may not be the involvement that you are looking for. Actually it may not be involvement at all but rather a reaction to the lack of it and an indication of a culture going down the drain. Positive bottom-up should be brought into the organization by top-down leadership and activity, establishing effective two-way communication channels. Top-management should want, ask for and enable bottom-up involvement to make it effective. Adequate (prompt, correct, positive) management response to problems and/or solutions and suggestions originating from lower levels of the organizational hierarchy is necessary.

Balanced approach

It is of great importance that the three supporting columns (PLAN-TRAIN-DO), carrying the level of performance, are developed in balance which each other. There must be a balance between the activities to be done, the training/instruction provided and the execution of the activities. If not, an unbalanced situation may occur with lower effectiveness and possible demotivation. Leadership should consider this: DO follows TRAIN follows PLAN follows OBJECTIVE.

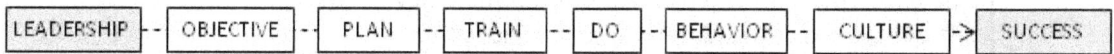

LEADERSHIP	OBJECTIVE	PLAN	TRAIN	DO	BEHAVIOR	CULTURE	SUCCESS

Through subsequent plans, the performance level will be raised to the level of the objective (of the management system).

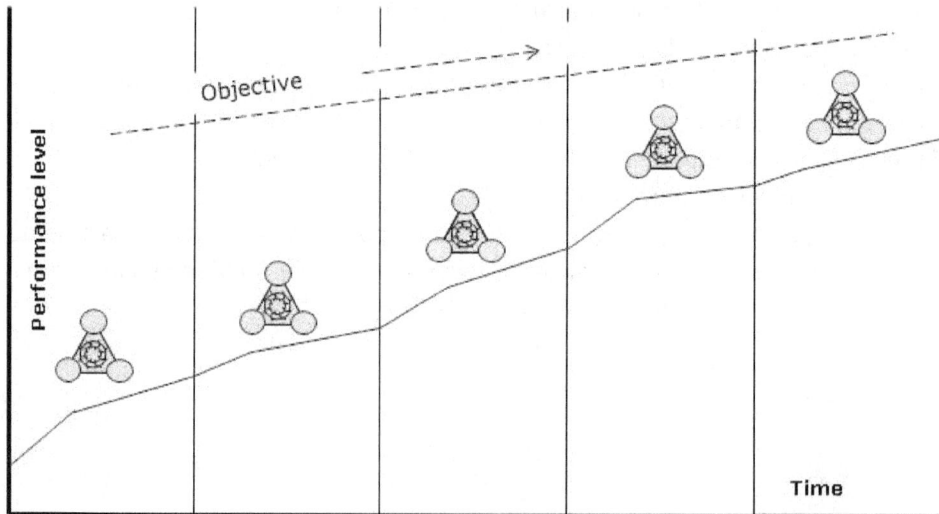

Picture 2.21 - Improvement: Plan-Train-Do; and keep on doing

2.3.2 The Process

I had my own (safety management) consulting firm during the eighties of last century; first under the name ILCI (International Loss Control Institute) Benelux, later under the name LCC (Loss Control Centre). My main activities were auditing (ISRS – International Safety Rating System), training and consulting; all based on the agreement that I had with Frank E. Bird, Jr. and his ILCI. My clients were mainly in the process industry. At that time, safety was not much of an issue outside that industry. It was only during the early nineties that I became involved in the area of contractor safety but even then those were mainly contractors supplying services to the process industry. In 1994, these contractor efforts evolved into the accredited certification scheme SCC/VCA – at present including about 14.000 valid certificates in The Netherlands; most of them outside the process industry.

As a consultant in the area of safety (management), my process industry clients were mainly paying me to help them to become safer. In the end that meant a lower injury frequency rate or keep it at the same – low - level. Soon I realized that the results they were looking for could only come from their own efforts, through a process that they should go through to help themselves. I also realized that, as a consultant, I should be able to let them know what that process should be. So I started developing a step-by-step process that would allow clients and consultants to agree on the process through which the client would be able to create their own success. With or without the help of the consultant, internally or externally.

W. Edwards Deming

If you can't describe what you are doing as a process, you don't know what you are doing."

W. Edwards Deming (1900 – 1993) statistician, professor, author, lecturer and consultant

First I came up with a process of 11 steps, then 13. Early nineties of last century, there were 16 steps to which I later added one more step to bring the total to 17. The number of steps, by the way, is not that relevant. It could be less or more, whatever is right for your situation. However, the process is essential and should include all steps that are critical to reach the desired performance level and objective; so be careful when leaving steps out.

The 17-step process is generic and will – at least in my opinion – apply to all efforts intended to bring change/improvement to the organization. Safety management, in which area I worked, is really not different from any other aspect of business. All management systems contain management activity areas to reach goals/objectives and all should have the structure to make sure that activities are carried out and results obtained. And remember that a management system is really no more than a plan to reach objectives, to produce results. As such the 17-step process could be the pathway to success; in business as well as in other parts of life.

Implementation of the process in a particular situation can be rather complicated due to a number of aspects, to include:

- Unclear objectives
- Lack of leadership
- Lack of resources
- People having other ideas

- Existing vested interests
- Resistance to change
- Earlier experience
- The culture

Many of the success barriers mentioned above can be eliminated or reduced using the 17-step process in an open and honest manner but, even then, it still may take an effort.

The 17-step process is not a "fill-out", "tick-off" type of guide. The process described is intended to put you on the right track; you will have to adapt it to your situation and opportunities which will change over time; what is not possible today may be possible tomorrow.

Organizational changes are almost always complex or complicated; people make them so. The principles and process, however, are relatively simple. So, when on your way, it helps to remember the basics. If done gradually and following the 17-step process – from the top down – these people related issues may be solved when on your way. Take your time, go as fast as you can but don't overdo it.

In a complex situation?

Go back to the basics
and get results from your management system

LEADERSHIP - PLAN - TRAIN - DO

In principle improvement should include all steps of the 17-step process, after a decision has been taken by top-management "to make a change". Preferably these steps should be taken in the order presented. However, depending on your situation, you may be able to combine certain steps while it may also be possible or necessary for you to add or delete some – the number 17 is not a holy number! But think twice before leaving steps out; they all have a meaning and purpose.

Lao-tzu

A journey of a thousand miles begins with a single step

Lao-tzu, The Way of Lao-tzu Chinese philosopher (604 BC - 531 BC)

Depending on the circumstances the order of steps may also be slightly different. For example: to obtain the necessary (top) management interest and motivation to lead the process, it may be helpful to first carry out a baseline assessment (step 7) or an opinion survey (step 6) and use the results of that in a management workshop (step 2). In that workshop you may then also use the maturity profile that you find in appendix B on page 224.

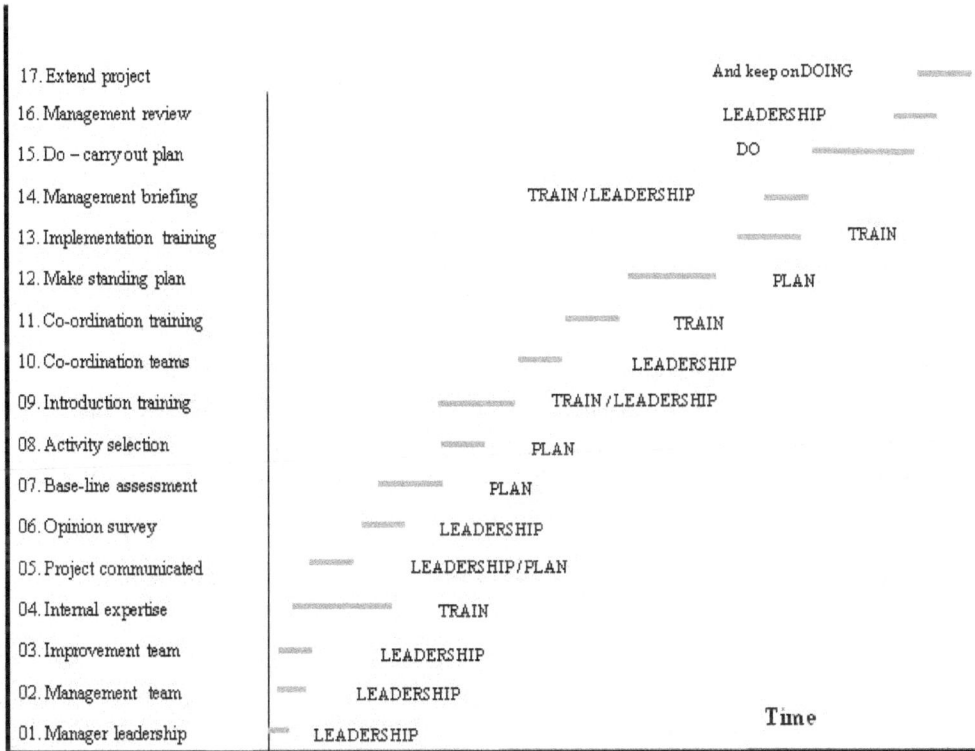

17. Extend project		And keep on DOING
16. Management review		LEADERSHIP
15. Do – carry out plan		DO
14. Management briefing		TRAIN / LEADERSHIP
13. Implementation training		TRAIN
12. Make standing plan		PLAN
11. Co-ordination training		TRAIN
10. Co-ordination teams		LEADERSHIP
09. Introduction training		TRAIN / LEADERSHIP
08. Activity selection		PLAN
07. Base-line assessment		PLAN
06. Opinion survey		LEADERSHIP
05. Project communicated		LEADERSHIP / PLAN
04. Internal expertise		TRAIN
03. Improvement team		LEADERSHIP
02. Management team		LEADERSHIP
01. Manager leadership		LEADERSHIP

Time

Picture 2.22 - The relation between the platform model en the 17-step process

2.4   17 STEPS TOWARDS YOUR FUTURE

PLEASE NOTE: each step of the 17-step process is provided with further detail in appendix F on page 267.

1.   Top Manager Leadership

Improvement - positive change - can only result from top-management leadership. In fact the greatest guarantee for success lays with the top person him-/herself, through his/her personal leadership, believes, commitment and actions.

Vital to the entire process is the choice of the objective. Obtaining the objective must be fully supported and desired by the top person. If not, it may be difficult to impossible to provide the necessary – visible – leadership and commitment.

Step 1 will clarify for the director that personal leadership at the top, transformed into commitment and actions, is a must to obtain desired success.

Purpose of this step is to make sure that the individual leadership, commitment and support is given by the senior executive of the unit being considered. (The "unit" here would most likely be a site or location but could be a subsidiary or whole company.)

2.   **Management Team Leadership**

The improvement process must be carried by the entire management team, from senior management to supervisory level. All levels are important but the involvement of the group that directly reports to the top manager is crucial. This is the first level where strategy and policy are being transferred into the management system for further detailing and implementation at lower levels in the organization. An important start of this leadership activity is a top management workshop during which the need for change, principles and the process described in this book are communicated. Using the management maturity profile – see appendix B on page 224 – may help to start the necessary discussion at this level to agree on the need for change.

Leadership from the top down is the foundation of the platform model and the source of success.

Purpose of this step is to make sure that the individual leadership, commitment and support will be provided by all members of the management team. The "management team", as meant here, consist of the managers directly reporting to the senior executive and could also include relevant staff personnel and employee representation.

3.   **Management Improvement Team**

Coordination at the top of the organization provides for the high level power source that is required to get the improvement process started and on its way to success. This is the team that will manage the process to give direction and meaning to strategy and policy. This team will lead and support, decide on main actions to be taken, evaluate progress and stimulate the entire organization to the desired level of excellence. Here the management team can be pro-active to identify, evaluate and control tomorrow's problems. The management improvement team reviews work done by the element coordination teams (step 11) and approves elements (step 12) before being put into practice (steps 13, 14 and 15).

An important function of the Management Improvement Team is also to periodically review management system implementation, in relation to activities carried out and result expected, and to stimulate the process of continuous improvement (steps 16 and

17). This team would include relevant staff personnel and worker representation and may also include external expertise.

Chairperson of this team should preferably be the top-manager or a board member taking personal responsibility for the success of the improvement process.

As applicable, individual management improvement team members should be given responsibilities for the operation of element coordination teams (step 10), possibly as team leaders. Doing it this way greatly facilitates the vital communication between management improvement team and the elements coordination teams. The detail of this depends on the size of the company or organization.

An important start of this step is a workshop similar to the one mentioned in step 2 and including the role of this team.

Purpose of this step is to make sure that leadership and coordination for the overall improvement process is structured at senior management level.

4. **Internal Expertise**

In-house expertise should be available to assist management in the improvement process. This in-house expertise should preferably consist of several persons to allow for the necessary continuity. This (multi-disciplinary) expertise is necessary in all stages of the process. If in-house expertise cannot be made available, external expertise could fill this gap, provided the external expertise will be there on a more or less continuous basis and reporting to a high level manager.

While in-house expertise would be preferable, external consultants could help during the entire process and more specifically in steps 1, 2, 6, 7 and 8.

Purpose of this step is to make sure that expertise is provided to assist and coordinate in the development and implementation of the management system to be set up as part of the improvement project.

5. **Project communicated**

Leadership needs to be demonstrated through commitment if it is to "pull and push" the organization into the desired direction. There is no better way to do this than letting everybody in the organization know what the plans are, what steps (of the 17-step process) can be expected and when. Leadership becomes tangible when put on paper and shared with everyone involved, from top to bottom. Leadership transferred into commitment and action is necessary in order to obtain the desired goal(s). It forms the foundation of the three columns: PLAN – TRAIN – DO on which the performance level rests, moving up towards the objective to be reached.

Communicating what is going to be may contain a certain risk; the risk that management becomes accountable – people will see what the actions are compared to what has been said. At the same time this communication also shows that management is serious about making changes and committed to make it a success. Very important in this respect is the objective to be reached which should have the full support of all high level managers. Making the change and the future cannot be done halfheartedly. Failure to carry out the process, the plan to reach success, will be counterproductive and will be seen as failure of (top) management to do what needs to be done.

The principle of emotional ownership (1)

People tend to be more willing to participate in planned change when they have (had) an opportunity to participate and influence the process leading to change

---

Purpose of this step is to assure senior management leadership and commitment by communicating to everyone in the organization through which process and which steps the improvement will be obtained.

6.   **Opinion Survey**

To further demonstrate the commitment and the desire to make things work, an opinion survey is a tremendous tool to find out how people in the organization - at all levels - feel about the related aspects. Surveys should be carried out at senior (top and middle) management, supervisory and operational level. It is a strong indication that management wants to know how others think and feel. If well done, in particular in combination with step 5, it helps to "loosen up" the organization, to lessen the resistance to change at a later stage of the process and provides further information about areas which may need special attention.

Preferably these surveys should be made anonymously and carried out by independent internal or external expertise. At one time, when I did audits with the ISRS (International Safety Rating System), I used to carry out these opinion surveys two months prior to the audit. That way I had a lot of information available about the operation of the (safety) management system before doing the actual evaluation; allowing interesting communications during the audit interviews. See a senior management survey example in appendix C on page 228. For similar examples directed at supervision and operational employees – see my website www.topves.nl and use the website search function with "safety opinion survey".

Purpose of this step is to collect subjective/objective information about the actual situation/culture related to the subject of the improvement process and the management system to be developed. To also loosen up the organization for the improvement process to come.

7.   Base-line Assessment

No improvement process can really start before an organization determines where it is. For the improvement process you need to know where you are, where you want to go and how you wish to go there. So you can build on what is already there.

```
The past is unchangeable but how it is seen is not,
making all future pasts at once thrilling and changeable
```

To know where you are means an assessment of the present level of activities; an "audit" of what you are doing in relation to the objective that you want to reach. Such assessment or audit should provide a picture of the management activities taking place and a good idea of the strength of present activities and of development needs. The assessment may also help to select management system elements for the first action plan (step 8).

If possible, the audit should be preceded by an opinion survey (step 6) as the information gathered through the survey can be used during the audit. Results of audit and opinion survey could be combined into one report. Together with the selection of elements in step 8 and the results of the survey (step 6) the results of this assessment provides a good framework for the introduction in step 9.

Purpose of this step is to obtain a good picture of the present situation as related to the project involved. This assessment is a foundation on which to build further.

```
The Principle Emotional Ownership (2)

The more ownership people have in the way a present situation has
developed, the more difficult it is to change
```

8.   Selection of Elements/Activity Areas

The base-line assessment (step 7) and the opinion survey (step 6) should provide the organization with a good picture of what the present situation is. The next step is to determine what elements or management activity areas should be included in the management system and which of those should be in the first action plan. Realizing that you cannot do everything at the same time, you need to set priorities. Criteria for selecting elements for the first plan would include issues such as:

- Importance of the element to the overall system objective
- Efforts to set up and execute the element activities
- Needed resources (time, expertise, money) to set up and execute these activities
- The (visual/measurable) effects that these activities have in relation to the objective of the management system

Preferably, the first plan should include elements directed at keeping problems outside the organization.

The principle of the critical few

In any given group of occurrences, a small number of causes will tend to give rise to the largest proportion of results

---

Louis A. Allen, management consultant and writer. Founder of Louis Allen Worldwide.

Element selection should be approved by the management improvement team (step 3) to include establishment of element objectives to guide the work of the element coordination teams (steps 10 – 12).

Elements selected should preferably allow results within 18 months after step 5 (communication of project); the shorter this period, the better. Having visible/measurable results within a limited time period is critical for motivation, cooperation and management leadership.

The larger the effect the elements and their activities have - with the least use of resources - the better to create the necessary momentum, motivation and support for the ongoing improvement process. Early success is important for continuing the process.

Peter Drucker

Management by objectives works if you first think through your objectives. Ninety percent of the time you haven't.

Peter F. Drucker (1909 –2005) - management consultant, educator, and author

Purpose of this step is the selection of management system activity areas or "elements" to be part of the first action plan, based on expected effectiveness and visible results.

9. Introduction Training

During this step the philosophy, concepts, models etc. are conveyed to all management, supervision and relevant staff personnel. The same or similar introductory training should also be given to employee representation and operational personnel. These introductions are not intended to generate specific action. They are meant to be informative about the project and objectives, to answer any questions that may be there and to remove concerns that may slow down the process later on.

Providing proper information to all people is of vital importance for the success of the following steps in the process. These sessions are intended to also bring the necessary leadership further down the organization. Such leadership is very much needed at the level of the "point of control" (normally the level of direct supervision and operational personnel).

If possible, these workshops should be provided by internal expertise (step 4), opened and closed by a member of the management improvement team and include participation of relevant members of management and supervision.

Preferably this introduction program should include the results of steps 6, 7 and 8 mentioned above. The use of the maturity profile (appendix B, page 224) should be considered to obtain further feedback about actual management system related activities.

These workshops are an excellent opportunity to demonstrate the leadership and commitment through upstream management participation and to collect suggestions that may facilitate implementation of the next steps of the process.

Purpose of this step is to make sure that all management, supervision, staff, worker or trade union representations and operational personnel are aware of the improvement process, know the terminology, models, concepts, etc. To "put the noses in the same direction".

10. Element Coordination Teams

Once the elements have been selected (step 8), these need to be further detailed to become meaningful for implementation. This would normally take place in an "Element Coordination Team" chaired by a top- or middle manager to allow for leadership, authority, support and the availability of adequate resources.

The element coordination teams should have direct lines of communication into the management improvement team; this could be obtained by having members of the improvement team act as element leaders.

The element coordination teams or simply "element teams" could include representatives of middle management, supervision and staff personnel as needed and should include operational personnel. The team membership should provide ownership and involvement throughout the organization and facilitate implementation at a later stage.

The size of the team will largely depend on the size of the organization and availability of people. In small companies this may just be a 2-person team or even a single person. In smaller companies a team or person may be responsible for coordinating more than one element.

Purpose of this step is to establish coordination for development of management system elements in preparation of the implementation thereof and to see that assessment of activities and their results will be done periodically.

11.   **Element Coordination Team Training**

This is vital training and instruction for a vital team. Element coordination (teams) will be THE authority when it comes to setting up system elements. These in turn will be the reference for the improvement process on its way to the overall system objective(s).

Good knowledge of what is expected of this team is essential and a lot of unnecessary work can be avoided if these people are properly instructed. Team members should know what they are expected to do and why, what they help to set up and coordinate. They will act as focal points when establishing and detailing the activities of the elements for which they have been given special responsibility. These activities shall be established in relation to the objectives set (step 8) by the management improvement team (step 3). Training should include subject content regarding the elements and knowledge of the generic structure of the elements to be part of the system. Special attention should be given to HOW the element activities are to be carried out.

This training should also consider the assessments of activities carried out and results obtained, an important part of step 15. The assessments are part of the element structure that I suggest for each element of the management system. This assessment training/instruction may be combined with the management briefing in step 14.

Purpose of this step is to assure adequate knowledge and skills are available for effective element coordination, development and successful implementation.

```
┌─────────────────────────────────────────────────────────────┐
│           Making Your Future is only 17 steps away            │
│                                                               │
│              One step, then the next and so on.               │
│                                                               │
│                 Or 3 jumps: Plan – Train - Do                 │
└─────────────────────────────────────────────────────────────┘
```

12.   Element Development - PLAN

Here is where the basis is laid for doing the right things in the right way, after element objective(s) have been established. Clear performance standards - supported by appropriate "how to do" guidelines and instructions - must be set up for the activities to be part of selected elements. For example: how inspections should be done, when and by whom; how to go about task analysis; what unwanted events to investigate, by whom and when. After selection of elements in step 8, this step is dealing with the more detailed "why, what, by whom, when and how" of activities that are specific to obtain the elements objectives. This step should also include designation of training to be provided prior to implementation (steps 13 – 15).

Carrying out the work that is part of the management system will often lead to further detailed work procedures and –instructions for operational personnel. These could be quite extensive. These operational instructions and procedures are part of the entire system to reach objectives and control unwanted events. Physical separation of these work procedures - the "how to do" - from the actual management system manual allows making changes to the procedures without having to alter the system manual itself.

A management system that is too detailed in relation to the environment in which it is to function becomes more a barrier to success than helping to reach desired goals. To prevent the system to become more detailed than necessary it is suggested to start with the most critical activities to reach the element objective. Changing element activities or adding activities can follow regular periodic evaluation of activities carried out and of results obtained. This type of "natural growth" is only possible if risks, to which your organization is exposed, allow this. This way of system growth is normally not possible in case of certification. Certification requires that a minimum level of specified activity must be reached to obtain the certificate while time for natural growth may not be there; normally a certificate is required by a third party and needs to be obtained within a limited time period - for commercial or other reasons.

While all 17 steps are important as part of the improvement process, this step is vital as it forms the basis for success which can only come from doing the right things in the right way. This is where the management system gets meaning and will act as a reference for implementation, after the approval by the management improvement team.

Purpose of this step is the development of selected management system elements (steps 8 and 16) and their activities by element coordination teams (steps 10 and 11), with approval by the management improvement team (step 3).

13. **Element Implementation Training - TRAIN**

After execution guidelines and instructions (what, why, when, by whom and how) have been set up for implementation of the specific activities and after approval by the management improvement team, relevant people must be provided with the necessary information and skill training. This would include supervision, middle management, specialist staff and operational personnel as required.

This training is essential and should only be given after step 12 has been concluded for the elements selected (step 8 or 16). This will then create the best position for proper implementation: motivated and knowledgeable people ready to carry out the work that is requested of them through the management system.

Element coordination teams may be a good source to provide trainers.

Purpose of this step is to assure proper training for execution of the activities contained in the plan elements.

14. **Management Briefings**

To properly carry out their leadership, coaching and support function, senior/middle management, supervision and others as applicable must know: (i) what the critical points are to evaluate execution of the system element activities, and (ii) what results those activities are expected to generate.

Asking the right questions about planned progress stimulates activity and shows where management puts its priorities. It focuses attention on result related factors.

When asking a question like: How is the training going? the answer may very well be: "Good" or "Not so good". If that is the only question a manager is able to ask, what contribution has he or she made? Additional questions should include: When was training given? To how many people? By whom? What have you learned? Related to inspections, a question like: How many deviations were noted during the last week's inspection and what was their risk classification? Is much better than just asking: "Have inspections been done?"

This training includes the aspects relevant to element effectiveness in step 15: assessment of activities carried out and results obtained. This training could also be provided to operational personnel within the framework of people empowerment and could be combined with the training mentioned in step 11 concerning the evaluation of activities and results.

Element coordination team members may be a good source to provide these briefings.

Purpose of this step is briefing managers, supervisors, staff and others regarding the critical aspects of element activity execution. To enable them to evaluate, stimulate, guide and coach the implementation of the activities in their area of responsibility.

15. Carrying out Element Activities - DO

This is where people go to work in accordance with the element standards/criteria and guidelines. This is where it all comes together. Here is where the plan is turned into practice; all the previous steps are there to provide the best opportunities for this step to be successful.

Here is where policy turns into action, affecting behavior and attitude, contributing to a new company culture. If it fails here, everything else has been futile but if done properly, success should be imminent. Here is where leadership gets practical meaning.

Evaluation is vital in this part of the process to include periodic assessment of element activities and results. Leading questions here are:

- Are activities carried out as described in the element plan?
- Are desired element results being obtained?

If element activities are not carried out as intended, cause analysis should uncover reasons for non-compliance and action plans shall be prepared to correct the situation.

If element activities are carried out correctly but element objectives are not obtained it shall be considered to alter or add elements activities such that objectives will be met.

All action plans following these evaluations shall be approved by the management improvement team and include assignment of responsibilities and a time path. Ongoing evaluations will be needed to assess and secure results obtained.

These element assessments could very well be combined to form the basis of the periodic internal audit report leading to the review by the management improvement team in step 16.

Purpose of this step is to carry out the activities as intended by the element plan (step 12).

16.   Review by the Management Improvement Team

Based on the assessments done in step 15 this review, by the management improvement team, should consider the results of the entire management system and the results of the supporting system elements.

If desired element results are obtained but the objectives of the entire management system are not reached, consider adding elements to augment the overall system chance of success.

This review should also consider any necessary adaptations to the management system following external requirements – technological, political, social.

To allow "natural growth", no improvement related management system should be built and made operationally effective through issuing one action plan only. Additional plans are necessary to add elements and activities. And no performance can be kept at a desired level without periodic evaluation and review.

Adding new elements in principle means repeating the 17-step process from step 8 onward.

Purpose of this step is to review the performance and results of the management system by the management improvement team and to assure proper resourcing, development and execution of additional action plans.

17.   Extend Project, Repeat Process

Each of the management system elements shall have its own specific objectives. Even though specific element objectives may be reached it does not necessarily mean that the objectives of the overall management system are there. As suggested under step 8, it will be good to have the first action plan contain the system elements through which visible results can be obtained within a limited period of time and with limited resources. It also means that other elements – which may require increased resources – may have to be added at a later stage depending on overall management system results as reviewed in step 16.

Abraham Lincoln (1809 – 1865) - the 16th President of the United States

Purpose of this step is to further extend the management system in relation to its overall goals/objectives, based on the assessments results obtained in step 15 and the review in step 16. Step 17 suggests repeating a number - not all - of the previous steps to bring the overall performance of the management system closer to the desired objective. Ongoing periodic evaluations need to take place to secure continuous improvement of already implemented activities.

In other parts of life

Making your future is not a onetime event as your future – nearby or further away – includes many aspects and therefore many opportunities to make plans to carry out. These opportunities to make plans for your future will start at an early age and will continue throughout your life. So it is important that you will learn how to make plans and carry them out successfully as early as possible.

I know that you probably will not read this book at an early age; you will probably be grownup when you do and if you do. But here is what you can do: involve children, yours or others, in the process. In your family start as soon as you think your kids will understand. First involve them in making your plans and start simple. After they have gotten the idea, give them roles to play in your plans. Even give them the leadership role with your support. Then have them make their own plans and draw their own mind-maps. You and other members of your family will then be their team members to help them to realize their plans.

This way you will help your children, and those of others as the case may be, to help themselves to make their plans and their future - they grow into the habit to create their future rather than wait and see what will be coming. You make them think before acting, you help the next generation.

2.5   CONTENT OF A MANAGEMENT SYSTEM – selecting elements

What I mean by "content" is basically answering the question: which activities areas should be included in our management system? These activity areas or "elements" depend on the objective of the management system.

Of course a first question would be: What are management activity areas? The easy answer to that question would be: "Those are areas of management activity". While this is the question in reverse, it is also the correct answer. These elements include activities to manage certain business aspects. These activities belong together to reach a sub-objective of the management system – the element objective. Together these elements produce the objective(s) of the management system that they are part of. Examples of (safety related) management activity areas or elements are: purchasing, design (of installations, work environment, procedures etc.), hiring and placement of personnel, inspections and maintenance, task risk identification/evaluation, incident investigation and analysis, training, work rules and permits, etc. These are elements of a safety management system but I think you will recognize that those also belonging in other systems such as related to quality, risk management, environment.

The objective of the management system not only determines the content of the system in terms of elements. It also determines the objectives of these elements. The hazard here may be sub-optimization. For example "design" as part of a safety management system may focus only on safety issues while the design function within a quality management system may be limited to quality issues. Or training for safety may be separate from training for quality while it concerns the same tasks. This does not seem very efficient but may just be practice when setting up separate systems or only one system dealing with only one business aspect. Is risk identification or problem solving different in these areas? Why is safety or loss control training separate from quality training? Are these aspects not part of the same job to be carried out?

By using the terms "manage" or "management", do I mean to say that personnel other than managers could or should not be involved? Certainly not! In fact, the involvement of operational people is a must to have desired management activities results; managers or staff specialists certainly cannot do it alone. These areas of activity shall be lead and supported by management – from the top down. These management activity areas often result in more detailed work procedures or instructions to guide the operational work at levels in the organization where the work is actually being done.

You will have to determine which elements should be included in your management system but you do not have to start from scratch. You can make use of experience gained by others which is available through various reference sources, including:

- Legislation
- Industry standards

- Certification norms
- Industry management system examples
- Commercially available audit systems

There are management system references for safety and health, for quality, for the environment, for business continuity, for social responsibility, food safety, risk management and more. As a company or organization you probably need or want to address more than one business area through a single management system approach. This may lead to an integrated system combining various business areas. The question then is: how far should you go? Should you incorporate everything into one management system? Could you? Maybe you first want to include the issues in your management system that are most important to your organization and, once that system is operational and successful, extend the system as desired.

A good start would be to set up a system looking at safety, health, quality, environment and risk management. Such system would affect your employees, your clients, neighbors and authorities, some very important stakeholder groups. At the same time, a management system dealing with those issues also protects your company against mishaps that might be serious to catastrophic. Taking care of those is also good for your (long term) shareholders. Should you wish to start more limited then start with safety and health and extend from there.

Because safety has been a major issue within the industrial environment since the beginning of the industrial revolution, many of the tools, methods and techniques that are being used in the quality and environment areas originated in the safety world. If you would look at audit systems as references for management system activity, you would find that safety related audit systems were there in the sixties of last century in the American Steel Industry. This knowledge was used by Frank Bird when he started the Total Loss Control system within INA (Insurance Company of North America) at the beginning of the seventies. In 1978 this TLC approach developed into the International Safety Rating System (ISRS) via an intermediate, the Loss Control Service Guide in 1976.

In appendix E on page 243, I provided a number of safety related references with their elements. These listings may not be entirely up-to-date any more but they give you a good idea what activity areas or elements were included. They may help you to select elements for your management system.

Various references – same elements

When comparing various content related reference documents (appendix E) you may come to the conclusion that many of these documents refer to the same elements or management activity areas. This should not come as a surprise; reaching objectives and preventing unwanted events, either pro-active or re-active, often share the same elements or activity areas. And it does really not matter whether you are looking at safety, or quality or other business areas that are vital to the success of an organization.

You have seen the picture below before; this is just to bring it back to your attention.

Check the boxes in the matrix to see if the consequences at the top could be due to performance deficiencies in the activity areas on the left.

	Product Loss	Quality problems	Property Damage	Waste	Liability Claims	Occupational Illness	Personal Injury	Environmental Damage	Personnel Turnover	Loss of Customer	Loss of Market share	Information Loss	Loss of Image	Etcetera
Training/Instruction														
Design of Installations, Workplace														
Purchasing of Goods, Services														
Hiring of Personnel														
Management/Supervision														
Inspections														
Learning from Unwanted Events														
Emergency Preparedness														
Post Emergency Plan														
Change Management														
Work Procedures/Instructions														
Communications														
Task Observation														
Risk/Problem Identification														
Etcetera														

Picture 2.23 - Different problems/losses – same causes

Let us take the elements of the safety management audit system that I used to work with and see if they could also be relevant to the other business areas indicated in the picture below. I am using the activity area descriptions of the safety audit system and its predecessor that existed between 1976 and 1994. You find these activity areas in the left hand column of the table below. I gave my opinion by ticking off the activity areas which I consider relevant for the business areas mentioned in the 5 columns.

Management System Activity Areas SYSTEM "ELEMENTS"	Safety	Quality	Risk Management	Environment	Cost Control
1. Management Leadership	✓	✓	✓	✓	✓
2. Management training	✓	✓	✓	✓	✓
3. Design engineering/change management	✓	✓	✓	✓	✓
4. Mechanical Integrity	✓	?	✓	✓	✓
5. Materials and services management	✓	✓	✓	✓	✓
6. Hiring and placement of personnel	✓	✓	✓	✓	✓
7. Rules and permits to work	✓	✓	✓	✓	✓
8. Risk/problem identification/evaluation	✓	✓	✓	✓	✓
9. Control of critical tasks	✓	✓	✓	✓	✓
10. Skill training	✓	✓	✓	✓	✓
11. Personal protective equipment	✓	?	✓	?	✓
12. Inspections and maintenance	✓	✓	✓	✓	✓
13. Communications	✓	✓	✓	✓	✓
14. General promotion	✓	✓	✓	✓	✓
15. Emergency preparedness	✓	✓	✓	✓	✓
16. Post event/post emergency planning	✓	?	✓	✓	✓
17. Off-the job (family) protection	✓	?	✓	?	✓
18. Product stewardship	✓	✓	✓	✓	✓
19. Environmental care	✓	✓	✓	✓	✓
20. Unwanted events investigation/analysis	✓	✓	✓	✓	✓
21. Culture and behavior modeling	✓	✓	✓	✓	✓
22. System evaluation and review	✓	✓	✓	✓	✓
23. Documentation, records and reports	✓	✓	✓	✓	✓

Picture 2.24 – Different business areas sharing the same management system elements

You may disagree with me concerning some elements, partly be because of differences in understanding what these elements include, but overall we would probably agree that most "safety" activity areas are also relevant to the other business areas listed.

You may also want to consider how you could structure a list of elements, such as those in picture 2.24, into an ISO type layout as presented in ISO Guide 83 "Higher Level Structure". When you do, keep in mind that ISO references are mainly there for certification purposes. Could those act as a management system reference? Yes they could. Do they provide the best layout? Not necessarily so, they may not have the best format or structure. Do you have to put your management system into an ISO structure? I don't think so; I think that you may be better off to set up your system to include management activity areas or elements as described in appendix E on page 243. If you want a certificate, you may want to make a matrix between your management system and the related certification reference, ISO or otherwise. That way you have the system that you like best while it may make it easier for the auditor and yourselves during the audit process. Making such matrix may also be helpful if you wish to communicate about your management system to external parties such as authorities or customers who may be more familiar with the ISO setup.

In other parts of life

In private life you would probably not talk about activity areas or elements. You would probably just refer to "things to do". But the principles are still the same. Your plan would include as many things to do that together they will allow you to reach the objective of your plan and it does not really matter whether the time period will be a few weeks or several years. You also need to be aware of possible events that may lead to failure so you can correct them well before they grow into real problems. You need to know what you should do if real problems arise and you should learn from what goes wrong so it does not happen again. Hopefully, you do that anyway when going through life but possibly that happens more or less intuitively. When looking at what can go wrong don't fall into the trap of overdoing it as that may prevent you from doing anything. Some people may tend to give too much attention to why things are not possible; they come up with many things why it <u>cannot</u> be done and forget that making your future requires focus on how it <u>can</u> be done. Don't be like those people!

Select the proper elements

As I said before, I used to know and work with safety audit systems between the beginning of the seventies and early nineties of last century. I know that is some time ago but I want to make a point that you may wish to consider when setting up your management system.

The audit system I used to work with most contained 20 activity areas or elements, each containing references (≈ activities) provided with a relative numerical value. (See appendix H on page 298 for an example audit reference using numerical values.) In total there were about 600 references. This allowed scoring of actual element activity of a company – see picture 2.25. The audit system also included 10 recognition or award levels based on the percentage score obtained in the elements during an audit.

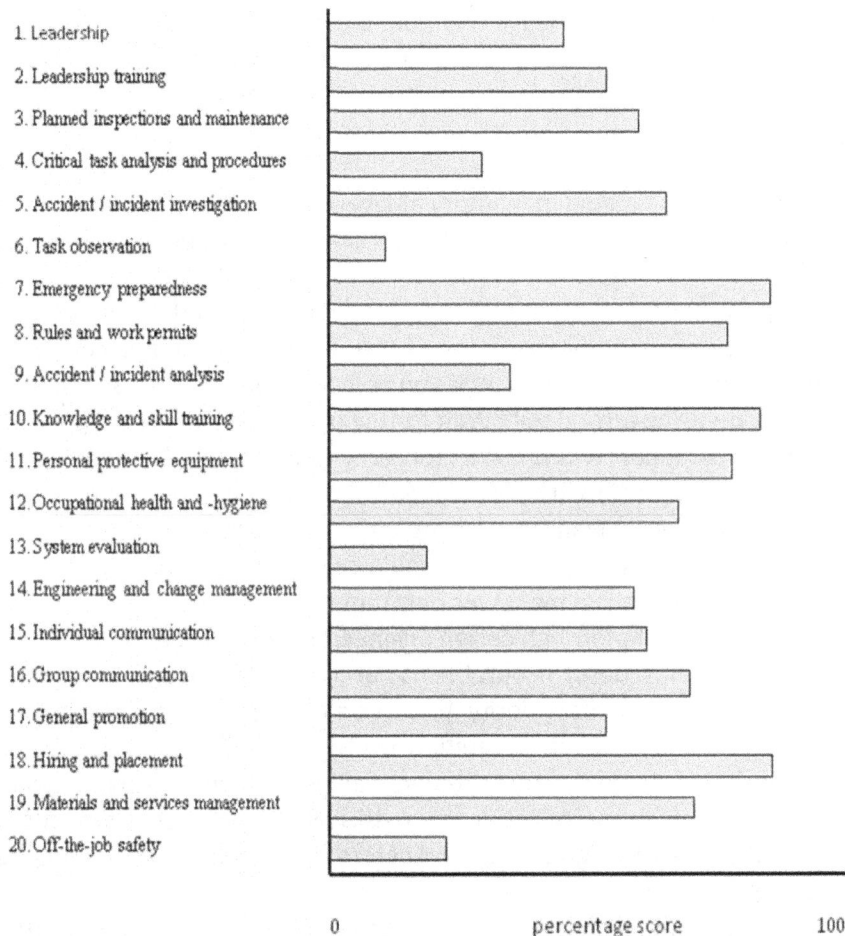

Picture 2.25 – Example of graphical summary of a safety system score

The elements to reach a certain award level were partly mandatory and partly by choice. At the two lowest award levels there were specified, mandatory, elements only. Moving towards higher levels, the number of specified obligatory elements increased while optional (choice) elements were added. At the highest level – level 10 – all elements were obligatory. Both the individual element score and the average score over all elements went up moving from level 1 towards level 10.

The recognition at the lower levels was easy to obtain as there were only few mandatory elements requiring low scores and thus easy to comply with. So a company could already receive recognition without much effort. The reasoning behind this was that early – and therefore: easy - recognition would stimulate companies to do more in order to obtain higher recognition levels.

While this may have been a good approach from a behavior point of view – "success breeds success"- it also invited companies to leave the more difficult, but sometimes very essential, elements out of their system until these became mandatory as part of the award system.

For example:

- Critical Task Analysis became mandatory at level 9. But critical task analysis is essential to identify and control task related risks. How can you train people if you have not first identified the critical tasks? Leave your people exposed to unidentified hazards?
- Critical Task Observations mandatory at level 10. The observations, however, are to learn from and/or correct the execution of critical tasks, essential to control of risks. How can you improve control of risks if you do not observe or discuss the way that critical tasks are being carried out? Wait for the unwanted event to happen?
- Emergency Preparedness was required for recognition at level 9. But emergency preparedness is essential to provide needed help to victims. It may also include the Post Event or Post Emergency Plan (PEP) to get operations back to normal after a major interruption. Emergency preparedness should be one of the first elements to set up.
- Engineering/Change Management was only required at level 10. However, this is essential to control risks through design engineering and changes to both technical and non-technical systems. Designing problems out of your facilities and the working environment should be a first priority. If you don't do that, you may be in for a surprise before you get to those higher recognition levels!
- Materials and Services Management required at level 10. Purchasing of goods and services (contractors) is essential to control risks by keeping them from entering your company. Why wait till a high award level before taking action to stop risks from coming into your organization?
- Hiring and placement mandatory at level 8. Essential to control people related unwanted events; keep the risk takers out of your company. When we are saying that "people make our business", we also indicate that they can break our business. So why wait until later to make sure that people are fit for the work they are going to do and bring the working environment in balance with their capabilities?
- System Evaluation only became mandatory at level 10. Evaluation of what is being done and what the results are is essential for making your system effective. So why wait until late before going out there to see if you are moving in the right direction?

All these elements are very basic to obtaining success and control of unwanted events and should be included as mandatory elements in any business management system – from the start or as soon as possible - they are the foundation of a sound (risk) management.

So here's the point I want to make: when setting up a management system, make sure to first include those elements that keep problems out of your company and do not wait until later unless there is a very serious reason to do that. It does not make much sense to keep on "solving" problems at one end while there are still coming in at the other end.

In the eighties an adapted version of the safety audit system was used in the mining industry in South Africa. At that time there were rather negative observations made in the media (press, TV) because of the high fatality rate in mines using the audit system while receiving high level recognition. This negative publicity culminated after the Kinross mine disaster took place in 1986, killing 177 people. I remember that very well. When visiting an offshore client in The Netherlands one day and before going into a meeting, I was shown the Granada TV broadcast "World in Action" about the Kinross disaster, recorded by one of the company's employees. That did not make my day, or maybe I should say: that made my day and some more after that – not in a positive sense as you can imagine.

The recognition system as I described above - leaving out essential risk control activities until the very high award levels - may very well have contributed to the South African mining situation that threw negative shades over an otherwise good tool. The changes that were made from the original version to meet the needs of the South African mining industry may have been another factor.

A tool, such as a management system (audit) reference, is only as good as the qualifications and intentions of those who are using it and that, of course, is an issue with any system, certification or otherwise, that recognizes performance. So, be aware of that. The end result of using a tool may be influenced by the environment – commercial, economic, social, political - in which the tool is being used. A good instrument can be used in the wrong way, also on purpose. During training sessions I used this simple example to make the point: a hammer is good tool to drive a nail into a piece of wood, but in wrong hands and with the wrong intention? So don't be fooled by the recognition that you get and look beyond that to find out what really brings improvement to your company or organization. That certainly also applies to certification – getting the certificate does not necessarily mean that you doing well or are better than the rest; it means that you met some minimum requirements …. as seen by the auditor working for a commercial certification body.

2.6   THE STRUCTURE – the management system engine towards your success

The management system or -plan consists of elements or sub-plans containing specific activities. To be effective, the activities contained in these elements must be properly carried out to reach the objectives of the element. Without this, the overall objective(s) of the management system may remain wishful thinking; the combined element objectives should bring the overall system or plan objective.

Each element should be structured to stimulate implementation and improvement of the activities that are part of the element. The assumption is that the activities are essential to obtain the objective(s) of the elements and that those together will deliver the objective of the management system.

The structure of each element includes the improvement loop or -wheel as an ongoing process to improve element contribution to the overall management system.

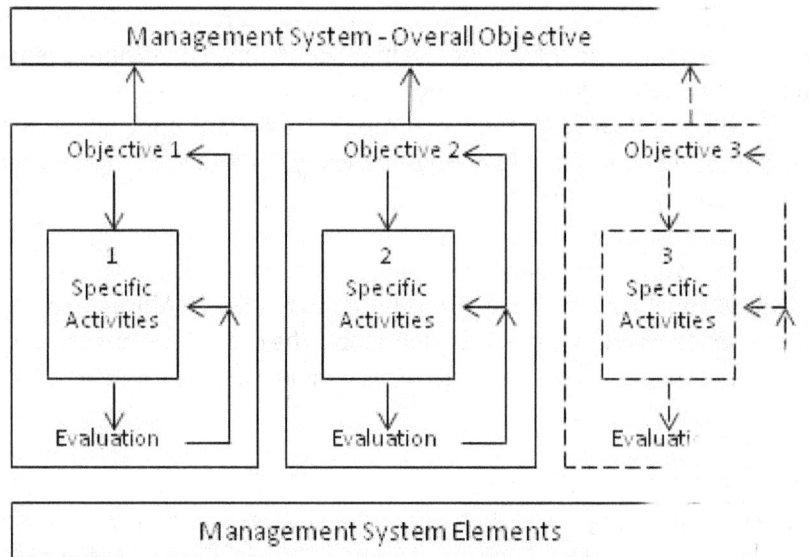

Picture 2.26 – Element structure as the engine towards success

The structure outlined below and further detailed later has the advantage that each element of the management system will have its own objective, activities and improvement loop. This way, the practical effect of the management system is multiplied by the number of elements. So if you would have 15 elements or management activity areas in your management system you will be able to also improve the organization in each of these 15 areas. So instead of having only one objective - that of the overall management system - you have an extra 15 objectives and as many improvement areas. It may also be easier to determine where activities are lacking in case the overall system objective is not being obtained.

Structure of a Management System Element – a bird's eye view

The structure basically represents the "improvement loop" which forms a process going from leadership and objective to the periodic assessment/evaluation of results.

The structure starts with the element management statement and coordination, then goes to the establishment of the element "standing" plan with the specific element activities that are considered relevant to obtain the element objective; training of people to be involved; execution of activities and ends with assessment of activities, evaluation of results and the periodic review and improvement.

The element structure shown below is repeated in more detail in chapter 2.6.1 on page 169 and beyond.

[1]   *Element policy or management statement*

Top management communication regarding: (i) the reason(s) why the element is important and, (ii) what objectives are expected.

Each management activity area shall have its own specific objective(s), different from the objective(s) of the management system as a whole.

[2]   *Element coordination*

Assignment of the responsibility for element coordination to an individual or team. Purpose of this coordination is to develop, maintain and improve the element plan. People selected to participate on the team shall have expertise and vested interests in relation to the element subject. To be chaired by a person with sufficient authority.

Element coordination should cover all structure related functions.

[3]   *Element plan development*

The element plan shall include specific activities to reach the element objective(s): WHAT must be done, by WHOM, WHEN and WHERE.

The element plan should also include (separate) procedures or guidelines describing HOW the activities shall be carried out, including tools and forms to be used.

[3.1]   *Review of legislation and standards for minimum requirements*

To establish minimum requirements for element activities set by legislation and applicable industry- and certification standards.

[3.2]   *Additional element activities as indicated by other sources*

Additional element activities obtained from sources other than those mentioned under 3.1.

[3.3]   *Employee participation in development of element activities*

Participation of personnel from relevant levels to develop criteria for execution of element activities. Making use of available expertise and experience and creating "emotional ownership" to facilitate implementation of activities.

The Principle of Emotional Ownership (1)

People tend to be more willing to participate in planned change when they have an opportunity to participate and influence the process leading to change

---

[4]   *Employee training to execute element activities*

After the element plan [3] has been completed and after approval by the management improvement team, this training or instruction should include: (i) implementation of element activities by relevant (operational) personnel, (ii) coaching and stimulation of activity implementation by managers and supervisors and, (iii) carrying out assessments of activities carried out and results obtained.

[5]   *Employee participation in executing element activities*

Include relevant, properly trained/instructed, people in the execution of element activities and in the improvement thereof.

[6]   *Communication to internal and external parties*

Communication of relevant information to stakeholders.

[7]   *Element plan assessment*

Periodic assessments of: (i) element activities carried out and, (ii) element results obtained

[8]   *Review and improvement*

Periodic review of element results [7] in relation to element objectives set and to generate improvement actions as appropriate.

Please note that the structure also includes the platform model essentials: (objective and) leadership [1], (element) plan [2] and [3], training [4] and doing what needs to be done [5], [7] and [8]. The presence of platform model aspects in the structure should not be a surprise;

making element plans is very similar to making a management system. After all: elements plans and management system are both plans.

I had my first ideas about the generic element structure during the late eighties of last century when I had my own consulting firm. After selling my firm to DNV (now DNV – GL) in 1991, I was able to introduce the structure into a process industry version of the ISRS (International Safety Rating System). That happened in 1993. Few years later I did get some knowledge about the structure of the Operations Integrity Management System (OIMS) of the Exxon Company (now ExxonMobil) to find out that there was quite a similarity between the structure of their system, the 1993 structure and the structure I suggest in this chapter.

The July 2009 ExxonMobil OIMS brochure, found on the Internet, list 11 system elements:

- Driver
    - Management Leadership, Commitment and Accountability
- Operations
    - Risk Assessment and Management
    - Facilities Design and Construction
    - Information/Documentation
    - Personnel and Training
    - Operations and Maintenance
    - Management of Change
    - Third-Party Services
    - Incident Investigation and Analysis
    - Community Awareness and Emergency Preparedness
- Evolution
    - Operations Integrity Assessment and Improvement

The ExxonMobil OIMS brochure also list 5 items under "The characteristics of management systems" representing the improvement loop from objectives to verification and feedback and improvement. Very similar to the structure I mention above (points 1 – 8). These 5 items and accompanying text are given below between "QUOTE "and "UNQUOTE".

> QUOTE
> Each operating unit must have in place properly designed and documented management systems that address all the Expectations set out in the OIMS framework. Management systems put in place to meet OIMS Expectations must incorporate the following five characteristics to be effective. It is important for all five characteristics to be documented.
>
> *Scope and objectives*
>
> Scope defines the System's boundaries and identifies interfaces with other systems, organizations and facilities. Objectives clearly define the System's purpose and expected results.

Processes and procedures

Processes address the steps that describe what the System does and how it functions. Procedures address the key tasks required by a process.

Responsible and accountable resources

Approval authorities, experience and training requirements that qualify people to carry out their roles and responsibilities are specified for both implementation and execution of the System.

Verification and measurement

A System must be checked to see whether it is functioning as designed and is achieving its stated purpose. There are two components. Verification determines that processes and procedures are functioning and being effectively executed. Measurement confirms the quality of System processes and determines that System objectives and results are being achieved.

Feedback and improvement mechanisms

These mechanisms help ensure that actions are taken to continuously improve the System. They use findings from assessments, and from verification and measurement activities, to enhance System suitability, capability and effectiveness."
END QUOTE

Relation between structure and the 17 steps

In the table below (picture 2.27) I indicate the relation between the structure and the steps of the 17-step process. You will note that there is a partial overlap.

It is not the idea to do things double. I suggest that you would include the structure in each element, limit the descriptions there as necessary/applicable and then extend on this as part of the 17-step process. For instance where it concerns training, it may be sufficient to mention in each element what training will be given and to whom and provide further detail when you arrive at the appropriate step of the process. You may be able to combine certain parts of the training, for example where it concerns instructing members of different element teams about their responsibilities and tasks.

When applying the structure per element, you may want to leave certain structure items out of certain elements as they may not apply depending on the element subject. Select the format that will suit you best; just take care to include the issues necessary to obtain success. For an example of the structure as part of a system intended for high hazardous industry, look at appendix G on page 289.

Structure Item	Process Step
1. Element policy or management statement	Top management leadership (steps 1, 2, 3)
1.1. Element need assessment	Element selection (steps 8, 16)
1.2. Specific element objectives	Element selection (steps 8, 16)
2. Element Coordination	Element coordination teams (step 10, 11)
3. Element plan development	Element plan development (step 12)
3.1. Legislation etc. – minimum activities	
3.2. Additional element activities	
3.3. Employees involved in making the plan	
4. Employee training to execute activities	Element training and briefings (steps 13, 14)
5. Employee participation in execution	Carrying out activities (step 15)
6. Communication to stakeholders	
3.6.1 Data collection and analysis	
7. Element plan assessment	Carrying out element activities (step 15)
3.7.1 Assessment of element activities	
3.7.2 Assessment of element results	
8. Element review and improvement	Review and extension of system (steps 16, 17)

Picture 2.27 – Relation between system element structure and the 17-step process

2.6.1   The structure in more detail

The structure that I suggest for each of the elements of a management system:

1.   *Element policy or management statement including:*
   1.1. Reason for element activity
   1.2. Objectives of element
2.   *Element coordination*
3.   *Element plan development*
   3.1. Review of legislation/standards for minimum requirements
   3.2. Additional element activities as indicated by other sources
   3.3. Employee participation in development of element activities
4.   *Employee training to execute element activities*
5.   *Employee participation in execution of element activities*
6.   *Communication needs to internal/external parties*
   6.1. Data collection and analysis
7.   *Element plan assessment*
   7.1. Assessment of element activities carried out
   7.2. Assessment of element results in relation to element objectives
8.   *Review and improvement*

The generic structure can be seen as a combination of the Deming circle PDCA (Plan - Do - Check - Act) and the Plan-Train-Do platform model that I use to show the main ingredients for success. The structure also contains elements of the 17-step process that I developed for management system building, implementation and improvement.

In other parts of life

In private life "structure" is basically the same as in business. Each of your plan elements or "things to do" should have its own objective. All those objectives together should bring you to where you want to be, the overall objective of your plan. Each of your plan elements shall consists of activities that you have to carry out together with the people that are involved in your plan. From time to time you need to see if those activities are done as they should and if they bring you closer to your objectives.

---

1.   <u>Element policy or management statement</u>

   1.1.   *Element need assessment*

Each activity area or element of the management system is vital to the performance of an organization – vital to reach management system objectives – and to maximize chances for success. The leadership by management from the top down and throughout the organization is one of the basic aspects for success as we also show in the platform model. This leadership must be clear in each of the elements of the management system.

The element policy or management statement should be based on a need assessment for the activity area concerned, answering the question: Why is this element necessary? It is only after this need has been established that it can – and should – be communicated by senior management This statement expresses why management feels that the activity area is important and provides the basis for allocation of necessary resources.

I feel it is important that each element of the management system should start with its own need assessment and management statement as each element represents vital activities to be carried out in relation to the management system objectives. If this support from high level management is not there, it may be the first step towards failure of the management system.

   1.2.   *Specific element objective(s)*

It is also important that each activity area has its own specific goals/objectives. These should not be the same as the objective(s) of the total management system. For example, while the objectives of a safety management system could be "zero accidents", the objectives of the elements making up the management system should not.

This requires some imaginative thinking but providing specific element objectives has the advantage of being able to improve the element activities as part of the overall management system. It also helps to find possible causes in case the overall management system objectives cannot be obtained. Elements such as inspections or accident investigation could have objectives such as: "better inspections" or "no class A deviations" and "better accident reports" and you should then be able to indicate what is "better". Preferably objectives should be measurable, quantitative. Examples of quality measurements of inspections and accident investigations or, rather, the measurement of the related reports, can be found in books such as: Practical Loss Control Leadership (Bird, Germain – 1986, ISBN 0880610549).

2.   Element coordination

Each activity area represents a vital part of organizational activity to obtain the overall management system objective(s). It is therefore important to make sure that things are done properly.

Element development, maintenance and improvement needs to be done by responsible and accountable people who have the necessary authority to act. Assignment of coordination responsibilities is vital to element development and success. If the coordination is not clearly assigned including proper mandate to act, chances for success will be limited as nobody will feel responsible for results to be obtained.

Coordination shall be assigned to a team or person with authority to allow proper development, implementation and improvement of all activities to reach element success. This team or person shall have:

- Adequate knowledge of the specific activities (the "content" of the element) necessary to reach element objectives
- Adequate knowledge of how to reach results. To include basic models, the 17-step process and the element structure
- Sufficient support from higher up the organization (management improvement team, step 3 of the 17-step process) as well as from the levels where the actual work will be performed (steps 14 and 15)

Adequate resources should be made available in terms of money, time and assistance to carry out the tasks required.

Coordination of element structure functions 3 - 8 mentioned below can best be done by a team including people from various levels and after they have been properly instructed about their roles, tasks and responsibilities (step 11 of the 17-step process). The team should be headed by a higher or middle management person, preferably a member of the management improvement team (step 3 of the 17-step process). In smaller organizations, coordination may be assigned to a single person possible coordinating more than one element. In that case, this person should consult with people at the operational level when carrying out element structure functions.

3.   Element plan development

In principle, we consider two different types of action plans: [i] single-use plans and, [ii] standing plans but please remember that the basic difference between those plans is only their duration; standing plans are there "forever" while single-use plans are not.

Element plans, like the management system itself, are "standing" plans, not limited in time and will normally exist during the life span of the undertaking or organization and even beyond that. Those plans will be adapted over time depending on results obtained as well as following changes in industrial, social, political and environmental conditions.

Activities to be included in the element plan shall provide the " WHAT shall be done and WHY, WHEN, WHERE and by WHOM. Those aspects will be included in the management system "manual".

HOW activities are to be carried out should preferably only be referenced in the description of the element activities. The more detailed description can best be done separate from the main system document, the "manual" (see pictures 0.04 on page 32 and 1.05 on page 54). These "How to" details shall include tools such as forms and methods to be used during implementation.

Application of element activities (step 15 of the 17 steps) may generate single-use plans to cope with specific issues. These "projects" could produce issues that you may want to add as element activities or to improve existing ones.

Following element objectives set, plan development should include: (i) what activities need to be carried out, why, when and how, (ii) which people will be involved in execution of activities, (iii) training/instruction to be provided, and (iv) assessment and review of what is done and of results obtained.

3.1.   Review of legislation and standards for minimum requirements

The minimum activity content of an element or activity area will include requirements put on your organization by third parties including:

- Authorities (legislation)
- Certification bodies (standards like ISO)
- Industry associations
- Insurance companies

These minimum requirements are often necessary to obtain operating licenses, certificates, association memberships, insurance coverage or for commercial reasons.

These minimum requirements need to be established when setting up management system activity areas. The sources of these requirements need to be reviewed periodically to assure that the external requirements will be met on an on-going basis. The review of external requirements which would influence the company's management system is also included in steps 8 and 16 of the 17-step process. They are of particularly importance if your organization requires a "license to operate". If minimum requirements are not met properly, the organization may lose its operating permit, clients and market.

Some of the external requirements may be mandatory such as legislation or industry practices (which may be like legislation). Other requirements may be "semi-mandatory" because the organization wants to meet third party criteria - like having an ISO certificate because of customer requirements. Other examples of these "voluntary" requirements are non-ISO contractor safety certification systems that are being used in parts of Europe, such as SCC in The Netherlands, Belgium and Germany and MASE in France. Without such certificate it may be very difficult for contractors to obtain jobs and work on projects in the petrochemical and other types of industry. Insurance related requirements may include those for coverage under a HPR (Highly Protected Risk) policy.

The review, to establish minimum activities, starts by determining which external requirements are applicable to the organization and what it is that these external sources want the organization to do and how. Following the inventory, requirements are to be translated into activities that people in the organization need to carry out to meet the objectives.

The responsibility for these reviews shall be assigned and a system shall be set up so that the requirements are communicated to the people responsible to make sure that they are met. Sometimes the review of sources can be done by an external party, possibly the industry association to which the organization belongs. However, the responsibility to meet requirements always remains with the organization and its management.

3.2.   *Additional element activities as indicated by other sources*

The requirements as determined through review of legislation, codes and standards etc. form the minimum basis for the description of the activities in each element. On top of that, further activities can come from other sources such as clients, suppliers, your head office, your own ideas, neighbor pressure groups, from projects and from unwanted event investigation/analysis.

3.3   *Employee participation in development of element activities*

While element coordination includes all aspects of the structure, particular attention should go to the WHAT, WHY, by WHOM, WHERE, WHEN and HOW of the element activities.

As mentioned earlier, the HOW should better be contained in separate documents with the advantage of keeping the management system description (the "manual" containing why, what, where, by whom and when) relatively small. This separation has the advantage that the "HOW to" documents can be altered based on practice and results while leaving the core manual unchanged.

Participation of employees from relevant levels is desired and in some case also required (by legislation or certification etc.). Participation helps people to associate with activities and will allow "emotional ownership" necessary for proper implementation.

> **The Principle Emotional ownership (1)**
>
> People tend to be more willing to participate in planed change when they have had an opportunity to participate and influence the process leading to change

Benefits of employee involvement include:

- Making use of their knowledge and experience concerning the activities to be carried out
- Obtaining their buy-in to reduce possible resistance to change that may occur during development and implementation

Employee involvement would be desired at the development stage where activities are being formulated as well as during any change/improvement process that may follow the actual implementation.

4.   <u>Employee training to execute element activities</u>

Training/instruction of employees (at relevant levels) is important to assure proper execution of element activities to obtain results and reaching element objectives.

The element plan needs to indicate what training is to be provided to those who will do the work and to those who will guide, coach and motivate the execution of activities.

Training/instruction shall include, as appropriate:

- Implementation of work – the HOW to do – that needs to be carried out in line with the activities described in the element. This training/instruction includes the use of tools, methods and forms of the work to be done (step 13 of the 17-step process).
- Management – guiding/coaching - of the activities as described in the elements by those persons who have a responsibility over a work area in which the activities need to be done. In principle, this training (called "management briefing" as step 14 of the 17-step process) will focus on the critical few issues which are part of the element activities. It allows asking the proper questions and – by doing so – evaluate and stimulate proper execution of activities carried out.
- Execution of work that is part of the "improvement loop" and includes the periodic assessment and evaluation of activity execution and their results and the preparation and follow-up of improvement plans.

5. Employee participation in executing element activities

This participation includes the actual involvement of relevant personnel in implementing the element activities. Include assignment of tasks, responsibilities etc. to those persons, after receipt of proper training/instruction.

The element plan should include which people should be involved in the execution and coaching of the work to be done; after proper training/instruction (point 4 above). Normally this should at least include the "point of control people", those who do the actual work and those who will supervise, coach and guide this.

6. Communication to internal and external parties

This includes required or desired communication concerning element activities to internal as well as external parties.

The element plan needs to indicate what information will be provided to the various stakeholders. Providing information to stakeholders should also include other-than-normal and emergency situations.

Establishing communication needs to include:

- Identification of relevant stakeholders/interest groups
- Information needs to inform these groups
- Collection, analysis and presentation of data for effective communication
- Communication channels, methods and frequencies

Internal parties may include various levels of management and supervision, staff, committees, employee representation and operational employees.

External parties may include authorities, insurance companies/brokers, pressure groups, neighbors, media, employee family members, customers and suppliers.

6.1. *Data collection and analysis*

For communication to various parties, relevant data needs to be collected, analyzed and put into the desired format for presentation. This may vary depending on the party involved and the element concerned. The plan needs to indicate responsibilities for collecting and analyzing data and the communication thereof to stakeholder groups.

7. Element plan Assessment

The assessment can be done by people from various levels in the organization: staff specialists, individual managers/supervisors, a team of managers or combination of managers and employees. It should be considered to have a first assessment done by people of the department or unit where the work is carried out. This follows the reasoning that self-management may be the most effective way of management given the fact that these people have also been involved in developing and/or carrying out element activities. As needed this first assessment may be followed by a more formal review or "audit" by an appropriate team of managers and/or experts, covering all areas, units or departments where the same element activities are being carried out.

The element plan needs to indicate when and by whom these assessments shall be carried out.

Information from these assessments needs to be communicated to the element coordination teams for further consideration and processing. Assessment results may be used in interdepartmental recognition programs.

7.1   Periodic assessment of element activities

Periodic assessment of what is being done within the framework of each element plan. The assessment compares "what is done" with "what should be done'.

7.2.   Periodic evaluation of element results

This is to determine the results obtained from activities carried out (point 7.1) and assumes that proper input, in terms of element activities, will result in desired output. Results are to be compared with objectives set for the element.

The results of the periodic assessments may also be included in the communications mentioned under point 6 above.

8.   Review and improvement

The periodic review will normally be carried out by a team in which participation of people from operational and higher management levels should be considered. Preferably, this should be done by the element coordination team having the overall responsibility for element performance, possibly in combination with the management improvement team (step 3 of the 17 steps). These element reviews are an important source of information for the overall system review mentioned in step 16 of the 17-step process and the starting point of extending system efforts, as appropriate, in step 17.

Purpose of this review is to discuss the results of the assessments (point 7) concerning: (a) the execution of activities carried out, in comparison with what should have been done (points 3.1 and 3.2 above) and, (b) the results reached, in comparison with objectives set (point 1.2 above). Are activities carried out as indicated in the element plans? Are the element objectives obtained?

If activities are not carried out as planned and objectives are not obtained, investigation should reveal why. Actions should be taken to correct the situation so that activities will be carried out as intended.

If activities are not carried out as planned but objectives are nevertheless obtained, you may want to review the objectives set; possibly objectives were not properly described or measurable.

If results are being obtained with activities carried out as planned then further extension of element activities may not be needed until future evaluations prove otherwise. This situation offers an excellent opportunity for management to recognize operational level efforts for results obtained and to demonstrate management support and commitment.

If activities have been carried out as intended but wanted results are not there then extension of existing activities or carrying out additional activities should be considered. This situation may be an excellent opportunity for communication between managerial and operational levels; to discuss relevant issues and come up with solutions such that wanted results will be obtained at a later stage. An improvement plan needs to be set up with assignment of responsibilities for action implementation, follow-up and completion dates.

2.6.2. The structure – some observations

Is the structure required?

For certification this may not be required. But if you want results from what you are doing then you should include that structure one way or another; in all elements that contribute to the overall results of your management system. So my answer would be "yes", the structure should be there unless you only want a certificate and nothing more.

Does the structure have to be as indicated above?

In principle, my answer is "yes" but you may be able to combine certain items so in practice it may look different. Not a problem, as long as the essentials are there.

One example, concerning a system with eight elements, is provided in picture 2.28.

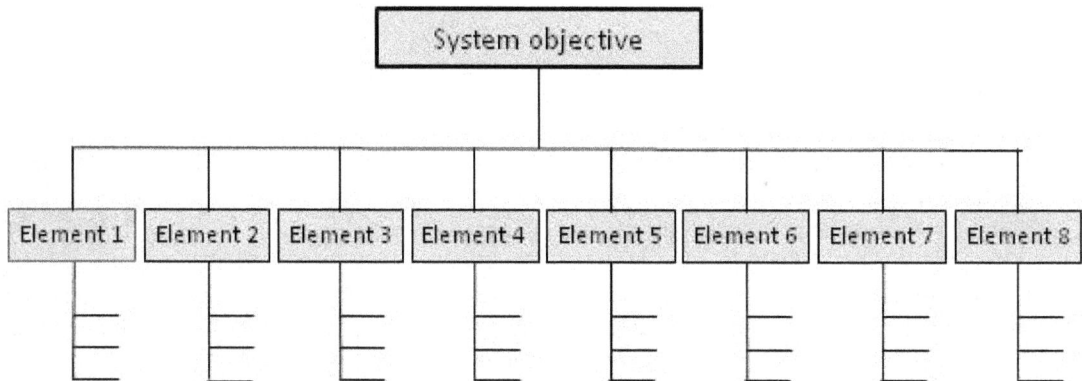

Picture 2.28 – Suggested structure of management system reference

The proposed structure of each element then looks as follows:

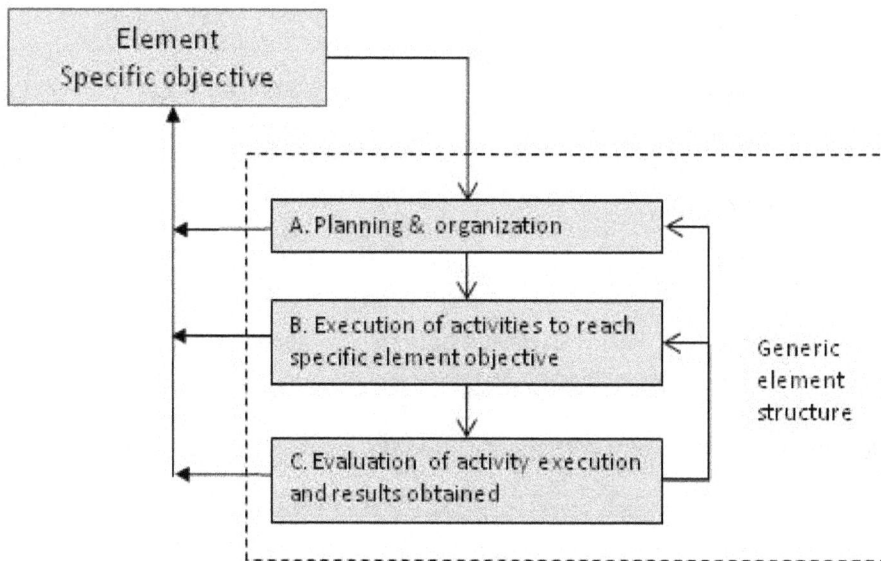

Picture 2.29 – Suggested generic structure of management system elements

Apart from the element specific objective, the element structure shown in picture 2.29 consists of the main items for success:

A. Planning and organization including three levels:
   1. Management (leadership) – why the element is there and the objectives to be obtained
   2. Coordination – assignment of responsibility and resources for element coordination

3. Operational - involvement of operational levels in developing and executing element activities
B. Execution of activities including the specific elements activities – what, whom, when and how – to reach the element objective
C. Periodic assessment of what is being done and of results obtained. Reports of findings to include suggestions for improvement in case desired results are not there

The structure basically includes the improvement cycle and is based on the platform model for change and improvement. The picture below shows this cycle as the "Improvement Wheel" where the element- or "standing" plan is contained in the axle which is driven by the "engine" built around it and fuelled (pushed and pulled) by management leadership, the foundation of the platform model: Plan – Train – Do.

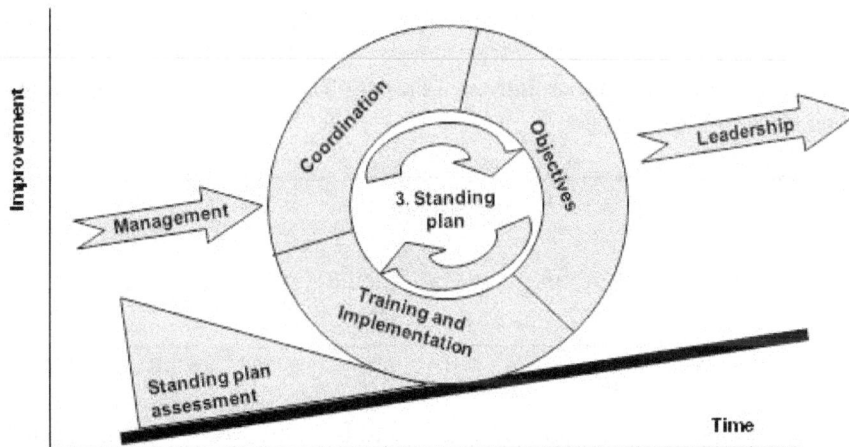

Picture 2.30 – The "improvement wheel" combining platform model and element structure

2.7   RATING THE 17-STEP PROCESS - indicator of improvement efforts

On the following pages, you will see a method that I made to put a numerical value on application of the 17-step process and its individual steps. Purpose of the rating is to have a (relative) numerical indication of the efforts towards success.

This rating method allows an evaluation of the 17-step process within a client's organization*).

*) From a consultant's point of view, the "client's organization" could actually be the organization by which the consultant is employed. In that case the internal consultant would likely be a staff member while the "client" would be (the management of) the organization. The rating method could also be used by an external consultant hired to assist (the management of) a company in an improvement or change process.

The rating may help to indicate to the client what his relative chances are for success. As such, this tool can be an important means of communication. It may also help to identify weaknesses in the process in case overall objectives (of the plan or management system) are not being obtained. The rating criteria used (see appendix F on page 267) also provide more specific detail for implementing each of the 17 steps.

Lord Kelvin

When you cannot measure, your knowledge is meager and unsatisfactory

---

William Thomson, 1st Baron Kelvin (1824 – 1907) British mathematical physicist and engineer.

The rating can be used in any situation. It can be used to find out how a management system related process has been set up. This would have value if results in a particular business area – safety, quality etc. – have been less than favorable. The rating can also be used prior to starting the process of 17 steps. That way the changes for success may be indicated before the process has begun. This would include development of criteria (appendix F) directly related to the roles of individuals in the process. Using the rating this way would allow scoring en route to success.

Putting value factors on Process Steps

I came to this rating method after I made the improvement process during the late eighties of last century. At that time I had my own consulting firm advising industrial clients – mainly process industry at that time – how to improve their safety performance. First the process had 11 steps, then 13 and in 1994 it had 16 steps. I increased the number of steps to 17 several years ago by introducing what is now step 16. (See pictures 2.33 and 2.34 on pages 186 and 187 for the original 16 steps.) The reason why I made the tool was that I wanted to have a means to communicate to my customers about their improvement efforts.

Setting up a rating system for the 17-step process was not really a difficult issue. I started by assigning a maximum value of 100 points to the entire process. Then I divided these 100 points over the 16, later 17, steps using my own judgment. The result of that is shown in picture 2.31 below providing a maximum score for each step. After that I developed criteria for each of the steps (see appendix F, page 267) to allow scoring of the actual efforts of a company between zero and the maximum value, thus arriving at a score or "rating" for each individual step. Putting a value on the entire process then was simply achieved by adding the individual step scores.

Looking back at the scoring now I would probably consider a higher maximum score for step 12 because this step includes the structure which I consider so important in relation to step 15. I might raise the maximum score of step 12 to 20 points or more of which I would assign 80% to the structure alone.

The maximum of 100 points makes it easy if to communicate percentages of what is possible. If the total score is substantially less than 100, that may indicate that important issues may be missing and the individual step score will indicate where additional action may be required.

Step	Description	Maximum Score
1	Top Manager Leadership - **LEADERSHIP**	4
2	Management Team leadership - **LEADERSHIP**	4
3	Management Improvement Team - **LEADERSHIP**	4
4	Internal Expertise	5
5	Project communicated	5
6	Opinion Survey	5
7	Base-line Assessment	5
8	Selection of Elements/Activity Areas	5
9	Introduction Training	6
10	Element Coordination Team(s)	7
11	Element Coordination Team Training	6
12	Element Development - **PLAN**	7
13	Element Implementation - Training- **TRAIN**	7
14	Management Briefing	6
15	Carrying out Element Activities - **DO**	10
16	Review by the Management Team	6
17	Extend Project	8
	Total maximum score	**100**

Picture 2.31 – The 17-step rating method, putting a number on efforts

I added the 4 essentials of the platform model to the process steps for illustration purposes only knowing that those aspects are also present in other steps; management leadership and communication (training/instruction) are issues in all steps.

This rating tool is my attempt to put numbers on efforts as part of the process of change and improvement. Therefore, assigning value factors or points to the various steps represent my personal views. The score provided is arbitrary and not based on any scientific or validated grounds. So you may wish to alter the numbers as you prefer. You may wish to do this with your colleagues or – if you are a consultant – with your client so you may have less discussion about the outcome of the rating later on. When doing this, you may also want to go through each individual step to decide which criteria shall be included in the scoring of each step. My (safety) related example of scoring criteria is shown in appendix F on page 267.

Dr. H. James Harrington

Measurement is the first step that leads to control and eventually to improvement.

If you can't measure something, you can't understand it. If you can't understand it, you can't control it. If you can't control it, you can't improve it

---

H. J. Harrington (1929), American author, engineer, entrepreneur and consultant

2.8 APLICATION OF PROCESS AND PROCESS RATING

The examples below are from the time that the improvement process included 16 steps and the scoring was slightly different from what it is today as the process now includes 17 steps.

Unfortunately, I have had limited personal experience using process and rating with clients. The reason for that is simple: I left hands-on consulting in 1991 when I sold my consulting firm while assuming other responsibilities with the company that bought my firm. I would have liked to have the 16-step approach accepted as THE way of doing consulting work but, unfortunately, that opportunity was not available then. Anyway, even with the limited personal experience, the examples show that the process may have its values, depending on the intention of the users, consultant and his/her client.

The examples below include the two ways in which to use the improvement process: (i) in a consulting job and, (ii) as the rating tool to assess in-company efforts.

1.   Use of the process in a consulting job – helping the client to become better

The picture below shows a copy of a letter that was received from a client and I guess any consultant would love to get a letter like this. The consultant XX, a colleague of mine at that time, used the 16-step process when he started with his client. That way the 16-step process really became the roadway to the success that the client was looking for. After receiving the letter, XX and I looked back at the process that was used to conclude that 15 of the 16 steps were taken as intended. Of course you need a client to agree to follow the process with your help.

The advantage of using a consulting approach such as the 17-step process is that you will be able to repeat it with other customers. That way you, as a consultant, could build your own approach based on the success of your previous customers. How much better would you want your marketing to be?

Unfortunately, the company that XX and I worked for at that time never accepted the approach as the standard reference for consulting to be shared by all consultants. The only reason I can come up with is that the company was not really a management consulting firm as the consulting provided was mainly focused on helping companies to get a certificate. And that is really different from helping a company to become better; certification and improvement are not really synonymous. At least that is what I found out working for that company during several years and that is still my opinion today.

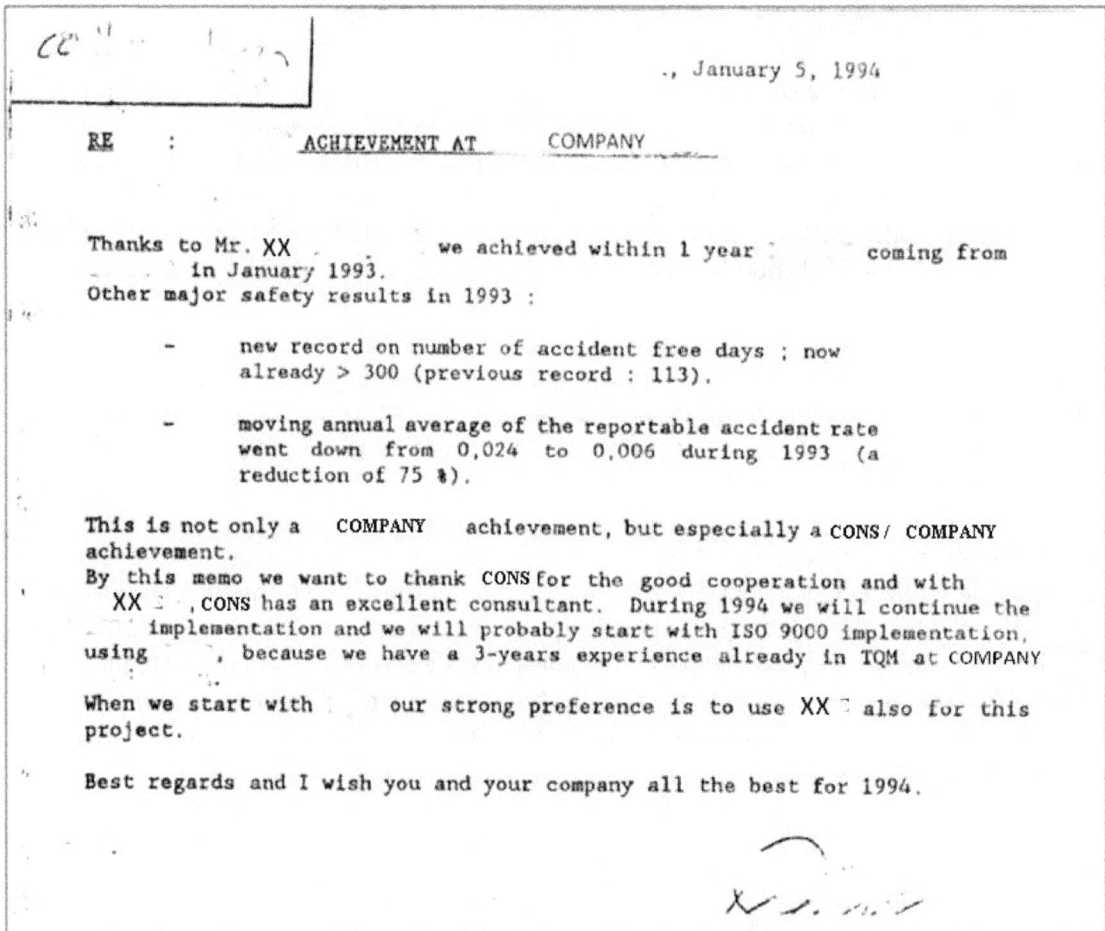

Company = Client; XX = Consultant; CONS = Company employing XX

Picture 2.32 – A letter that any consultant would like to get from her/his client

2.   Use of the rating tool – assessing in-company efforts to improve

I have knowledge of two exercises, one with my direct involvement and one without.

Chemical company

This was an exercise using the rating tool in relation to a chemical company in The Netherlands.

Following increased attention by the Dutch authorities due to the not so good accident rates, the company wished to improve the safety record. Within that context, we looked at the efforts the company had taken to reach results in the areas of safety, quality and environment. Note that the company did not make use of the 16-step process when setting up the efforts that were evaluated with the 16-step rating method.

Sitting around the table were five people: the quality manager, the safety manager, the environmental manager, their boss the SHEQ manager and I. We used the 16-Step rating tool as a reference which was given to them prior to the meeting. Knowing the efforts in their area of activity these people provided their judgment when establishing the scoring in each of the 16 steps. The evaluation criteria for each step – see appendix F, page267 – were used for that purpose. The whole session took about 3 to 4 hours to come up with the results.

The table in picture 2.33 shows the score obtained per step for safety, environment and quality while the maximum score per step is provided in the column "Max score per step". The score in safety was the highest because, at that time, the focus of the company was on bringing the accident rate down. Safety scored 43%; environment came second with 34% and quality reached 26%. I then added the three areas together to obtain the combined average score which resulted in 103 points out of a maximum of 300, or just over 30%.

Now remember: these numbers do not represent absolute values – they are relative to the reference that I made. Yet the score showed that there was sufficient room for improvement, even when applying a margin of 50% or more.

As a consultant an evaluation system like this rating provides a means to uncover possible weaknesses in the improvement process within your client's organization. Without a proper process, success may just be wishful thinking and at some time your client may be asking you some serious questions about results. If that happens, the 17-step rating method is a tool to show your client what they should do, or should have done, to create their own success. But better: do things beforehand and sit down with your client to establish what the step objectives are and the criteria by which to measure their progress; this then can become the "working agreement" between you and your client.

STEP	MAX SCORE PER STEP	SAFETY ACTUAL SCORE	ENVRNMNT ACTUAL SCORE	QUALITY ACTUAL SCORE	COMBINED MAX SCORE	COMBINED ACTUAL SCORE
1 – Top mngr leadership	5	3	2	1	15	6
2 – Mngmnt team leadership	5	3	3	4	15	10
3 – Mngmnt improvement team	5	4	1	0	15	5
4 – Internal expertise	5	4	2	1	15	7
5 – Project communicated	6	1	5	0	18	6
6 – Opinion survey	5	0	0	0	15	0
7 - Base-line assessment	5	4	3	1	15	9
8 – Selection of elements	5	3	4	1	15	7
9 – Mngmnt intro training	6	4	3	0	18	7
10 – Element coordination	7	6	1	2	21	9
11 – Element coordination training	6	1	1	1	18	3
12 – Element development	8	3	3	4	24	10
13 – Element implement. training	8	1	1	0	24	2
14 – Management briefing	6	0	0	1	18	1
15 – Carrying out activities	10	4	4	5	30	13
16 – Repeat process	8	2	1	5	24	8
TOTAL	100	43	34	26	300	103
16-STEP assessment 02/24/1995						

Picture 2.33 - Results of using the 16-step rating on a chemical plant in 1995

Contractor to process industry

In this case, the 16-step rating was used as part of a small project in which I was asked to evaluate the safety activities of a contractor firm supplying services to the process industry. Purpose of the project was to generate improvement actions to maintain their favorable accident frequency rate which was of vital importance for continuation of the good relation with their clients.

Without my involvement the rating was carried out internally by people of the contractor firm. Like the chemical company, this company also had no previous experience with the 16-step process and had not used this process to set up, maintain and improve its safety management system.

STEP	MAX SCORE PER STEP	SAFETY ACTUAL SCORE
1 – Top mngr leadership	5	4
2 – Mngmnt team leadership	5	3
3 – Mngmnt improvement team	5	2
4 – Internal expertise	5	4
5 – Project communicated	6	4
6 – Opinion survey	5	3
7 - Base-line assessment	5	4
8 – Selection of elements	5	4
9 – Mngmnt intro training	6	3
10 – Element coordination	7	5
11 – Element coordination training	6	5
12 – Element development	8	6
13 – Element implement. training	8	7
14 – Management briefing	6	5
15 – Carrying out activities	10	7
16 – Repeat process	8	6
TOTAL	100	72

Picture 2.34 – Results of the 16-step rating use on a contractor company in 2007

After reviewing the results of the exercise, my opinion was that the score provided was rather on the high side which can be expected in case of an internal evaluation. My own score would have been lower, in particular concerning steps 10, 11, 12 and 14. Main reasons to lower score were:

Step 10 – no coordination assigned
Step 11 – no training/instruction provided
Step 12 – no element structure provided
Step 14 – no critical element criteria provided to evaluate and stimulate activities
Step 15 – limited periodic assessment related to certificate required activities only

No coordination and no coordinator training, no element structure and no criteria for daily management coaching and no proper periodic assessments and reviews could have reduced the total score with 25 points or more, further highlighting areas for improvement. It also indicates that the involvement of an objective knowledgeable person (facilitator) could be of value in the evaluation process.

The contractor firm, by the way, did carry out periodic internal audits using a contractor certification scheme. Their reports mainly indicated non-conformities noted in comparison with the scheme that did not entirely reflect their own management system related efforts. The certification scheme also did not include the structure that I suggest for proper implementation and improvement. So their internal audits referred to non-conformities in comparison with a reference that was lacking an essential aspect for improvement. The external audit producing the certificate was likewise.

I did not want to be involved in any consulting work based on my own evaluation report as I do not like tie-in sales. So I do not really know how the company continued after my involvement other than that they hired another person to further assist them. A brief search on the Internet showed that they seem to do pretty well safety wise.

CHAPTER III   IMPROVING THE MANAGEMENT SYSTEM

PLEASE NOTE. The means to maintain and improve the management system as described below will not be discussed in much detail. I have only listed a number of ways to do this to illustrate some of the possibilities.

Once you have started to improve your organization's performance you probably want to maintain and improve your efforts and results and when you do, keep in mind that:

- Desired results, organizational behavior and culture may only be obtained after considerable time
- The environment in which your organization operates will not be static, it will change over time and because of this, today's performance level may not be sufficient anymore tomorrow

When improving activities and performance I consider two different situations:

- Improving your existing efforts and the results thereof if you have not yet reached the management system objectives set. This would be the normal situation when you start small and let the system grow based on results.
- Improving your system once you have reached your initial objectives. This would probably always be the case as the world around us will change requiring periodic adaptations of the management system, its level of performance and objective(s). You may regard this as maintenance of the system to stay at a desired performance level in a changing environment.

These improvement efforts are very similar. Yet, when it comes to doing audits as one of the main methods for improvement, I recognize two different types as we will see below under "audits".

There are two main ways along which you can maintain and improve your management system:

- Pro-active. Carry out audits, evaluations or assessments to establish: (i) what is being done to reach objectives and, (ii) what the results are of what is being done. Both aspects are included in the 17-step process as part the assessment of element activities and results (in step 15) and the in review by the management improvement team (step 16). The latter considering overall management system results also in relation to the environment – political, social, technical, economic – in which your organization operates.

- Re-active. Learn from unwanted events that result from management system inadequacies. The events may occur because of: (i) incompleteness of the management system due to missing elements or insufficient activities within existing elements and, (ii) non-compliance with element criteria/activities of an otherwise adequate management system.

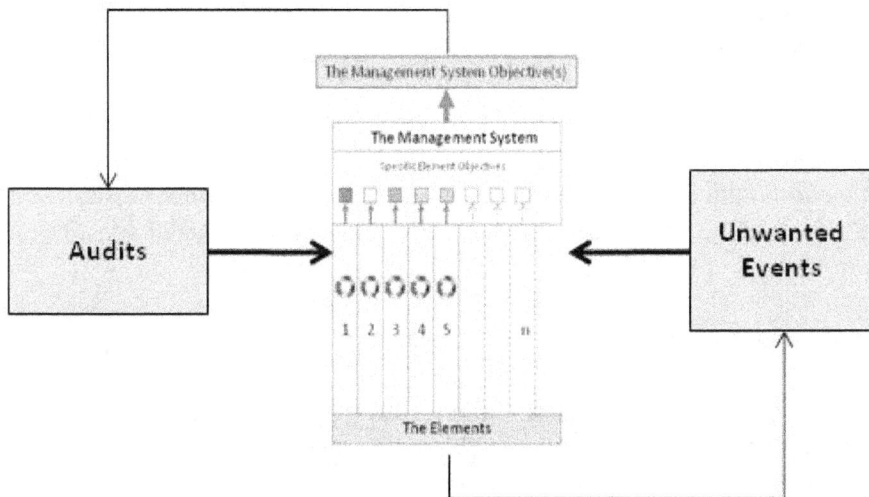

Picture 3.01 – Two main ways to maintain and improve the management system

In addition to audits and unwanted events there are also some other sources that you may want to consider when improving what you are doing:

- Total system result and individual element results achieved
- Inspections
- Observations
- Projects or single-use plans
- Exit Interviews

Audits - of total system and individual system elements

Purpose of a management system audit is to assess activities being carried out.

An audit is carried out using a questionnaire that has been set up using one or more reference sources containing information relevant to the objective of the management system.

I would divide audits into two categories based on their use:

- Internal audits based on your own management system, its elements and activities. Purpose of these audits is: (i) to improve execution of activities and results if the performance level for which your management system has been set up has not yet been obtained and, (ii) to maintain the performance level once that has been reached. Step 15 of the 17-step process relates to this type of assessments which are also part of the recommended element structure.
- External audits which are related to your management system objective. They can be used in case your system does not allow you to reach the objective(s) that you are looking for. The external system needs to be selected with care; it needs to be more extensive and detailed than your present system to allow adding elements and/or activities. External audits can be used in step 7 and 8 of the 17-step process. They can also prove to be helpful when setting up and extending the management system in step 12, 16 and 17.

A bit more about audits later.

Unwanted events – learning from what goes wrong

Unwanted events are important as they may indicate failures of the management system to control events that are in the way of reaching system element objectives. Although they are after the fact, and therefore not a preferred source, they can provide vital information to improve efforts provided that cause analysis goes all the way back to the basic and root causes and into the management system.

To use accidents, mishaps or other type of unwanted events for improvement, you need to have those reported and people in your organization have to be aware of this. A good protocol is a must. Risk classification, part of the protocol, will help to get the attention for investigation and cause analysis of the events that deserve that. A protocol example is provided in appendix J on page 331.

More about unwanted events later.

Results of system and elements

A good starting point to determine the effectiveness of a management system is to regularly assess and measure results and evaluate those against objectives set or to the objectives that you really may be looking for.

The result measurements include:

- Specific results of the individual elements that make up the management system
- Overall management system results; the combined results of the elements

These result measurements are included in the suggested element structure and part of steps 15 and 16 of the 17-step process.

The overall objective of a safety management system could be having no more than a certain number of accidents. The overall results of a quality management system could be to have no more than a certain number of product failures or customer complaints. Results measured higher than these objectives could indicate improper functioning of the management system or of one or more system elements.

When only the results of the overall management system are being measured, it may be hard to identify what may have led to those, less than desired, results. Comparing results obtained against the specific objectives set for each element will give a better indication of what may be causing the less than expected effects of the system. This, of course, assumes that the elements are relevant to obtain the objective(s) of the system as a whole.

Both result measurements – of overall system and of specific elements - should be done and analyzed for improvement opportunities.

Be careful by giving commendations in relation to end results only. This may have a counterproductive effect. If having no accidents or complaints will be the basis for giving awards of gifts, the effect may be that accidents or complaints may not be reported. Rewarding people, departments or companies on end results should preferably be combined with input performance measurements; what is being done and the results thereof

Inspections – uncovering substandard conditions

Basically, inspections are to find deviations from standard (= good) conditions or situations that may have been caused by accidents, not following standard work practices, improper maintenance, inadequate design or purchasing, etc.

Deviations noted during inspections should be treated as unwanted events to include risk classification and cause analysis, as applicable and possible. These deviations are very similar to accidents and should receive the same attention. Often, however, situations found during inspections are corrected immediately or through a work order system, without risk classification and cause analysis. If (basic) management system related causes are not treated it is very likely that, one day, the same or similar will happen again possibly with entirely different consequences.

Observations – uncovering substandard acts/behavior

Basically the same as inspections but now directed at what people do and their behavior, general behavior as well as specific behavior, during the execution of work, in particular critical tasks. Deviations from "standard" work practices or behavior should be considered as unwanted events and treated as such.

Inspections and observations are good opportunities to apply "accident imaging" – see page 208. Simply put, those principles boil down to asking the question "what if?", what could happen if situations were different from actual? Best done in a team approach using brainstorming techniques under guidance of a facilitator.

Projects – single use plans dealing with problems or opportunities

Projects can originate from various sources and for various reasons and often deal with problems or opportunities. They may generate information that would help to improve the management system so future problems may be prevented and opportunities not missed. Inspections, observations, audits, exit interviews, and accidents or unwanted events are amongst the sources that lead to single-use projects.

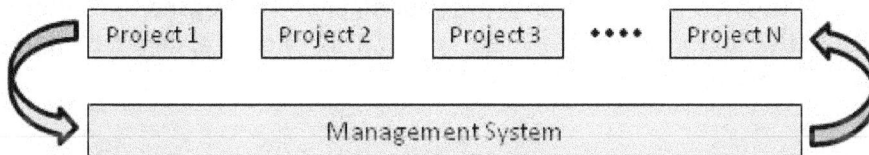

Picture 3.02 – projects feeding the management system

Exit interviews

Exit interviews can be a good source to learn about the operation of your company and its management system(s). Exit interviews are similar to opinion surveys to find out what people think about what you do. People/companies – including people leaving your company, temporary workers, contractors and suppliers - experience what you do. They may be a source to find out about unwanted events that took place but did not get reported. They may give you feed back on how your management system, or parts thereof, is working. Exit interviews may be a valuable source to learn what went right and what went wrong. They may help your company to become better, build a good relationship with suppliers and improve its market image.

Customers, of course, are also a good source to obtain information about the functioning of your management system, most likely your quality system; don't wait till your customers are on their way to the exit.

And what about end-users? You and me and all of us? Do we not wonder sometimes why people or companies provided the product or service the way they do? That's also applies to the services or products that your company provides. We do not consider these issues under "exit interviews" but the idea is still the same: ask people about products and services being delivered. Why wait for complaints to spread around and damage your company's image and market. Be pro-active and learn from the experience of those that are vital for your continuing success. This is should not be limited to business-to-business providers only but be extended to include end-users of companies as well as political and social institutions.

3.1   THE AUDIT – pro-active, pre-event improvement

Depending on the reference you are using, the audit basically has two objectives:

1. When using your own management system as a reference, the audit is to verify that the activities, specified in each of the activity areas or elements, are carried out as intended and that desired results are being obtained. As such this type of audit is a tool to improve your organization to the limit provided by the management system objective; but not really a reference to extend beyond the objective level set.

2. If using an external reference the audit may uncover missing elements or element activities. This may help you to improve your organization beyond the performance level and objective set for the management system. This, of course, depends on the extent and quality of the audit reference used.

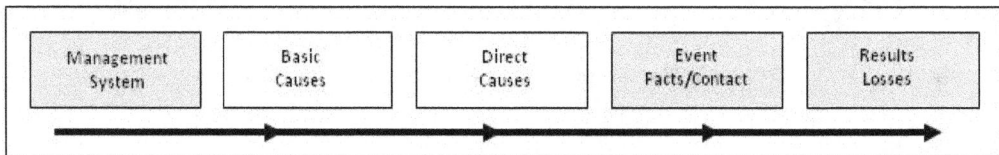

Management System	Basic Causes	Direct Causes	Event Facts/Contact	Results Losses

3.1   The audit checklist or questionnaire

Basically, the audit is done using a checklist or questionnaire covering the items that are relevant in relation to the objective of the management system to be audited. The checklist may have been developed from external reference documents such as:

- Legislation
- Industry standards
- Certification norms
- Any combination of those and other references

Using external reference documents, the steps involved in making useable audit questionnaires will include:

- Transferring each item or sentence of the reference document into a question. This allows the auditor to ask the questions. This is the easy part of the process.
- Deciding which answers to each of the questions will be acceptable. This is the difficult part of the process but a vital one as requirements should be clear for audit results to be consistent between auditors. Interpretation margins should be as narrow as reasonably possible and desired.

Audit references may be provided with value factors to allow scoring. This would be very helpful when communicating audit results to relevant internal and external parties and when setting targets for further implementation and improvement. Please see an audit scoring example in appendix H on page 298 and in picture 2.25 on page 161.

3.2   The auditor

To get consistent and reliable results from different auditors, these people should have adequate knowledge including:

- The audit process – from opening meeting to closing meeting and what to do before, in between and after that
- The subjects being audited – objectives of the (management) system and its elements
- The checklist – questions to be used when doing the audit
- What the acceptable answers are to the audit questions

The last bullet point is critical. There must be a good understanding between auditors about what the acceptable answers are otherwise the audit results may vary widely between auditors. If that is the case, it may result in a questionable value of the certificate and undermine the purpose of the certification process and that of certification as a whole. That purpose is to be a reliable indication about the minimum performance level of the certificate subject for stakeholders using the certificate in their decision-making processes. Stakeholders may include customers, suppliers, consumers, the legislator, insurance companies, neighbors, consumers and the public in general.

In case of accredited certification, interpretation between auditors of different certification institutes may be a crucial issue. Certification Institutes are commercial organizations and competition may tempt them and their auditors to seek the lower ranges of the interpretation margins.

Auditors should be given adequate training and retraining to stay in tune with developments concerning the audit checklist, the audit process and the acceptability of answers to the audit questions. Auditors should also have adequate knowledge of the type of industry they are auditing.

Auditors should be given sufficient time to properly carry out audits and to make the audit report. This too may be an aspect of concern in case audits are carried out by auditors working for commercial certification institutes.

3.1.3   The auditing process

Between the opening and closing meeting, the audit process would normally consist of:

- Review of management system documentation (may happen prior to on-site visit)
- One or more site or location visits
- Verification of the working of the management system both in the office and on location

I used to carry out audits with the ISRS (International Safety Rating System) and predecessors between 1975 and 1991. ISRS, by the way, is less sensitive to competition issues as ISRS is a proprietary product (from 1978 ILCI and since 1991 DNV, Det Norske Veritas, now DNV-GL). I used to carry out opinion surveys prior to the actual on-site audit. This provided me with valuable information about the way people felt about their safety management system, before going through the process of verification. See appendix C on page 228 for an ISRS related opinion survey questionnaire that I used. To my knowledge such opinion surveys are not (normally) done in case of accredited certification but I think they would be a great help to make sure that the (management) system being audited actually works as intended.

Verification of the management system would include:

- Review of system manual and related documents to verify contents and structure of the management system
- Interview of persons assumed to have knowledge of the system and execution of activities
- Review of registrations containing data in relation to the execution of management system activities

- Site/location visits to observe physical conditions, the behavior of people during their work and to further interview people that are at the receiving end of the management system

If the audit is done by an external auditor, and if not already required through by the external audit process, internal audits should be done prior to the external audit to assure positive external audit results. Further review and verification will be done by the external auditor leading to the certificate. Internal audits, when done properly, also allow involvement of own company personnel in the process and adds to the learning about the effectiveness the organization's own management system. For that learning process, it is recommended to include both managerial and operational people in the internal audits as well as the use of an expert "facilitator"

3.1.4 The audit report

The findings of the audit will result in an audit report containing:

- A description of the audit process and planning
- Audit reference used (internal/external)
- Sites/locations visited
- Persons interviewed
- Commendation of positive findings
- Deviations found (and recommendations to correct)

As applicable for later review, the auditor should keep notes of audit findings in addition to those presented in the report.

In case of a certification audit, the report may also serve as the basis on which the certificate will be issued or withheld. The value of reports generated after the certification audit may be limited due to competition issues between certification institutes and the limited time allowed for report preparation. Improvement recommendations are not normally included in the audit report in case of accredited certification. Certification reports may just be limited to reporting non-conformities. In that case it is to be assumed – by the reader of the report – that all other issues are properly implemented and complied with. Whether that is actually so may depend on the qualifications and credibility of the auditor.

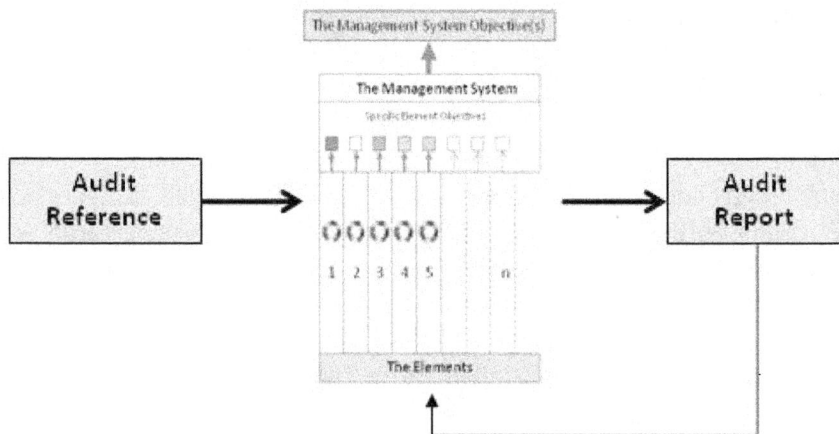

Picture 3.03 – Auditing the management system is proactive control

Some remarks

When auditing a management system all aspects: content, structure and "how to" should be looked at. The latter may be done on an at random basis but critical documents should be reviewed in detail.

Most audit systems I am aware of pay attention to content and "how to". Including the element structure, however, may be a different matter and is probably not present in most audit (and management) systems. I consider that a serious shortcoming. If you would leave out the structure, you are leaving out what I consider the "engine" that drives element activity implementation towards results. Without that you are leaving out an important driver towards success. I would even defend that, if the structure is not there, the management system cannot really be effective or at least it will be difficult to get the wanted results or it may take much longer to get there.

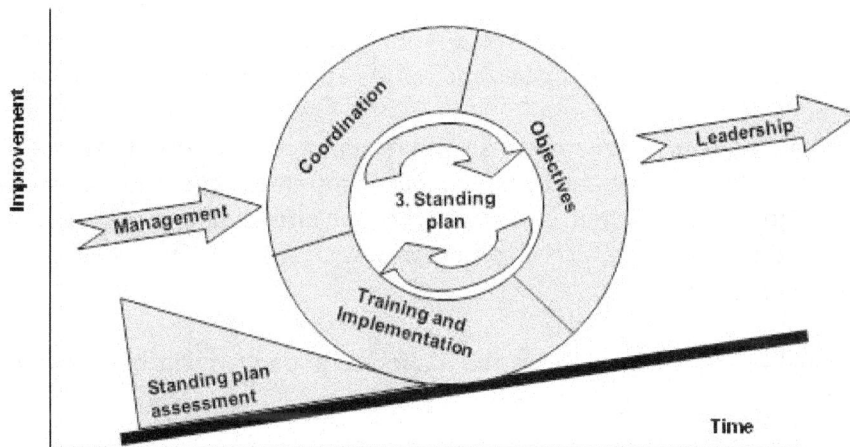

Picture 3.04 – The "improvement wheel" containing the platform and structure items

3.1.5   Higher abstraction level audits

Referring to the last paragraph above: when eventually success will be there and you would look back, it may very well be that all or the majority of the structure items will have been taken care of. That should only be logical. After all, how can you get lasting success without the ongoing support and involvement of all or most of the people in the organization? And without making sure that necessary activities to reach your objective(s) are being carried out and adapted whenever appropriate?

This is how I came to the "higher abstraction level audit" (See example appendix I, page 326) which would concern (internal) improvement directed audits and would most likely not apply to certification audits which may have a limited purpose: to get the certificate.

NOTE: When referring to higher abstraction level audits I do not refer to the ISO Guide 83 "Higher Level Structure".

If you want to have a relatively quick impression of a management system to see if the system is designed to work as it should, you may consider carrying out audits at a higher abstraction level by concentrating on the presence of:

- A sufficient number of elements or (management) activity areas that are relevant to reaching the objective of the management system
- The structure of those elements, similar to that mentioned in chapter 2.6 (page 163) including objectives, activities, the involvement of relevant personnel from all levels and the assessment of activities carried out and results obtained

The reasoning behind this approach is that it would be very unlikely, or at least very difficult, to reach desired management system results if the "improvement loop" - the structure from element objectives to evaluation of activities and results - is not there or incomplete.

If the structure is not there or incomplete, the main recommendation after the audit should probably be to install the structure and complete it in all the elements of the management system. It is only after implementation of the structure and after finding that success is still not there, that you need to look further at the content of system and elements to see if activities need to be changed or added.

These audits should not necessarily replace the traditional in-depth audits but rather be in addition to those.

One of the prerequisites of doing these higher abstraction level audits is that objectives of elements and the overall management system are as specific and well defined as necessary and possible. The in-depth audit, going into the element details regarding the activities - what, when, by whom and how - may only be required if the clearly defined objectives are not obtained. A good approach may be to have an in-depth audit once every 3 years with annual higher abstraction level audits in between. Of course, the latter assumes presence of the structure and the audit would verify the proper working thereof, in particular when comparing results obtained with element objectives.

An example that relates to the above from my own experience. In 1993 I was involved in making a process industry version of an existing safety audit system including issues relevant to the process industry. This process industry version included the element structure while the original system did not. Both audit systems included scoring opportunities resulting in a level award for the entire management system ranging from 1 to 10 with 10 being the highest possible level. Both audit instruments were used parallel to each other when auditing a chemical plant in Spain. The audit using the original system resulted in a level 8 rating while the audit using the process industry version with the structure did not go beyond level 1. A precondition to assigning award levels using the latter version was that the improvement cycle represented by the structure, had to be a closed loop which, I think, was only a logical requirement.

Although my example may not be hard evidence that the structure should be included, it is only logical to make it part of the audit reference and management system. If not for anything else, leaving the structure out of the audit may indicate a high quality level management system while it actually does not have the necessary arrangement to make it work effectively. After all, the structure is there to assign responsibilities and verify that activities are carried out and results obtained – what else is the purpose of a management system and its audit reference? In the case of my example, using the audit without the structure would tell the customer that they did a very good job. Using the audit without the structure tells them that they have not even begun to make it work. Which one would you think will give the right message? And which one, do you think, they would prefer – the one with the higher award level or the one with the better change for success?

3.2   LEARNING FROM UNWANTED EVENTS – post event improvement

You may have heard the saying that "all accidents are preventable". While, in theory, that may be true, in practice this will not be possible depending on your definition of accident and unwanted event and the availability of resources. So it is probably more correct to say: "all accidents are preventable but not all can be prevented". Theory versus practice. Anyway, accidents and other type of unwanted events and their losses are "excellent" sources to learn from and to improve the management system and to further the control of risk and loss.

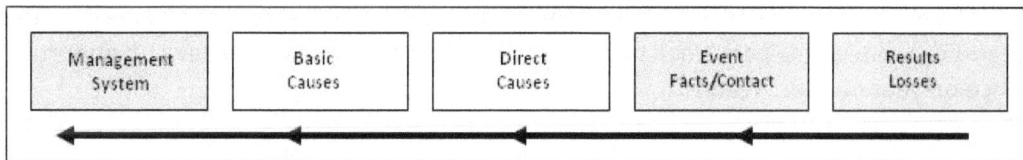

"Excellent" sources to improve but maybe not preferred as results of unwanted events may be serious or catastrophic and you really do not want to learn from those.

SANKOFA - "return and get it", learn from the past

3.2.1   Learning from unwanted events that DID get reported

Learning from unwanted events requires that they are reported and information obtained to allow cause analysis all the way back to the management system.

You need to have a process to learn from unwanted events; a process based on a protocol similar to the example provided in appendix J on page 331.

Learning from unwanted events with serious consequences is a must but not the preferred way as you may be learning from events that are irreversible. Learning from unwanted events with relatively minor consequences, or no consequences at all, is the better way. You need to have a risk classification method (see chapter 1.5.3 on page 70 and appendix J) to select the important ones and to give those the attention and resources required; to gather data, analyze causes and take remedial actions including management system improvements.

Risk classification could also be used when evaluating deviations noted during inspections or (behavior) observations. Substandard conditions or acts observed during inspections and observations could represent actual losses or could have resulted in loss if the circumstances would have been different. Substandard acts and conditions are (potential) unwanted events and should be treated as such.

Should you investigate all minor losses and no-loss events?

I do not think so. But you may want many of those events reported and you may want to record them for trend analysis. You may want to know what these small losses cost you per month or per year. Even though they are small on their own; together they may still have an important influence on your business results.

After a small loss or no-loss event has been reported, use risk classification to find the high potential (HIPO) events that could lead to serious loss and carry out an in-depth cause analyses on those.

BE AWARE: giving (too) much attention to events that will not and cannot generate more than minor losses may demotivate people, including management. Investigation of unwanted events uses resources (time, money, attention) so try to limit the investigation to the important events and use your risk classification method to highlight those that need attention.

Accident Analysis - to uncover causes for remedial actions

When analyzing unwanted events, consider two routes:

- From the event going "upstream" to uncover why the event took place – cause analysis
- From the event going "downstream" to find why losses are what they are or could have been – (potential) extent of loss analysis to evaluate the effectiveness of the after the event (emergency) actions.

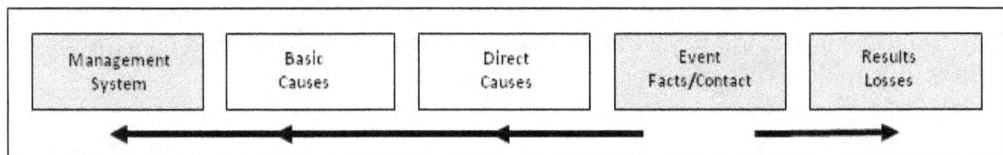

Event Cause Analysis – "upstream analysis"

Analysis of unwanted events is directed at finding the causes that have lead to the event and its consequences.

Cause analysis would normally be directed at three levels:

- Direct causes - see chapter 1.6.4, page 87
- Basic causes – see chapter 1.6.5, page 91
- Management system aspects – see chapter 1.6.6, page 94

Basis causes and management system aspects can be considered the "root causes" of unwanted events. Root causes are at the practical end of causes analysis; "practical" meaning that the causes can (still) be controlled through efforts and resources that are in proportion to the expected or desired results.

Based on the level of risk, the investigation protocol (example appendix J on page 331) shall indicate when to carry out a cause analysis. When establishing the risk level – using your risk classification method - consider circumstances that are (slightly) different from those that caused the unwanted event.

Extent of Loss Analysis - "downstream analysis"

The extent of loss analysis should consider:

- Presence and efficiency of barriers between the event and its (possible) consequences
- The availability and quality of private and public emergency means
- The presence and effectiveness of a post event or post emergency plan to also limit secondary, "indirect", losses including commercial losses such as loss of market and company image

Could the consequences of the event be much different or larger under other circumstances? Consider issues like: if the fire would have occurred during another time of the year, would the loss have been much greater? If the fire brigade could not reach your plant in time because there was an accident blocking the road or because the bridge was open, what would have been the consequences? If, for whatever reason, there would not be enough water at the right pressure to extinguish the fire, what then?

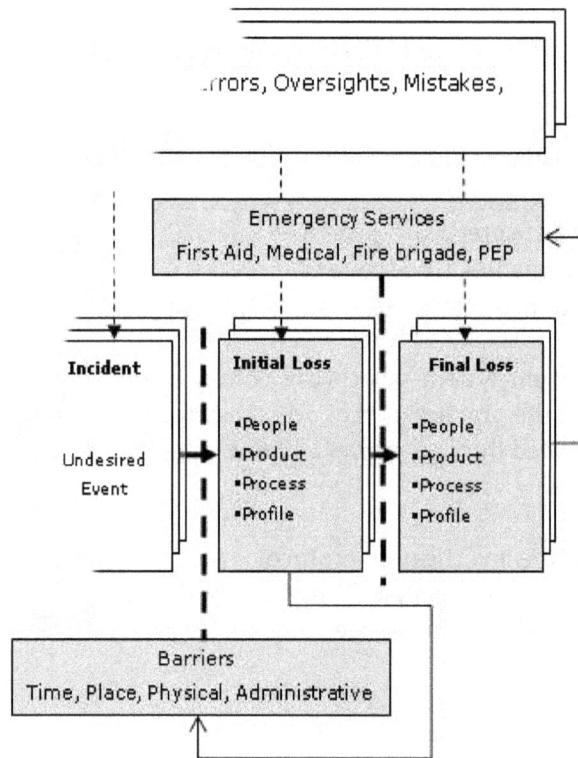

Picture 3.05 - Downstream, extent of loss, analysis

Unwanted event analysis – upstream and downstream - can be an important source of information to improve the management system and all related aspects.

This is why these analyses should preferably be done using a team approach under the guidance of a "facilitator"; someone with sufficient knowledge and expertise about the analysis method used. The role of this person is of particular importance if the data will be put in a database for future use and retrieval of information.

Remedial actions

Remedial actions – following either upstream or downstream analysis - should preferably be developed through a team approach including the following people as team participants:

- Relevant management and supervision
- People from department where the event took place
- People carrying out the activities that took place prior to or during the event
- Staff people from maintenance, human resources and other relevant departments

- People involved in emergency actions including external sources as appropriate
- Facilitator to guide the process of investigation, event cause analysis and remedial action development

These team exercises are examples of projects that are generated by the management system element "learning from unwanted events."

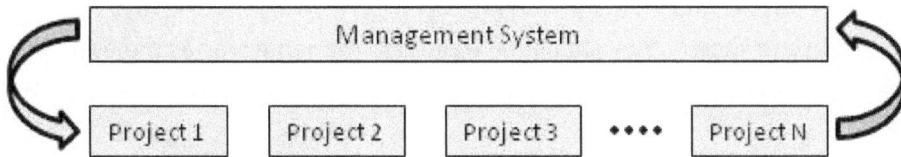

Picture 3.06 – The management system generating projects

To make sure that remedial actions will be carried our properly and within the established period, consider the following functions:

- Event owner - person responsible for everything that is related to the event, including the actions to be taken. Probably the head of the department where the event took place. Or higher up the organization depending on the (potential) impact of the unwanted event.
- Action owner - person responsible to assure that a particular action, or a set of actions, will be carried out. This could be the person who actually carries out the action or someone who makes sure that somebody else, possibly outside the company or organization, carries out the work.

An event would normally have one event owner but could have several action owners, depending on the number and diversity of actions.

3.2.2 Learning from unwanted events that <u>DID NOT get reported</u>

Accident ratio studies (see triangle picture 1.18 on page 82) suggest that many unwanted events do not get reported for one reason or another. These include the events that did not result in visible loss or they may not get reported simply because in-company procedures do not require that events other than injuries be reported.

Reasons for not reporting may also include:

- Fear of discipline
- Concern about the record
- Concern about reputation

- Fear of medical treatment
- Dislike of medical personnel
- Desire to avoid work interruption
- Desire to keep personal record clear
- Avoidance of red tap
- Concern about the attitude of others
- Not understanding the importance

Once these events are known, they should be treated in the same way as the events that did get reported. In order to learn from them they need to be known and there are several ways to find out about them:

Inspections

During inspections substandard of unsafe conditions may be noticed. These conditions did not occur by themselves - they were caused, most likely because someone did something or because someone did not do something (right). Deviations noted during inspections may not be analyzed for their causes. Risk classification on deviations noted during inspections may normally not be done. Normal practice may be that they are corrected, probably noted on a form and that's about it. If that is the way it is done, opportunities are lost to prevent the same conditions from happening again, possibly with much different consequences.

Observations

Behavior observations are like inspections. Only now they are directed at what people do and how they do it. In practice, however, the people carrying out behavior observations often tend to focus on conditions rather than on what people do. Focusing on conditions is easier than observing and addressing people about what they do and why. But even when directed at behavior, these observations tend to consider more general behavior such as rule compliance, often because of the background of the people carrying out the observations.

Critical task observations are directed at how critical (risk sensitive) tasks are being carried out. These observations also are part of (initial) training/instruction to verify that the training has been effective and are also a good way to see if these tasks are properly carried out according to procedures or work instructions, the "standard way of doing the work". Critical task observations are an excellent source to find deviations that could lead to unwanted events and are a good means to see if existing procedures, work environments or tools need to be adapted.

Observations of critical tasks are directed at the execution of specific (elevated risk) tasks and require thorough knowledge of how the task should be performed. An alternative to observing critical tasks, with similar or better results, is to have group discussions involving people carrying out the tasks involved.

Observation of critical tasks is part of a process to control risk during the execution of work. This process includes:

- Listing of all functions in the organization
- Determination of tasks per function
- Identification of risks involved when executing tasks – use risk classification
- Control of identified risks including:
    - Possible elimination of risk
    - (Technical) risk reduction measures
    - Measures leading to task or work procedures, instructions or rules to properly handle the risks that remain after elimination and reduction
- Training of people using work procedures etc. including performance observation to check training efficiency
- Periodic observation or discussion of the execution of critical tasks
- Feedback from accidents, incidents and other unwanted events

The last two points are important to improve work procedures including adaptation necessary because of introduction of new tools, changes in the working environment etc. The last point allows identification of critical tasks that were not considered before. These should be added to the "critical task list" for further processing following the process steps mentioned above. These last two points are also good opportunities to find out whether up stream activities such as design, purchasing and training are being carried out as they should.

Please note that the process above is not limited to operational work only; it can be applied to all functions, all disciplines at all levels in the organization and including decision-making.

Behavior of management and supervision plays an important role in creating the behavior of people at lower organizational levels; either general behavior or behavior during the execution of specific tasks. So if the behavior at lower levels is less than desirable, look at the behavior of upstream people and also look at the management system and at the way people have been and are involved in making that system work as it should.

Incident Recall

Incident Recall is a structured process of communication/interviewing to uncover events that could have resulted in unwanted consequences - events that have been reported and may be used for learning before they will be forgotten.

The interviewing could be done by a supervisor/manager or by a staff person more experienced in interviewing techniques. The interviewer should have a good knowledge of the work involved and the conditions under which this is done.

Incident recall could be done on a one-on-one basis or as a group exercise. The latter is probably the better approach but requires a no-blame fixing culture in which people are attuned to helping each other to get better and prevent unwanted events.

3.2.3   Learn from unwanted events that <u>COULD happen</u> – accident imaging

Basically "accident imaging" is: imagine what could happen. When you do that, look at the broad picture and include all possible unwanted events and consequences. Accident imaging is answering the question "what if?", "What could happen if the situation was different from what it is now?" Look at possible deviations from what is normal. Look at possible causes as well as possible consequences. Consider changes in existing process- or work procedures following (temporary) deviations in the normal work environment. Imagination is the only limiting factor.

Accident imaging could provide important information to secure continued operation of your company or organization and improve the management system.

Accident imaging should take place during design stages of installations, work environment and procedures. It can and should take place during inspections and investigation of unwanted events. It can take place during all or most business processes. What if we would lose that particular supplier? What if the warehouse would burn down? What if we would lose one of our key people? What if we lose our power supply, would we lose customers? What if we would have a fire, how much would we lose? WHAT IF?

Two examples of "what if?"

1.   The Moerdijk Fire –The Netherlands 2011

        In January 2011 a fire occurred at a chemicals processing plant at Moerdijk, The
        Netherlands. An employee used an open flame to defrost a flammable liquid pump with
        the end result that the total plant burned down and went into bankruptcy later on; no
        injuries.

        On 16 January 2012 DutchNews.nl reported: "Management failings are to blame for last
        year's massive fire at a chemicals packaging company in Moerdijk, near Rotterdam,
        according to a safety council report on the blaze, NOS television reports. The report,
        which has not yet been officially published, says Chemie Pack failed to meet operating
        permit conditions and did not keep to its own policy or procedures. This led to the
        company failing to take any safety measures to manage the fire."

2.   Cardboard manufacturer - Belgium 1970

My own experience includes a cardboard manufacturer and this happened in 1970 when I was working as a technical representative for INA, the US insurance company. My job was to look at factories and give my opinion about the insurability of the operation concerned. Central to this was the question: "What if". In relation to property damage and consequential loss (business interruption).

With cardboard rolls stored end on end, close to the ceiling, no sprinklers and smoke detectors no longer operational due to previous frequent alarms caused by diesel fueled forklifts, my advice was simple and straightforward: not recommended for insurance with an estimated maximum property loss of 90% of sum insured. Two months later, the plant burned down killing six people and with an almost total property loss, saving only the space separated power plant representing 10% of sum insured.

Two examples of what happened when the unwanted - but foreseeable - "what if" event occurred.

The quality of a management team is determined by:

1. Knowing in advance what problems could occur in their organization or unit
2. The number and size of those problems
3. Knowing what the causes of those problems could be
4. Knowing what actions to take to minimize the negative consequences

A quality management team should only have known problems with limited consequences

---

Philip B. Crosby (1926 – 2001) - US quality consultant, business philosopher and author

The process of accident imaging would include the following steps and considerations:

(1) Assuming a deviation from existing circumstances, which situation could lead to an unwanted event?
(2) What type of unwanted event?
(3) What could be the likely or possible consequences of that event?
(4) How often could the unwanted event occur?
(5) What are the likely or possible causes leading to the unwanted event?
(6) What preventive and contingency actions can be taken?
(7) What would be the results of these actions?

(8) What would be the costs of these actions?

(9) Who is going to do what and when?

Risk classification is important in this process, to estimate event frequency and consequences in steps 3 and 4 as well as in step 7 and 8 when considering potential action results and costs.

Accident Imaging - remember Murphy's Law: "What can happen, will happen". A matter of chance; not doing anything may be like playing Russian roulette.

When carrying out accident imaging – possibly as part of doing inspections or maintenance – try using a team approach as mentioned above under "remedial actions" (page 204). Involve people of the level where the action is – the point of control level.

The principle of point of control

The greatest potential for control tends to exist at the point where the action takes place

---

3.2.4   Selecting events for further processing

When known, all unwanted events, independent of their source, should be risk classified and - if above a certain level – investigated and analyzed to include aspects improving the management system whenever possible and applicable. What caused the event and why are consequences what they are? Or, as part or risk assessment - what could the consequences have been?

Learning from unwanted events accumulates in the management system giving direction to procedures and instructions. Determining how work places and installations are to be designed and equipment is to be purchased. How work procedures are to be set up and people are to be trained/instructed to properly carry out their work - safely and without undue loss. This way the management system - by creating a better working environment, better communication and influencing behavior of people - helps to mold the culture of the organization while at the same time obtaining better cost control and sustainable profitability.

```
┌──────────────────┐        ┌──────────────────┐
│                  │        │     Unwanted     │
│   Management     │ ◄───── │      Events      │
│    System        │        │    and their     │
│                  │        │      Losses      │
└──────────────────┘        └──────────────────┘
         │                           │
         ▼                           ▼
┌─────────────────────────────────────────────────┐
│  procedures, work methods, inspection system,     │
│  inspection checklists, maintenance, workplace    │
│  design, engineering, purchasing, training,       │
│  personnel selection, communications, risk        │
│  assessment, emergency preparedness, etcetera     │
└─────────────────────────────────────────────────┘
```

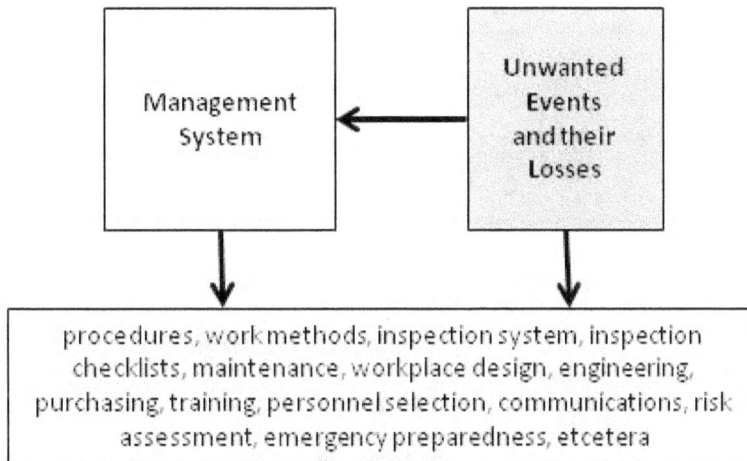

Picture 3.07 – Learning from events is reactive, after the event, control

Management system, audits and unwanted events – your success, your future

Your plan, evaluating results of what you are doing and learning from the things that may keep you away from your success and your future belong together – in business as well as in private live. They go hand-in-hand; two sides of the same coin.

Your future and success is determined by:

- What you should do - your plan or management system
- What you actually do and how - your behavior, your motivation

It is all in your mind, your heart, your hands, your plan, and your management system

```
          ┌─────────────────────────────────────────┐
          │     YOUR FUTURE, YOUR OBJECTIVES         │
          └─────────────────────────────────────────┘
                           ▲
                           │
          ┌─────────────────────────────────┐
          │     WHAT YOU DO and HOW          │
          └─────────────────────────────────┘
                           │
          ┌───────────────────────────────────────────────────┐
          │  procedures, work methods, inspection system,      │
          │  inspection checklists, maintenance, workplace     │
          │  design, engineering, purchasing, training,        │
          │  personnel selection, communications, risk         │
          │  assessment, emergency preparedness, etcetera      │
          └───────────────────────────────────────────────────┘
                           │
       ┌──────────────┐  ┌──────────────────┐  ┌──────────────┐
       │   AUDIT      │  │   YOUR PLAN      │  │   EVENTS     │
       │  Check what  │→ │   and resources  │← │ Learn from   │
       │   you do     │  │                  │  │ what happens │
       │              │  │   YOUR           │  │              │
       │              │  │   MANAGEMENT     │  │              │
       │              │  │   SYSTEM         │  │              │
       └──────────────┘  └──────────────────┘  └──────────────┘
```

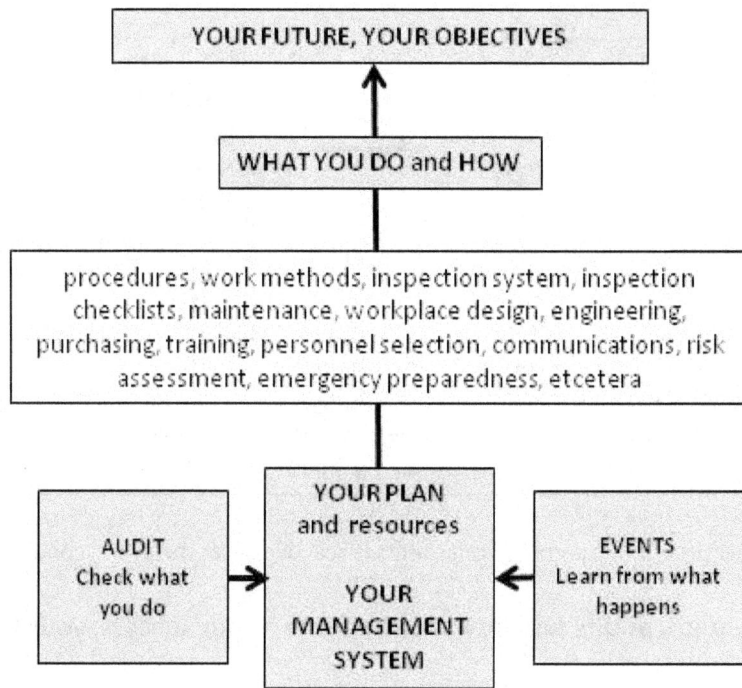

SUCCESS IS THERE FOR THOSE WHO DO NOT GIVE UP

(But be realistic: if you have done all you can and success is not even around the corner then you may want to start looking for something else. BUT DO NOT GIVE UP EASILY!)

THINGS TO REMEMBER

After closing this book, I hope you will remember a few things on your way to your next future:

1.   THE PLATFORM MODEL for change/improvement

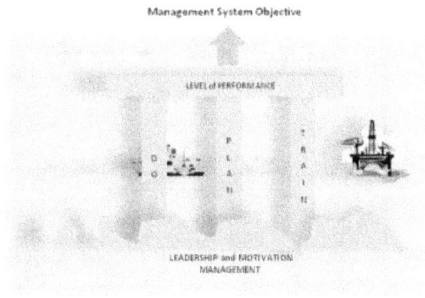

2.   THE 17 STEPS– process towards improvement and success

3.   THE STRUCTURE – the engine driving activities, fueled by leadership

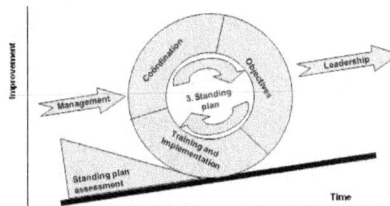

4.

> **One of the main aspects of the management function is to control loss**
>
> To close the gap between "how it is (done)" and "how it should be (done)"

5.   DO IT TOGETHER – involve those who need to be involved

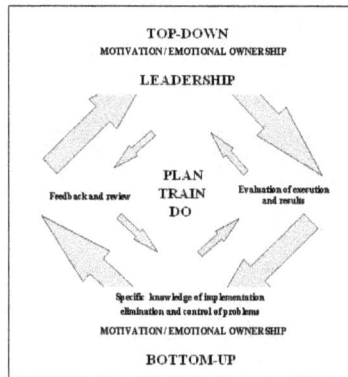

TOP-DOWN
MOTIVATION / EMOTIONAL OWNERSHIP

LEADERSHIP

PLAN
TRAIN
DO

Feedback and review

Evaluation of execution and results

Specific knowledge of implementation
elimination and control of problems

MOTIVATION / EMOTIONAL OWNERSHIP

BOTTOM-UP

If you really want (to do) something, you will find a way.

If you don't, you will find an excuse.

E.J. Rohn (1930 –2009) was an American entrepreneur, author and motivational speaker

LOOKING BACK

I apologize for not being complete, for repeating certain items (which, by the way, I did on purpose but you may feel that I did too much of it), for typing errors and for possibly incorrect use of the English language which is not my native tongue.

I hope that I have been somewhat consistent using the terminology throughout the book although you will have noted that I sometimes use terminology rather freely as I do not wish to be too limited by definitions. Examples are the use of terms such as: standing plan, management system, management activity area, element and terms like accident, incident and unwanted event.

If I have infringed on copyrights or any other rights, I also apologize; it is not my intention as I like to give credit to those who deserve it. If you have noticed any infringements, please let me know so I may be able to correct that.

Other than that, I am solely responsible for what I wrote in this book while making an honest attempt to share some of my ideas and experience with you. Should you have any comments and suggestions to improve the content of this book, I would gratefully receive them at my email address.

Above all, I hope that you will be able to use at least some of the ideas presented in this book in your efforts to improve your organization or that of your client. If that is the case, I will be quite satisfied knowing that I did not write this book in vain.

Breda, The Netherlands

Willem Top
Website: www.topves.nl
Email: willem@topves.nl

ABOUT ME

I was born in 1940 and am living in The Netherlands where, in 1965/66 I got my BS degrees in Chemical Engineering and Industrial Engineering. I have been working in the area of safety and risk management since 1968, related to industrial insurance as well as to certification and worked for Dutch, English, American and Norwegian companies.

In 1985, I set up my own (safety) management consulting firm, Loss Control Centre, involved in management system auditing, consulting and management training. My activities were based on a cooperation with Frank E. Bird, Jr. founder and owner of ILCI (International Loss Control Institute), world safety leader during the second halve of last century and originator of the International Safety Rating System (ISRS). Following the sales of ILCI by Mr. Bird in 1989, I also sold my firm to DNV (Det Norske Veritas) in 1991.

I was given the opportunity to help introducing the ISRS into Europe and in 1989 took the initiative that led to the creation of the contractor safety certification system (SCC/VCA) that became accredited in 1994 and is used in The Netherlands, Belgium, Germany, Austria and Switzerland.

I wrote several articles between 1976 and 2013; most in Dutch, some in English and you can find these articles on my website. I also wrote two small books in Dutch in 1988 and 1989.

Apart from "Making Your Future" I wrote another book with the title: "Risk Management, Safety and Control of Loss – Protecting Your Organization – an Introduction" (ISBN 978-90-820411-3-2). The object of that book was to make clear the similarity of these three subjects as part of the management function and the role these areas play in the ongoing success of companies and other organizations. I like to see my books as short courses on management. While both contain the same ideas and principles, they more or less stand on their own each with a different focus.

Just one last thing before I say goodbye. After you came this far, you may wonder: Hey, Willem, what did you do to make your future? Were you successful?

The answer to that question? Yes and no. Rather than going into details, let me share you this with you:

- For most of my life, I did not really have a well-defined plan. As is probably the case with most of us, my route through life was largely determined by the opportunities, or the lack thereof that I found on my way. I made right decisions and wrong ones as I found out later. But even with a plan, there were successes and there were failures.

- I was successful when I could take the lead in what I wanted to do but when I had to depend on others success was not so evident. Maybe it is just me but maybe also there is a message in this: if you want to be successful, try to be in the leadership position. It just may be easier if you do not have to depend so much on others to reach your goal. But even if you would depend on others, as is often the case, this book may give you some ideas that will help you to get these others to work with you to reach your goals and make your future together.

Looking back at what I have down so far, I think that making a good plan while being in charge would probably provide the best conditions for success. That is also why I think that making your future should be taught at schools and in particular at those institutions that educate people to become managers and lead people later on.

I think that the 17-step process is a good pathway to success, in particular when you have to work with people to obtain your success.

For more information about me and my ideas, please visit www.topves.nl.

Besides articles in Dutch and English, I wrote two books:

- Risk Management, Safety and Control of Loss – Protecting Your Organization, an Introduction (2014, ISBN 978-90-820411-3-2)
- Making Your Future – in Business and Other Parts of Life (2015, ISBN 978-90-820411-4-9).

I like to think that my books form a unity when it comes to improvement, reaching objectives while, at the same time, controlling unwanted events.

Although each of these books stands on its own, they also belong together and include the same ideas, principles, tools etc. and a necessary overlap between them.

APPENDICES

On the next pages I provide several examples to illustrate issues that I have mentioned in this book.

PLEASE NOTE: The information contained in the appendices is provided as example only. If you want to use these in your organization, you need to adapt the contents to your specific needs and situation.

The appendices are:

APPENDIX A – Management system – some questions and answers

I asked myself some questions which, I think, you may also have. And then I also gave the answers.

<u>What is a management system?</u>

Please read the box below for a, very non-scientific, description of what the real meaning of a management system is.

What a Management System

In essence, a management system is a PLAN: "this is where we want to be and the way we will get there".

To make it effective in reaching the desired objective you need three things: (i) process, (ii) content and (iii) structure

A management system is a leadership tool, a plan or guide to direct an organization and its people towards objectives set.

<u>Why a management system?</u>

You probably will have some elements of a "management system" in your organization. However, it may not be written down which will make it more difficult to communicate to stakeholders. It may not be very good and it may not produce much or any results. But there should at least be some activities that can be the start of a management system that will produce results.

So the question may be: Why should we have a management system that works? The answer is very obvious to me: Why not have a management system that produces results that you want? You are doing certain things anyway, so why not doing them in a way that they work better? And involve people who know what to do, when and how?

A management system is a plan to reach objectives. No objective – no plan – no results – no future. Without it you may just wait and see what will be coming. Why not have a plan to make the future better?

You may also want/need a "management system" because your customers require you to obtain a certain certificate. That may not be the type and quality of a management system that I would be looking for. If you are just looking for a certificate, you may even find a consultant who will help you to set up a "management system" to meet minimum certification requirements. And that consultant may also help you to find a certification institute that will issue a certificate meeting those minimum requirements. That will provide you with a certificate but that may not produce the results you could have had and which your customer, or other stakeholder, may expect.

Does the Management System have to be in writing?

No, not necessarily. But if your organization is a little larger than very small it may be difficult to communicate the contents - who shall do what, why, when and how – to people in your organization or company. It also may be difficult or close to impossible to communicate to external parties if it is not put on paper.

If you want a certificate based on your management system it is a requirement to have it on paper so your system can be properly audited.

Does a Management System make the working of your organization rigid?

Could be, depends how complex you make it and sometimes that may be needed depending on the type of industry you are in. If you cannot afford unwanted events, no matter what, then your management system or plan may have to be rather detailed and, if you want to call it that: rigid.

For the average industry if you start small and let your system grow based on results you should end up with the management system that fits your organization: not too large and not too small, just right for you. But, please, when starting to build your management system, take care to select the elements that are essential in reaching the objective of your management system while, at the same time, keeping risks outside your company.

If you develop the management system using the 17-step process described in this book, it is likely that you end up with a system that is supported throughout the organization. The detail of that system will also depend of the qualifications of the people. That would fit in nicely with a concept such as people empowerment.

When is a management system a MANAGEMENT SYSTEM?

A management system includes management activity areas or "elements" which you may want to call differently like "chapters", "work processes" or "programs". The elements - such as purchasing, design, training, management of change – contain specific activities indicating WHAT shall be done, WHY, WHEN, by WHOM and HOW.

A management system is a MANAGEMENT SYSTEM when:

- There is a clear overall objective to which the system is directed
- There is enough content - a sufficient number of relevant management activities or elements - to reach the objective of the system
- Each element is structured to stimulate the execution of activities and reach element specific objectives

And, of course, to be effective:

- The system has been developed through a process to allow participation by people of all levels in the organization. So it will be a system of management all the way down to where the work is being done.

What to expect of a management system?

Short answer: everything you expect from it. If only certificate, then your management system should deliver that. If you want your system to comply with legislation, then that should be the results of your management system. If you want more than a certificate or compliance with legislation then it all depends on what you want and you should make your management system to deliver that.

Certification has a minimal performance level which, in practice, will often also be the maximum level.

Leadership – the basis for improvement – does not have a minimum or maximum. Leadership doesn't know any borders!

What form or shape should the management system have?

It does not really matter as long as it is clear what shall be done, why, when, by whom and how. And that it has the structure to make sure that necessary activities are being carried out and desired results obtained.

Many organizations build their management system parallel to certification requirements which is OK for getting a certificate. However, if you want improvement on top of that you want a management system that will suit you best to include the activity areas necessary to obtain the results you are looking for.

If you build your management system different from the layout of the certification reference, then it may help - for certification purposes - to make a matrix showing where the certification issues can be found in your management system. It may make it easier for the auditor. In fact, you may want more than one cross reference matrix if you want more than one certificate or to comply with various legislative requirements while your management system covers more than one business area.

What should be in it?

The content of your management system will be determined by what you expect it to do. If you want an ISO 9001 certificate, refer to ISO 9001, if you want an OHSAS 18000 certificate then refer to OHSAS 18000, and so on. If you want your management system for other reasons then include the activity areas and their specific activities that you think will bring the desired results.

In most cases you will include activity areas that are more or less generic to any objective that you may want to reach. Those include areas like: hiring and placement of people, design of installations and work environment, design of products, training of management, training of operating personnel, purchasing, management of change, etc.

What structure should the composing elements have?

Any structure that you think is suitable as long as the structure would stimulate implementation of activities and obtaining results. The structure suggested in chapter 2.6 on page 163 will help you to do that.

To facilitate execution of activities that are part of your system, it would certainly help if you build your management system along a process that will facilitate involvement and cooperation of relevant people. The 17-step process is a route to management (system) success.

Remember this principle of emotional ownership: "People tend to be more willing to participate in planed change when they have had an opportunity to participate and influence the process leading to change."

APPENDIX B - Safety and loss control management maturity profile

Instructions

The profile shown on the next pages is an adaptation by Mr. Frank E. Bird, Jr. of the Quality Management Maturity Grid made by Mr. Philip B. Crosby.

The profile allows you to give your personal ideas about the Safety and Loss Control Management situation in your company. Eight relevant issues are being considered (left-hand column) and you can evaluate these efforts on 5 different levels going from "Uncertainty" to "Certainty".

> Loss Control is broadly defined as "the control of losses". This definition can and does include injuries as well as property damage, production delays, product losses, environmental incidents, loss of clients, liability claims (including those arising out of product use/misuse), security losses, etc.
>
> The use of the term Loss Control bridges the gap between traditional (injury related) safety and risk management, total quality management and business excellence

The best way to do the assessment is to read the text provided in each row and determine which you feel best describes the situation in your plant. Put an "X" in the middle of that box.

The end result of your assessment is a graphical profile made visible by connecting the X's that you put in. The profile helps to obtain a picture of how you experience the safety and control of loss efforts in your organization.

You may also want to put values on each of the 5 columns, for example the value 1 on the column "Uncertainty" and the value 5 on the column "Certainly" – see top of columns. That way you will also be able to put a numerical score on the results obtained, per individual or average per group.

You can do this exercise with people from various levels in your organization. That will give an impression as to how people at various levels feel about the loss control efforts of the organization. That in itself can lead to an interesting communication and may assist in getting a proper perspective when looking to improve your efforts.

The profile is a good instrument to use at the start of meetings to get people to discuss the quality of their (safety and) loss control efforts. This may be the beginning of an improvement process using the 17-step, or similar, approach. This profile could be used in steps 2, 3 and 9 of the 17-step process.

Safety and Loss Control Management Maturity Profile

Level Category	Uncertainty (1)	Awakening (2)	Enlightenment (3)	Wisdom (4)	Certainty (5)
Management understanding of Safety/Loss Control	Comprehension of Safety/Loss Control as an important management tool is lacking.	Monetary losses capture the attention of key managers. Beginning to recognize the role of safety in the management system, but….	"We cause our own problems." "We can control most losses" "Losses are greater than anticipated."	"The savings are far greater than expected." "We are seeing results of efforts in all areas".	"We will survive and succeed because of our continuing efforts to control losses."
Management Attitude towards Safety/Loss Control	Tendency to blame others for accidents/losses. "That is why we have insurance".	Reluctant to devote time and effort to safety/loss control. Motivated only by (contractual) responsibilities to customers, employees, community, government.	Safety/loss control is essential to effective management and profitability. "We cannot prevent all losses, but we can control them … tell us what we can do more."	Positive and enthusiastic. Frustration is an emotion of the past and is replaced by confidence. Control of loss is the guiding principle.	Loss control is an absolutely vital part of our management system.
Management behavior In relation to Safety/Loss Control	Management behavior is a re-active, after-the-fact response to accidents and losses. Much finger pointing. Getting tough on offenders (of rules).	Much sincere, concerned discussion, but … less action. Trying motivational approaches – speeches, slogans, posters, etc. Top management is NOT visible.	Top management is listening and responding with support and action. Visibility (of Top management) is noticed.	Genuine participation and Involvement by management. Top management is recognizing its personal role in continuing emphasis (on safety and loss control).	Continued growth, maintenance and refinement (of the safety/loss control efforts) are key goals.

Safety and Loss Control Management Maturity Profile

Level / Category	Uncertainty (1)	Awakening (2)	Enlightenment (3)	Wisdom (4)	Certainty (5)
Management position towards Safety/Loss Control	Accidents and losses are part of doing business. Low priority (of safety) in relation to other business interests.	Questioning…. "Is it necessary to have injuries and losses?" "Are we meeting legislative requirements?"	We are committed to improving our management system through control of losses	Safety/loss control is a part of what we do and is permanently engraved in our philosophy and strategy. Safety/loss control performances are considered in management appraisals and recognition.	We know why we have few problems with control of losses
Safety/Loss Control position in management structure	Safety is a part-time function within other disciplines (personnel, engineering, maintenance).	Strong program coordinator appointed. May still be part of another discipline. Line management is getting involved.	Safety/loss control activities interact with all business functions. The safety/loss control function is visible in the management structure…. Line managers are "doers" and are held accountable.	Safety/Loss Control staff advisement from power base with high reporting relationship (to senior manager). Safety/Loss Control involvement in all major areas of business.	Safety/Loss Control staff advisement for loss control is a senior position. Prevention and control are vital organizational concerns.
Critical Safety/Loss Control problem approach	Problems are dealt with as they occur. The approach is essential after-the-fact. "Quick-fix" is the standard remedy.	Problems are dealt with in meetings with key personnel. The interest is "symptom oriented". Short term solutions to chronic problems.	(Potential) critical problems are identified and are openly confronted. Input is obtained from a variety of levels and resources. Basic causes are being identified to control recurrence.	(Potential) critical problem identification at the lowest possible organizational level. Specific techniques used to identify potential problems. Problem solving teams of capable people being used.	Prevention and control efforts are effective. Potential critical problems are noted and corrected before they occur.

Safety and Loss Control Management Maturity Profile

Level Category	Uncertainty (1)	Awakening (2)	Enlightenment (3)	Wisdom (4)	Certainty (5)
Safety/Loss Control measurement system	No systematic measurement of losses. An injury log is maintained as required by law.	Increasing concerns for frequency and severity rates and trends as well as for compensation and insurance costs.	Property damage costs and rates are part of the measurement system. Incident reporting gets attention.	Accurate measurement, analysis and communication of losses. Various loss types ("output") are being measured. Vital management system criteria ("input") in the measurement system.	Continuing refinement of both output and input data is being used to improve performance.
Safety/Loss Control system Improvement efforts	Improvement is not considered an option.	Safety programs begin to take shape and show results. Standards are being set and responsibilities for results are being assigned.	Continuing to develop and implement the necessary (management system) control elements. Increase of effectiveness is also being obtained through systems assessments.	Utilizing comprehensive assessments of the Safety/Loss Control system to assure effectiveness and to assist in further improvement (of the system).	Improvement of the safety/loss control system is a normal and continuing activity.

APPENDIX C- Safety and loss control opinion survey - management personnel

This questionnaire can be used to obtain an impression about the way people participate in, and feel about, the safety activities of your organization.

Questions have been developed at three organizational levels: (1) senior and middle management, (2) direct supervision and (3) operational employees. To a large extent questions are the same going from one group to another.

PLEASE NOTE: The example provided is directed at senior management. To see the questionnaires for supervisory and operational personnel, please visit www.topves.nl and use the website search facility looking for: "safety opinion survey".

I have used these questionnaires in conjunction with audits that I did with the International Safety Rating System. The surveys with these questionnaires were done prior to visiting the location and provided me with quite a bit of information before starting the actual audit.

By comparing the responses from the three groups an impression can be obtained about the way the safety program is working in an organization. If all works well then there should only be minor differences between the three levels. If differences are substantial then the conclusion may be that the safety activities are not properly identified, communicated and/or carried out. It may also indicate that the "management system" and its activities is more dictated by management – top down – than a mutual effort of management and employees together.

If differences between organizational groups are substantial, you may wish to carry out a safety audit to further identify strength and weaknesses. You may also want to do an evaluation using the 17-step process rating method (appendix F, page 267) to identify weaknesses in the process that was used to build the management system.

The overall results of these opinion surveys may be considered parallel to the results of the safety and loss control management maturity profile (appendix B on page 224) which is better suited for classroom activities. The opinion surveys will provide more detailed information about several safety and loss control activities in the organization.

The surveys are included as step 6 of the 17-step process.

1.	How often, in communication with your people, do you refer to the safety policy/program/guidelines of your organization?	a. weekly b. monthly c. annually d. never
2.	Have your safety responsibilities been clearly defined?	a. yes b. no
3.	How often do you participate in safety meetings with operational personnel?	a. weekly b. monthly c. once per quarter d. annually e. never
4.	How often do you participate in planned inspections concerning the part of the organization under your responsibility?	a. weekly b. monthly c. once per quarter d. annually e. never
5.	To what extent are your safety activities part of your (annual) appraisal?	a. none b. 0 – 10 % c. 11 – 20 % d. more than 20 % e. don't know
6.	In which specific safety activities do you participate? (These are activities that are not part of your normal job.)	a. none b. specific activities are: _____ _____

7.	What is your opinion about the way the following people in your organization feel about safety:	Not important				Very important	
	a. operational employees	0	2	4	6	8	10
	b. supervision	0	2	4	6	8	10
	c. middle and senior management	0	2	4	6	8	10

8.	How do you feel about the quality of the safety program of your organization?	Non existent				Excellent	
		0	2	4	6	8	10

9.a.	Do you know that work can be interrupted or refused in case of hazardous conditions?	a. yes b. no					

9.b.	If "yes", do you know the work interruption/refusal procedure?	a. yes b. no					

10.	What do you feel are the main causes of accidents that have occurred in your department or organization?	Not important					Very important
	a. unsafe acts of operational employees	0	2	4	6	8	10
	b. unsafe conditions of materials, equipment or work environment	0	2	4	6	8	10
	c. inadequate or insufficient training/instruction	0	2	4	6	8	10
	d. improper man – machine relation	0	2	4	6	8	10
	e. fatigue – monotonous work – stress	0	2	4	6	8	10
	f. use of alcohol, drugs, medication	0	2	4	6	8	10
	g. improper design of tools/equipment	0	2	4	6	8	10
	h. inadequate maintenance	0	2	4	6	8	10
	i. purchasing of unsafe tools, equipment etc.	0	2	4	6	8	10
	j. inadequate supervisory quality	0	2	4	6	8	10
	k. lack of management interest	0	2	4	6	8	10
	l. inadequate communication	0	2	4	6	8	10
	m. improper motivation of operational personnel	0	2	4	6	8	10
	n. improper motivation of direct supervision	0	2	4	6	8	10
	o. improper motivation of middle/senior management	0	2	4	6	8	10
	p. insufficient quality of safety department	0	2	4	6	8	10
	q. insufficient/improper safety rules/guidelines	0	2	4	6	8	10
	r. inadequate machine guarding	0	2	4	6	8	10
	s. improper machine controls	0	2	4	6	8	10

11.	How do you rate the safety training that you received when you joined the organization?	Inadequate				Excellent	
		0	2	4	6	8	10

12.a.	How long ago did you receive the last safety training?	a. last quarter b. last year c. 2-3 years ago d. > 3 year ago

12.b.	How do you rate the quality of that training?	Inadequate				Excellent	
		0	2	4	6	8	10

13.a.	Do you know that you have to report unsafe conditions?	a.	yes
		b.	no
13.b.	If "yes" do you know how to do that?	a.	yes
		b.	no
13.c.	Who do you think has the first responsibility to correct unsafe conditions at the work floor?	a.	senior management
		b.	safety coordinator
		c.	maintenance
		d.	supervisor
		e.	don't know
14.	How often are you informed about the status of the inspection program of your department or unit?	a.	monthly
		b.	once per quarter
		c.	semi-annual
		d.	annually
		e.	never
15.	When was the last time you were involved in the investigation/analysis of an injury or damage accident?	a.	last quarter
		b.	last year
		c.	don't know
		d.	never been involved
16.	Have you ever had instruction in concerning the investigation of injury or damage accidents?	a.	yes
		b.	no
17.	How often are you informed about the status (quality and extent of reporting) of the accident investigation program of your organization or unit?	a.	monthly
		b.	once per quarter
		c.	semi-annually
		d.	annually
		e.	never
18.a.	Do you participate in emergency plan exercises?	a.	yes
		b.	no
18.b.	If "yes", when was the last time this happened?	a.	last month
		b.	last quarter
		c.	last year
		d.	don't know
		e.	does not happen

19.	When was the last time you received accident statistics of your organization, department or unit?	a. last month b. last quarter c. last year d. don't know e. does not happen
20.	How do you rate the use of personal protective equipment (PPE) by: a. operational personnel? b. supervision? c. middle/senior management? d. contractors?	Inadequate Excellent 0 2 4 6 8 10 0 2 4 6 8 10 0 2 4 6 8 10 0 2 4 6 8 10
21.	How often are you informed about compliance with PPE rules in your organization, department or unit?	a. monthly b. once per quarter c. annually d. never
22.	Are chemicals or materials used in your department or unit that represent a health hazard?	a. yes b. no c. don't know
23.	How often do you receive safety/health information concerning materials/chemicals used in your department or unit?	a. monthly b. once per quarter c. annually d. never e. not applicable
24.	Do you regularly read magazines concerning safety/health issues? If "yes" which magazines do you read?	a. yes b. no _____ _____
25.a.	Do you periodically undergo medical texts because of your work?	a. yes b. no
25.b.	If "yes" how long ago was the last test?	a. < 6 months b. one year c. two years d. five years e. more than 5 years

26.	Did you receive information about the results of your last medical test?	a. yes b. no c. not applicable
27.a.	Have you received first aid training?	a. yes b. no
27.b.	Do you have a valid First Aid diploma?	a. yes b. no
28.	Have you received training/instruction concerning individual communication techniques?	a. yes b. no
29.	Have you received training/instruction concerning group communication techniques?	a. yes b. no
30.	What was the subject of the last safety campaign in your organization?	a. no campaigns b. don't know c. the subject was: _____ _____
31.	Do you regularly receive a newsletter of company magazine containing safety subjects?	a. yes b. no

32.	Which percentage of "near-miss accidents" do you think are reported in your department or unit?	None					All
		0	2	4	6	8	10

33.	How important do you find it for the following groups to have knowledge about methods to investigate accidents:	Not important					Very important
	a. operational personnel?	0	2	4	6	8	10
	b. supervision?	0	2	4	6	8	10
	c. middle management	0	2	4	6	8	10
	d. senior management	0	2	4	6	8	10

34.a.	How important do you find it for the following groups to know how safety inspections are carried out:	Not important					Very important
	a. operational personnel?	0	2	4	6	8	10
	b. supervision?	0	2	4	6	8	10
	c. middle management	0	2	4	6	8	10
	d. senior management	0	2	4	6	8	10

34.b.	How important do you find it for the following groups to know about the results of safety inspections:	Not important					Very important
a.	operational personnel?	0	2	4	6	8	10
b.	supervision?	0	2	4	6	8	10
c.	middle management	0	2	4	6	8	10
d.	senior management	0	2	4	6	8	10

35.	Should work procedures only relate to safety aspects or should they include all possible problems that may occur during the execution of work?	a. only safety
		b. all problems

36.	How much on-the-job training of operational personnel is provided by:	None					All
a.	experienced colleagues?	0	2	4	6	8	10
b.	direct supervision?	0	2	4	6	8	10
c.	training staff personnel?	0	2	4	6	8	10

37.	Concerning experienced colleagues who provide on-the job training, to what extent do they:	None				Best		Don't Know
a.	make use of task procedures/work instructions?	0	2	4	6	8	10	X
b.	make use of effective instruction techniques?	0	2	4	6	8	10	X
c.	motivate people to learn?	0	2	4	6	8	10	X
d.	observe the execution of the work and coach for improvement?	0	2	4	6	8	10	X
e.	Provide tips to do the work safer, better or easier?	0	2	4	6	8	10	X

38.	Concerning direct supervision who provide on-the-job training, to what extent do they:	None				Best		Don't Know
a.	make use of task procedures/work instructions?	0	2	4	6	8	10	X
b.	make use of effective instruction techniques?	0	2	4	6	8	10	X
c.	motivate people to learn?	0	2	4	6	8	10	X
d.	observe the execution of the work and coach for improvement?	0	2	4	6	8	10	X
e.	Provide tips to do the work safer, better or easier?	0	2	4	6	8	10	X

39.	In your department or unit, how is the compliance with:	None				Excellent	
	a. safety rules/guidelines?	0	2	4	6	8	10
	b. personal protective equipment rules?	0	2	4	6	8	10
	c. safe work procedures?	0	2	4	6	8	10

40.	How important, do you think do direct supervisors find the compliance with safety rules and instructions?	Not					Very	Don't Know
		0	2	4	6	8	10	X

41.	How often, do you think, do direct supervisors commend their people for complying with safety rules?	a. daily b. weekly c. monthly d. annually e. never

42.a.	Do you know the purchasing policy of your organization in relation to safety aspects?	a. yes b. no

42.b.	Do you think that safety is an important item within the purchasing policy?	a. yes b. no c. don't know

43.a.	Do you have contacts with suppliers apart from purchasing?	a. yes b. no

43.b.	If "yes" is that part of your function?	a. yes b. no

43.c.	If "yes" does this include items that have never been purchased before?	a. yes b. no

44.a.	Do you (sometimes) make work procedures?	a. yes b. no

44.b.	If "yes", do you have these checked by experts regarding safety aspects?	a. yes b. no

44.c.	Or do you do that yourself?	a. yes b. no

45.	How useful do you consider the safety meetings that take place in your organization?	Not					Very	Do not exist
		0	2	4	6	8	10	X

46.a.	Do you regularly receive information about the cost to your organization of off-the-job accidents?	a. yes b. no						
46.b.	Do you receive other information concerning off-the-job accidents?	a. yes b. no						
46.c.	Would you like to receive information concerning off the-job safety?	a. yes b. no						
47.	How well do operational personnel report damages to tools, machines, equipment, buildings, etc.?	None 0	2	4	6	8	All 10	Don't know X

48. If the answer to question 47 is less than 6, what then are the two most important reasons why the reporting is not better?

_____

_____

49. What are the three strongest points of the safety program of your organization?

_____

_____

50. What are the three weakest points of the safety program of your organization?

_____

_____

51. What are the most important things that you do to improve safety?

_____

_____

52. What can be done to better involve operational personnel in safety improvement?

_____

_____

53. What can be done to better involve management and supervision in safety improvement?

_____

_____

54. How useful do you find the safety statistics that you get for improving safety?

    a.   I do not get these

_____

_____

55.   How is your work in relation to safety measured and evaluated?

a.   This does not happen

_____

_____

56.   How do you measure and evaluate the work of your people with regard to safety?

a.   I do not do this

_____

_____

57.   Do you have any further comments to make subject the safety efforts of your organization?

a.   No further comments

_____

_____

PLEASE NOTE: To see the entire opinion survey questionnaire and those for supervisory en operational personnel, please visit www.topves.nl and use the website search facility looking for: "safety opinion survey".

APPENDIX D – How to make rules

"How to obtain compliance with rules" or "When to apply disciplinary action"

The process indicated by the 24 points below not only relates to the making of rules but can also be used as a guide to prepare procedures which should include the following headings:

- Objective
- Importance of the procedure
- Owner
- Coordinator
- Actions/work to be done
- Training/instruction involved
- Approval, signature(s)
- Date of issue, ID
- Implementation, including periodic compliance review
- Periodic review with stakeholders

Preparation

1. Rules only when necessary
2. Involve people concerned in rule making
3. Explain why rules are necessary
4. Make rules as simple as possible
5. Rules must be justified and correct
6. Make rules to comply with "normal" human behavior
7. Rules must not contradict each other
8. Make rule compliance attractive, make non-compliance unattractive

Presentation

9. Give worker preview of rules prior to instruction
10. Provide proper instruction
11. Test knowledge of rules
12. Keep rules accessible to users

Application

13. Provide "try-out" period to test rules in practice
14. Be clear in daily application of rules
15. Provide sufficient time for proper rule application
16. Be positive about rule compliance
17. Be negative about non-compliance

18. Proper example by supervision and management
19. Maintain rule knowledge
20. Periodically evaluate rule compliance
21. Periodically evaluate effect of rules
22. Keep rules up-dated
23. Be clear about consequences in case of non-compliance
24. Be consequent in case of non-compliance

Some comments are offered to the 24 points involved:

Preparation

The preparation stage is the period in which people are being made aware of the possible need for new rules or a new procedures rule. In this stage people are being involved in the making of rules or procedures. Obviously this can only take place when rules are being developed: once rules are implemented this worker participation is no longer possible.

1. Rules only when necessary
   Keep rules at a minimum. Rules should be prevented if possible. If we can avoid them we also avoid the problem of getting people to comply with them. Rules and procedures are administrative controls. They shall be on the end of the problem- or risk identification process after elimination and reduction. See also the task risk analysis process on page 70 or 207.

2. Involve people concerned in rule making
   Apply principle of participation - give "emotional ownership" whenever possible.

3. Explain why rules are necessary
   Give reasons for rules, it helps when people see the reasons behind them.

4. Make rules as simple as possible
   Apply "KISS" principle. It will be difficult for people to remember long and complicated rules. Use the language that will be understood by the end-users.

5. Rules must be justified and correct.
   Contents of rules must be correct and in line with the present situation.

6. Make rules to comply with "normal" human behavior
   Keep rules as practical as possible. Rules deviating from normal human behavior will be difficult to follow and may be the cause of a constant battle to have people comply with something that is far from "being natural". Apply the Principle of deviation from normal behavior.

7. Rules must not contradict each other.
   Various rules must be such that they reinforce each other rather than contradict. Should the latter happen, it would be extremely difficult to people to comply.

8. Make compliance with rules attractive, make non-compliance unattractive
   Prepare rules such that it will be attractive to follow them. Make it unattractive not to comply with rules.

   Each time a rule is made ask the questions: "Is it rewarding, one way or the other, for people to comply with rules? Or is it possibly attractive for them not to comply?"

Presentation

This stage is the period in which people are introduced to the "rules of the game". The usual instructional techniques can be used: "motivate - tell & show - test - check".

9. Give worker preview of rules prior to instruction
   "Motivate" is the first step of the instruction process: let people know what they are going to learn and why, what does it mean to them, how does this rule relate to his/her job.

   Make rule booklet available to each individual worker.

10. Provide proper instruction
    Use "Show & Tell", the second step of the instruction process. Whenever possible make rules "visible" by showing "how" and telling "why".

    Provide adequate means in line with applicable rules.

11. Test knowledge of rules
    "Test" initial knowledge of rules. Find out if the message has come across, if the instruction has been successful.

    Have each worker sign for receipt and understanding of rules and keep signed receipt in personal file.

12. Keep rules easily accessible to workers and supervision.
    Provide each worker with his own rule booklet whenever practical. Make more complex rules (such as Material Safety Data Sheets) available per department or area.

Application

This stage is the "normal" working situation: after rules have been set up and people are instructed the only thing left is to apply them.

13. Provide "try-out" period to test out new rules
    Allow a certain time for people to get used to new rules, get feedback, adapt rules when necessary. Use positive behavior reinforcement more heavily during this period.

    This period is primarily to get the bugs out of new rules and see how they work without having to apply the disciplinary policy right away.

    This period is only for new rules, not for new employees learning existing rules, except for the positive behavior reinforcement.

14. Be clear in daily application of rules
    "Check" people frequently in the proper use of rules. Exercise proper supervision including rule compliance maintenance. This daily supervision can be supported or enhanced by periodic formal observations directed at behavior of people (see 20).

15. Provide sufficient time for proper application of rules
    Provide sufficient time for people to carry out work such that rules can be applied as required.

16. Be positive about rule compliance
    Positive attitude of supervision and management towards compliance with rules - make rule compliance possible through proper decision-making - set the "right atmosphere". Use positive behavior reinforcement when applicable.

17. Be negative about non-compliance
    Disapprove of non-compliance by letting people know each time you see it. Every time non-compliance is noted and not acted upon, it is being reinforced.

18. Proper example by supervision and management
    Not your words count but your acts.

19. Maintain rule knowledge
Retraining, group meetings, personal contacts, task observations, tests, quizzes - test maintenance of rule knowledge.

20. Periodically evaluate rule compliance
With proper feed-back for correction, or commendation/motivation. Behavior observations (such as Unsafe Act Auditing) may be used here.

21. Periodically evaluate effect of rules.
Use information from accident/incident analysis whenever proper application of rules has, or could have, resulted in less injury, etc.

22. Keep rules up-to-date
Regularly review rules. Relate accident investigation to rules.

23. Be clear about consequences in case of non-compliance
Disciplinary policy: oral warning(s), written warning(s), time off without pay, dismissal or immediate discharge, depending on the violation.

24. Be consistent in case of non-compliance
Apply discipline only when needed: after all the above has been properly addressed to and in the proper order. The disciplinary policy in fact is only there to deal with people who knowingly, willfully, and without "legal" reason, violate rules.

Be consequent about application of discipline. Avoid "measuring with two yardsticks". Be objective. If necessary "built your case" by recording violations, dates, actions, etc. Don't forget: the disciplinary policy is there first of all to deal with the willful violators - the end station of discipline is discharge. And this will not be accepted without proper foundation.

APPENDIX E – The content of the plan or management system

The content of a management system consists of management activity areas or "elements" that are considered vital to obtain the objective(s) of the management system. The content determines the direction of the system towards the objective(s). The content boils down to "doing the right things" so the objective(s) of the management system can be obtained.

The content is considered in steps 7, 8, 12 and 16 of the 17-step process.

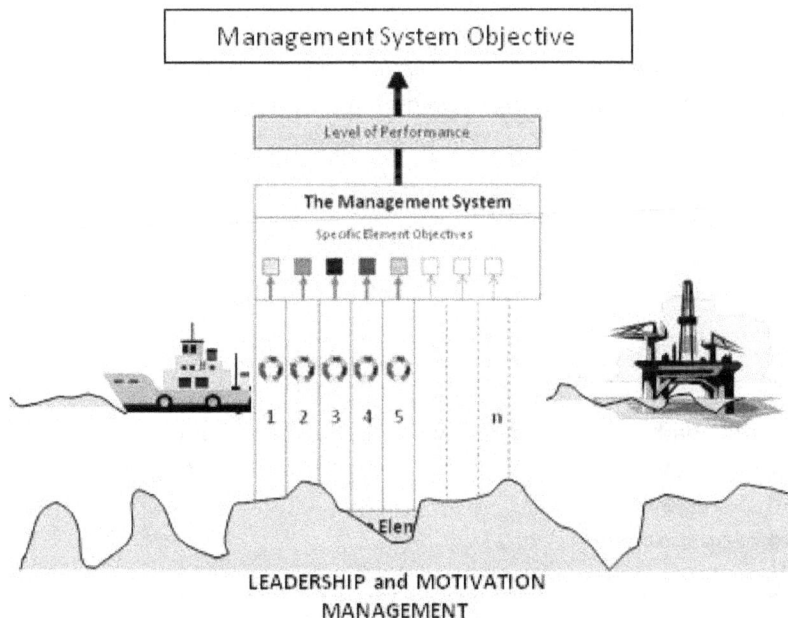

LEADERSHIP and MOTIVATION
MANAGEMENT

The management system contains a number of elements with their specific objectives and activities described in sufficient detail to be meaningful - to those who need to implement, supervise and evaluate the system. Elements should have a structure to contain and stimulate activities being implemented and improved. This structure is visualized in the picture above by the circle in each of the elements.

Sources of management activity areas or "elements" include:

- Legislation - national, international
- Industry standards
- Industry practice
- Certification norms or references
- Head office requirements
- Your own experience and ideas

A management system needs a number of relevant elements to reach the system objectives. To define the content of a management system, following steps need to take place:

1. Define the objective(s) of the management system
2. Determine what management activity areas or elements need to be part of the system to reach those objective(s)
3. Define the objective(s) of each of the elements
4. Determine the specific activities to be carried out to reach the objective(s) of the individual elements

You don't have to re-invent many wheels. Look at formal references – legislation, industry- and certification standards and what elements others use in their management systems. Whether that suits your organization is something that you need to decide together with your colleagues. The only advice I can give here is that you should be looking for elements that:

- Are required (by law or otherwise)
- Keep problems out of your organization
- Will be most effective to reach the objective of the management system

Some advice:

1.   When starting with your first action plan - the beginning of your management system - it is important that you will be able to get results within a period preferably no longer than 18 months, after step 5 of the 17-step process. If it will be much longer it may not motivate people. Shorter is better.

The principle of economic priorities

A manager will usually give priority response to items possessing the potential for the greatest proportion of results from the least investment of available resources.

---

2.   If you can afford it - depending on your situation, type of industry or activity - then don't start too big and grow "naturally", based on (initial) success. Start with a lean system and a limited number of elements and build it up based on experience and results. That way you end up with a system that addresses the needs and specific situation of your organization while reaching objectives with the least effort. But, at the same time, do not do too little or you may be caught by surprise. Preferably, start with activity areas that will keep possible problems/risks from entering your organization – if they don't come in, you don't need not to deal with them later on.

I realize that the approach "start small, grow slow and build on results obtained" may not be possible from the start as you may be looking for a certificate that you need "tomorrow", possibly for commercial reasons. If that is the case, get the certificate first and, once you have that, go back and start the process toward real improvement.

Some external Sources to add Content to your System

As my background is in safety, I mention a number of (mostly) safety related sources. When considering those, please keep in mind that I am using the broad scope of safety and loss control which covers injuries, property damage (any type), environmental damage, product losses, related liability situations, etc. Please think reaching objectives and controlling "unwanted events" that keep you from getting where you want to be.

No doubt there are many more sources available that you may be able to use to build your management system and addressing subjects other than safety. But by looking at the sources on the following pages, you may at least get an idea what to look for before you start inventing your wheels.

Besides the content of the management system, the structure of the elements is also very important as well as the process to make the system. Both process and structure help to develop and implement activities, obtain results and improve the system towards success.

PLEASE NOTE that references listed below may change over time and the information provided may not be the most recent. For up-to-date information contained in the sources listed, including information helpful for selection of specific element activities, please search the Internet.

Sources providing examples of elements that could form the content of a (safety) management system include:

A. Legislation – some major legislation
B. International standards - industry and certification
C. Industry examples – from several companies/organization
D. Commercial audit systems

A. LEGISLATION
Minimum content suggestions for your management system

Below, some examples are provided of legislative requirements which can be used to select management activity areas or elements of a management system.

OSHA 29 CFR 1910.119 – Process Safety Management of Highly Hazardous Chemicals. US legislation for the control of major hazards in the process industry.

- Employee participation
- Process safety information
- Process hazard analysis
- Operating procedures
- Training
- Contractors
- Pre-start-up safety review
- Mechanical integrity
- Hot work permit
- Management of change
- Incident investigation
- Emergency planning and response
- Compliance audit
- Trade secrets

SEVESO II – European legislation. Guidelines on a Major Accident Prevention Policy and Safety Management System, as required by Council Directive 96/82/EC (SEVESO II)

- Organization and personnel
- Hazard identification and evaluation
- Operational control
- Management of change
- Planning for emergencies
- Monitoring performance
- Audit and review

OSHA VPP – US legislation covering safety and health in the workplace

- Management leadership and employee involvement
- Management commitment
  - Employee involvement
  - Contract employee coverage
  - Safety and health management system annual evaluation
- Worksite analysis
  - Baseline safety and industrial hygiene hazard analysis
  - Hazard analysis of routine jobs, tasks, and processes
  - Hazard analysis of significant changes
  - Pre-use analysis
  - Documentation and use of hazard analyses
  - Routine self-inspections
- Hazard reporting system for employees
  - Industrial hygiene (IH) program
  - Investigation of accidents and near-misses
  - Trend analysis
  - Hazard prevention and control
  - Certified professional resources
  - Hazard elimination and control methods
  - Hazard control programs
  - Occupational health care program
  - Preventive maintenance of equipment
  - Tracking of hazard correction
  - Disciplinary system
  - Emergency preparedness and response
- Safety and health training

The principle of definition

A logical and proper decision can be made only when the basic or real problems are first defined

---

EPA 40 CFR 68 - Protection of the Environment, Chemical Accident Prevention Provisions - US environmental legislation

- Hazard assessment
- Process safety information
- Hazard review
- Operating procedures

- Training
- Maintenance
- Compliance audits
- Incident investigation
- Process safety information
- Process hazard analysis
- Operating procedures
- Training
- Mechanical integrity
- Management of change
- Pre-startup review
- Safety audits
- Incident investigation
- Employee participation
- Hot work permit
- Contractors
- Emergency response program
- Accidental release prevention
- Risk management plan
- Record keeping requirements

MES - Metatechnical evaluation system - Belgian interpretation of Seveso II

- Prevention Activities
  - The process installation
    - Specifying the process installation
    - Implementing the process installation
    - Maintaining the process installation
  - Operational procedures and instructions
    - Specifying operational procedures and instructions
    - Implementing operational procedures and instructions
    - Maintaining operational procedures and instructions
  - Measures for hazardous work
    - Specifying measures for hazardous work
    - Implementing measures for hazardous work
    - Maintaining measures during hazardous work
  - The emergency planning
    - Specifying the emergency planning
    - Implementing the emergency plan
    - Maintaining the emergency planning
  - Personal protective equipment
    - Specifying personal protective equipment

- Implementing personal protective equipment
- Maintaining personal protective equipment
- System activities
  - Policy
  - Organization
  - Document management
  - Selection and training
    - Own personnel
    - Third parties
  - Investigation of incidents and accidents
  - Information management
    - Regulations
    - External empirical data
  - Audit

B. INTERNATIONAL STANDARDS
Content requirements that cannot be avoided

Below, the management activity areas of a number of International Standards are provided. Please note that the information may change over time and the activity areas mentioned may not be the most recent ones. Please use the Internet to obtain most recent information regarding information sources provided, including information helpful for selection of specific element activities.

ILO-OSH 2001 - International Labour Office Guidelines on OSH (Occupational Safety and Health) Management Systems

- Policy
  - Occupational safety and health policy
  - Worker participation
- Organizing
  - Responsibility and accountability
  - Competence and training
  - Occupational safety and health management system documentation
  - Communication
- Planning and implementation
  - Initial review
  - System planning, development and implementation
  - Occupational safety and health objectives
  - Hazard prevention
  - Prevention and control measures
  - Management of change

- o Emergency prevention, preparedness and response
- o Procurement
- o Contracting
- Evaluation
  - o Performance monitoring and measurement
  - o Investigation of work-related injuries, ill health, diseases and incidents, and their impact on safety and health performance
  - o Audit
  - o Management review
- Action for improvement
  - o Preventive and corrective action
  - o Continual improvement

API 750 – an American Petroleum Institute recommended practice to manage process hazards

- Process safety information
- Process hazard analysis
- Management of change
- Operating procedures
- Safe work practices
- Training
- Assurance of the quality and mechanical
- Integrity of critical equipment
- Pre-start-up safety review
- Emergency response and control
- Investigation of process-related incidents
- Audit of process hazard management systems

The principle of multiple causes

Accidents and other loss producing events are seldom, if ever, the result of a single cause

---

API 581 - an American Petroleum Institute recommended practice for Risk Based Inspection

- Leadership and administration
- Process safety information
- Process hazard analysis
- Management of change
- Operating procedures
- Safe work practices

- Training
- Mechanical integrity
- Pre-start up safety review
- Emergency response
- Incident investigations
- Contractors
- Assessment

RESPONSIBLE CARE Codes – conduct guidelines for the chemical industry

Responsible Care is the copyrighted name under which efforts are described to upgrade the safety and environmental efforts of the international chemical industry. The initiative comes from within the industry itself and a logo is used to identify companies that make use of the voluntary program.

There are a number of different descriptions which may vary per country. Below I am showing the contents of the program as it was promoted by the American Chemistry Council.

The program consisted of six codes:

- Employee health and safety
- Process safety
- Community awareness and emergency response (CAER)
- Pollution prevention resources manual
- Product stewardship
- Distribution

These codes used to be contained in manuals which one could buy from the American Chemical Manufacturers Association. That was some time ago. Browsing the Internet, I could no longer find them but I give below the activity areas or elements of each of the codes as I used to know them. If you want to know more about Responsible Care, I can only advise you to search the Internet. Starting point may be the site of the International Council of Chemical Associations (ICCA). I understand that the number of codes has been reduced from the previous six (mentioned above and below) to presently three: the Operations Code, the Accountability Code and the Stewardship Code. The listing of activity areas as given below may no longer be up-to-date.

Process Safety Code

- Commitment
- Accountability
- Performance measurement

- Incident investigation
- Information sharing
- CAER Integration (CAER = community awareness and emergency response)
- Design documentation
- Process hazard information
- Process hazard analysis
- Management of change
- Siting
- Codes and standards
- Safety reviews
- Maintenance and inspection
- Multiple safeguards
- Emergency management
- Job skills
- Safe work practices
- Initial training
- Employee proficiency
- Fitness for duty
- Contractors

Employee Health and Safety Code

- Management commitment
- Employee participation
- Contractor selection and oversight
- Written programs
- Program assessments
- Data collection and analysis
- Hazard identification
- Hazard evaluation
- Medical fitness
- Medical surveillance
- Design and operations review
- Health and safety equipment
- Preventive maintenance and housekeeping programs
- Incident investigation
- Site security
- Emergency medical assistance
- Communications
- Training programs

Community Awareness and Emergency Response (CAER) code

- Employee concern assessment
- Communications training (internal/external)
- Employee education and emergency response plan and HSE programs
- Ongoing employee dialogue and outreach
- Evaluation of employee communication efforts
- Ongoing assessment of community concerns
- Outreach program on emergency response program and community risks
- Ongoing dialogue with local citizens
- Policy of openness
- Regular evaluation of community communications
- Ongoing assessment of risks from accidents
- Written emergency response plan
- Ongoing employee training on response responsibilities
- Emergency exercises to test emergency response plan
- Communication to local emergency planning committee
- Familiarize emergency responders to facility
- Coordination of facility emergency response plan with community plan
- Participation in testing community emergency response plan
- Sharing emergency response plan information with other facilities

Pollution Prevention Resources Manual

- Management commitment
- Quantitative inventory
- Impact assessment
- Education and dialogue
- Priorities, goals and plan for release reduction
- Implementation of reduction activities
- Measurement of progress
- Communicate progress
- Waste and release in research and design
- Promotion and support of waste and release reduction by others
- Periodic evaluation of waste management practices
- Selection etc of contractors and toll manufacturers
- Ground water protection programs
- Addressing past practices

Product Stewardship

- Leadership
- Accountability and performance measurement
- Resources
- HSE information
- Product risk characterization
- Risk management system
- Product and process design and improvement
- Employee education and products use feedback
- Contract manufacturers
- Suppliers
- Distributors
- Customers and other direct products receivers

Distribution

- Risk management
- Compliance reviews and training
- Carrier safety
- Handling and storage
- Emergency preparedness

CCPS - Center for Chemical Process Safety

CCPS is affiliated with the AIChE (American Institute of Chemical Engineers). The Center is committed to developing practices to control accidental release of chemicals and their consequences.

There are several publications by CCPS that refer to management system contents. These publications include: "Guidelines for Auditing Process Safety Management Systems", "Guidelines for Implementing Process Safety Management Systems" and "Guidelines for integrating Process Safety Management, Environmental, Safety and Health into a Quality Management System". From these publications the following list of topics can be distilled:

- Commitment and accountability
- Management system
- Process safety information
- Process hazards
- Hazard assessment
- Operating procedures / safe work practices
- Training
- Pre-startup review

- Maintenance / mechanical integrity
- Hot work permits
- Management of change
- Accident / incident investigation
- Emergency planning and response
- Audits

SCC - Safety Certification of Contractors

The SCC (Safety Certification of Contractors) originated in The Netherlands as the VCA and in 1994 started as the first accredited safety certification scheme that I am aware of.

The SCC contains 12 chapters:

- Safety, health and environmental (SHE) policy and organization, management involvement
- SHE risk analysis / plan of action
- Training, information and instructions
- SHE behavior
- SHE project plan
- Environmental protection
- Preparations for emergency situations
- SHE inspections
- Company health service
- Purchase and inspection of materials, equipment and tools
- Procurement of services
- Notification, registration and investigation of incidents

The operation of SCC/VCA is supervised by SSVV, including the CCVD-VCA, the Central Committee of Experts and its sub-committees.

The principle of shared results

The outcome of an organization is the combined work of many people at different levels and at different times. They all share responsibility for the company's success or failure.

ISO 26000 - Social responsibility

- Organizational governance
- Human rights
    - Due diligence
    - Human rights risk situations
    - Avoidance of complicity
    - Resolving grievances
    - Discrimination and vulnerable groups
    - Civil and political rights
    - Economic, social and cultural rights
    - Fundamental rights at work
- Labour Practices
    - Employment and employment relationships
    - Conditions of work and social protection
    - Social dialogue
    - Health and safety at work
    - Human development and training in the workplace
- The environment
    - Prevention of pollution
    - Sustainable resource use
    - Climate change mitigation and adaptation
    - Protection and restoration of the natural environment
- Fair operating practices
    - Anti–corruption
    - Responsible political involvement
    - Fair competition
    - Promoting social responsibility in the sphere of influence
    - Respect for property rights
- Consumer issues
    - Fair marketing, information and contractual practices
    - Protecting consumers' health and safety
    - Sustainable consumption
    - Consumer service, support, and dispute resolution
    - Consumer data protection and privacy
    - Access to essential services
    - Education and awareness
- Community involvement and development
    - Community involvement
    - Education and culture
    - Employment creation and skills development
    - Technology development

- o Wealth and income creation
- o Health
- o Social investment

ISO 14001 – the ISO standard concerning the control of environmental incidents

- Environmental policy
- Environmental aspects
- Legal and other requirements
- Objectives and targets
- Environmental management programs
- Structure and responsibility
- Awareness and competency
- Communication
- Environmental management system
- Document control
- Operational control
- Emergency preparedness and response
- Monitoring and measurement
- Non-conformance and corrective and preventive actions
- Records
- Environmental management system audits
- Management review

OHSAS 18001 – an ISO type standard concerning the occupational health and safety risk

- OH&S Management system elements
- General requirements
- OH&S policy
    - o Planning
    - o Planning for hazard identification, risk assessment and risk control
    - o Legal and other requirements
    - o Objectives
    - o OH&S management programs
- Implementation and operation
    - o Structure and responsibility
    - o Training awareness and competence
    - o Consultation and communication
    - o Documentation
    - o Document and data control
    - o Operational control
    - o Emergency preparedness and response

- Checking and corrective action
  - Performance measurement and monitoring
  - Accidents, incidents, non-conformance and corrective and preventive action
  - Records and records management
  - Audit
- Management review

OHSAS 18001 is presently being replaced by ISO 45001

C. INDUSTRY MANAGEMENT SYSTEMS
Examples of what others did

Below, examples of (safety) management systems and their elements of a number of companies are provided.

Oil and chemical company

- Management leadership, commitment and accountability
- Risk assessment and control
- Design and construction of installations
- Information and documentation
- Safety of personnel
- Health
- Training
- Operations and maintenance procedures
- Work permits
- Inspection and maintenance
- Reliability of HSE critical systems
- Environmental care
- Regulatory compliance
- Management of change
- Third party services
- Incident reporting, analysis and follow-up
- Emergency preparedness
- Community awareness
- Operations integrity assessment and improvement

Oil and chemical company

- Leadership
- Training for leadership
- Operational objectives and action-plan

- Selection and coaching
- Job introduction
- Technical training
- Task analysis and work instructions
- HSE Rules, permits and PPE
- Study of HSE risks
- Technical control during planning, construction and commissioning
- Maintenance and inspection
- Control of changes and improvement projects
- Product control
- Work by contractors
- Health
- Internal communication
- External communication
- Control of emergency situations
- Investigation and analysis of incidents
- Measurement and evaluation of HSE
- HSE audits
- Control of documents and HSE records
- Development and innovation
- Purchasing of products
- Handling of products
- Marketing and sales

Chemical company

- Safety, health and environmental commitment
- Management and resources
- Communication and consultation
- Training
- Materials hazards
- Acquisitions and divestments
- New plant, equipment and process design
- Modifications and changes
- She assurance
- Systems of work
- Emergency plans
- Contractors and suppliers
- Environmental impact assessments
- Resource conservation
- Waste management

- Soil and groundwater pollution
- Products stewardship
- SHE performance and reporting
- Auditing

Electronic company

- Management commitment and responsibilities
- Safety training
- Safe work practices
- Self assessments
- Government inspections and surveys
- Accident, incident and illness reporting
- Safe environment
- Mechanical safety
- Maintenance safety
- Contractor safety
- Electrical safety
- Fire prevention, fire protection and emergency response
- Chemical control program
- Process hazard reviews
- Materials handling safety
- Ergonomics
- Industrial hygiene exposure assessments
- Asbestos management
- Hearing conservation
- Ionizing and non-ionizing radiation protection
- Laser safety
- Ventilation
- Personal protective equipment
- Motor vehicle safety
- Meetings in non-Company facilities
- Sports safety program

Oil and chemical company

- Leadership and administration
- Management training
- Planned inspections
- Task analysis and procedures
- Accident/incident investigation

- Task observation
- Emergency preparedness
- Organizational rules
- Accident/incident analysis
- Employee training
- Program evaluation system
- Engineering controls
- Personal communications
- Group communications
- General promotion
- Hiring and placement
- Purchasing controls
- Off-the-job safety
- Hazard awareness
- Personal protective equipment
- Health protection
- Drug and alcohol abuse
- Environment
- Security

Chemical company

- Process safety information
- Operating procedures and safe practices
- Management of technology change
- Process hazard analysis
- Quality assurance
- Pre-start-up safety reviews
- Mechanical integrity
- Management of facilities change
- Training and performance
- Contractors
- Incident investigation and reporting
- Management of personnel change
- Emergency planning and response
- Auditing

Oil company

- Leadership and commitment
- Policy and strategic objectives
  - Strategic objectives

- o Policy statement
- Organization, resources and documentation
  - o Structure and responsibilities
  - o Management representative
  - o Resources
  - o Competence
  - o Contractors
  - o Communication
  - o Documentation and its control
- Evaluation and risk management
  - o Hazard and effects management process
  - o Identification of hazards and effects
  - o Evaluation
  - o Recording of hazards and effects
  - o Objectives and performance criteria
  - o Risk reduction measures
- Planning
  - o Asset integrity
  - o Procedures and work instructions
  - o Management of change
  - o Contingency and emergency planning
- Implementation and monitoring
  - o Activities and tasks
  - o Monitoring
  - o Records
  - o Non-compliance and corrective action
  - o Incident reporting
  - o Incident follow-up
- Auditing and reviewing

Food company

- Leadership and administration
- Hazards to the environment and identification of critical issues
- Environmental program
- Organizational rules and permits to operate
- Analysis of critical tasks/work activities
- Hiring and placement
- Training
- Communication and motivation
- Engineering controls
- Purchasing controls
- Health control

- Formal inspections
- Environmental performance monitoring and assessment
- Personal protective equipment
- Emergency preparedness
- Reporting/investigation and analysis of undesired events
- EH&S program evaluation

University

- Management leadership, commitment
- Operational risk management
- Communication, participation
- Documents and records
- Purchasing & contractors
- Emergency preparedness
- Incident reporting
- Management system audit
- Monitoring and reporting H&S
- School /service management review
- Legal compliance
- Occupational health
- University management system audit
- University management review

Oil and Gas Industry

- Leadership and administration
- Management training
- Planned inspections
- Task analysis and procedures
- Accident/incident investigation
- Task observation
- Emergency preparedness
- Organizational rules and regulations
- Accident/incident analysis
- Employee training
- Personal protective equipment
- Health control and services
- Program evaluation
- Purchasing, engineering controls
- Personal communication
- Group communication
- General promotion

- Hiring and placement
- Program administration
- Off-the-job safety

Contractor to Oil and Gas Industry

- HSE policy and HSE system
- HSE organization
- HSE communication structure
- HSE responsibilities
- Audits and job site inspections
- Project evaluation / HSE close-out report
- Subcontractors and suppliers
- HSE information, education, training and promotion
- (Near-miss) incidents and unsafe acts and conditions
- Risk analysis and work permits
- Environment
- Personal protective equipment (PPE)
- Location access
- Procurement and control of materials, equipment and services
- Reward and disciplinary policy

D. COMMERCIAL AUDIT SYSTEMS
External reference sources

Below, examples of commercially available audit references for management systems are provided.

Audit System 1

The management activity areas or "elements" below are from the 6th edition of the International Safety Rating System™ (ISRS).

- Leadership and administration
- Leadership training
- Planned inspections and maintenance
- Critical task analysis and -procedures
- Accident/incident analysis
- Job observations
- Emergency preparedness
- Rules and work permits
- Accident/incident analysis

- Knowledge and skill training
- Personal protective equipment
- Health and hygiene control
- System evaluation
- Engineering and change management
- Individual communications
- Group communications
- General promotion
- Hiring and placement
- Materials and services management
- Off-the-job safety

Meanwhile, the ISRS is in its 8th edition and comprises 15 elements:

- Leadership
- Planning
- Risk evaluation
- Human resources
- Compliance assurance
- Project management
- Training and c
- Communication and promotion
- Risk control
- Asset management
- Contractor management and purchasing
- Emergency preparedness
- Learning from events
- Risk monitoring
- Results and review

For further information about the ISRS contact Det Norske Veritas (DNV).

Audit System 2

- Leadership, commitment and accountability
- Training
- Process safety and management of change
- Environmental management
- Organizational culture and behavior management
- Product stewardship
- Task and operating procedures
- Recruitment and placement
- Occupational health

- Inspection, maintenance and work permits
- Procurement and services
- Information and documentation
- Internal communication
- Emergency preparedness
- Incident investigation, follow-up and prevention
- Security

Audit System 3

The following activity areas or "elements" are from the "Common Audit System" (CAP) which used to be available through IRCA USA. To check present status contact IRCA USA.

- Planning and leadership
- Training and communications
- Job /operation analysis and controls
- Change management.
- Purchasing systems
- Work rules and operating permits
- Inspections
- Occupational health and hygiene systems
- Personal protective equipment
- Incident investigation and analysis
- Emergency preparedness
- Audits and reviews
- Corrective and preventative action systems
- Environmental management systems
- Quality management systems

OPTIONAL TECHNICAL ELEMENTS

- Hazard Identification and risk assessment
- Security management
- Fire protection
- Product stewardship
- Seismicity
- Fleet management

APPENDIX F – Rating the 17-step process

This appendix contains the 17-step process based rating method in more detail. Please consider that the method provided comes from my safety related background. Please add, delete or change the rating criteria as you see fit for the purpose that you want to use it for.

The rating per step will vary between zero and the maximum value, depending on the extent to which the criteria of each step are met.

Step	Description	Score Range
1	Top Manager Leadership - **LEADERSHIP**	0 - 4
2	Management Team leadership - **LEADERSHIP**	0 - 4
3	Management Improvement Team - **LEADERSHIP**	0 - 4
4	Internal Expertise	0 - 5
5	Project communicated	0 - 5
6	Opinion Survey	0 - 5
7	Base-line Assessment	0 - 5
8	Selection of Elements/Activity Areas	0 - 5
9	Management Introduction Training	0 - 6
10	Element Coordination Team(s)	0 - 7
11	Element Coordination Team Training	0 - 6
12	Element Development - **PLAN**	0 - 7
13	Element Implementation - Training- **TRAIN**	0 - 7
14	Management Briefing	0 - 6
15	Carrying out Element Activities - **DO**	0 - 10
16	Review by the Management Team	0 - 6
17	Extend Project	0 - 8
	Total score	**0 - 100**

The scoring method is to help the assessor to establish a score for each step. Each of the 17 steps is provided with a number of criteria to consider when providing the actual score for the step concerned. All or most criteria listed need to be considered to allow final judgment but not all may apply to your specific situation. Please bear in mind that the score is subjective.

Putting a score on each step could be done by an individual but could also be done in a small group as part of a training exercise. When done in a group, it is important that this will be done under guidance of a facilitator who has acquainted him-/herself with the method prior to carrying out the exercise. When done as part of a training exercise, this may include all steps or a selection. The scoring of a company's improvement efforts shall be done in communication with the company; preferably after agreeing on the relevance of the scoring criteria.

Dr. H. James Harrington

Measurement is the first step that leads to control and eventually to improvement.

If you can't measure something, you can't understand it. If you can't understand it, you can't control it. If you can't control it, you can't improve it

H. J. Harrington (1929), American author, engineer, entrepreneur, and consultant

Please consider the size of the organization when using scoring criteria. The organization considered in the rating process should be as small as possible so that the evaluation will include participation of people at all levels in the making and improving of the management system.

In a large multi-location organization the actual management system manual could be at the corporate level while providing guidance to the development of local improvement processes which should then be the subject of scoring using the 17-step rating method. This way the specific environment – legal, social, cultural - of the location and the specific work to be done may be considered to the extent possible. The corporate manual would include the system objective, the (minimum) mandatory content or elements and the element structure.

The rating could be used prior to starting the 17-step improvement process. In that case, the rating criteria need to be looked at in advance and altered as appropriate to guide the developing process.

If the rating is used on an existing situation in which a clear process has not been used to develop the management system, the assessment should preferably be carried out under guidance of a person knowledgeable with the rating method and the 17-step process.

1.   TOP MANAGER LEADERSHIP – "LEADERSHIP"

Main purpose of step

Purpose of this step is to make sure that the individual leadership, commitment and support is given by the senior executive of the unit being considered. (The "unit" here would most likely be a site or location but could be a subsidiary or whole company.)

Please consider following items for scoring (add or delete as necessary/desired):

- Objective of the management system set
- Policy statement signed by the top manager
- Opens/chairs management team workshop (2)
- Chairs Management Improvement Team (3)
- Project (5) endorsed by the top manager and communicated
- Signature on system elements developed (12)
- Prepares and schedules site tours
- Periodic site tours made by the top manager
- Knows and applies behavior observation techniques
- Personal compliance with relevant rules
- Periodic communications issued by the top manager to (all) employees
- Addresses issues during important internal meetings
- Promotes system performance in- and externally in seminars, etc.
- Relevant important training sessions opened by the top manager
- Attended management briefing (14)
- Recognizes outstanding performance of individuals and/or groups
- Makes necessary resources available to carry out activities
- Participation in management system evaluations/reviews (16)

Assessor's notes

Score 0 - 4

Rating this Client

2. MANAGEMENT TEAM LEADERSHIP – "LEADERSHIP"

Main purpose of step

Purpose of this step is to make sure that the individual leadership, commitment and support will be provided by all members of the management team. The "management team", as meant here, consist of the managers directly reporting to the senior executive and could also include relevant staff personnel and employee representation.

Please consider following items for scoring (add or delete as necessary/desired):

- All top managers attended workshop to get informed about project
    - Content of workshop to include:
        - Workshop opened/chaired by Top manager
        - Reasons for change; maturity profile (appendix B, page 224)
        - Basic model for change – Platform model: Plan, Train, Do
        - Basic principles related to (management) system – objective(s), elements
        - Description of process and plan – 17-steps, content, structure
        - Agreement on system objective
        - Responsibilities of top managers
        - Leadership statement signed by individual members
- Participation on Management Improvement Team (3)
- Top managers chairing element coordinating teams (10)
- Prepare and schedule site tours
- Periodic site tours carried out by top managers
- Personal compliance with related rules
- Know and apply behavior observation techniques
- Attended management briefings (14)
- Chairing related meetings with their sub-ordinates
- Participating in related external events
- Participating in important management system activities
- Participation in management system evaluations/reviews (16)

Assessor's notes

Score 0 - 4

Rating this Client

3. MANAGEMENT IMPROVEMENT TEAM – "LEADERSHIP"

Main purpose of step

Purpose of this step is to make sure that leadership and coordination for the overall improvement process is structured at senior management level.

Please consider following items for scoring (add or delete as necessary/desired):

- Management Improvement Team established
- Chaired by top manager or board member (1)
- Top- and middle managers on team (2)
- Participation of employee representatives
- Description of tasks, objectives of team
- Participation of related internal/external expertise
- Training of Management Improvement Team members to include:
    - Reason for change/improvement process
    - Maturity profile (appendix B on page 224)
    - Basic principles related to system subject
    - Description of process and plan
    - Generic structure of management system elements
    - Project plan for approval prior to communication (5)
- Meeting frequency
- Meeting agenda's
- Minutes of meetings (contents, action lists, etc.)
- Management system elements approved by Management Improvement Team
- Specific initiatives by team to support project activities
- Management system evaluations/reviews (16)

Assessor's notes

Score 0 - 4

Rating this Client

4.   INTERNAL EXPERTISE

Main purpose of step

Purpose of this step is to make sure that expertise is provided to assist and coordinate in the development and implementation of the management system to be set up as part of the improvement project.

Please consider following items for scoring (add or delete as necessary/desired):

- Presence and qualifications of persons to facilitate throughout all process steps (project, overall management system):
    - Job/task description of individual(s)/department
    - Place in the organization (reporting lines to top management)
    - Formal basic education
    - Experience
- Type and quality of training regarding improvement process:
    - Subject matter related to system subject matter
    - Improvement process
    - Measurement/auditing
- Participation on Management Improvement Team (3)
- Taking part in training of Element Coordination Teams (11)
- Participation in management system evaluations/reviews (16)

Assessor's notes

Score 0 - 5

Rating this Client

5.   PROJECT COMMUNICATED

Main purpose of step

Purpose of this step is to assure senior management leadership and commitment by communicating to everyone in the organization through which process and which steps the improvement will be obtained.

Please consider following items for scoring (add or delete as necessary/desired):

- Written plan for improvement project prepared (less than one year ago)
- Contents of project plan including all major steps of 17-step process
- Time schedule included
- Plan discussed with relevant management levels prior to communication to all employees
- Project plan discussed with (and having consent of) employees representation
- Project properly resourced
- Project plan signed by the top manager (1)
- Project plan communicated to, and discussed with, all personnel
- (Yearly) updates of project plan (17)

Assessor's notes

Score 0 - 5

Rating this Client

6.   OPINION SURVEY

Main purpose of step

Purpose of this step is to collect subjective/objective information about the actual situation/culture related to the subject of the improvement process and the management system to be developed. To also loosen up the organization for the improvement process to come.

Please consider following items for scoring (add or delete as necessary/desired):

- Opinion survey done (no more than 3 years ago)
- Formal questionnaires used
  - Factual information regarding system performance
  - Subjective information on quality aspects
  - Use of scoring methods to allow quantification of opinions
- All levels in organization involved
  - Top- and middle management
  - Supervision
  - Operational employees
- Survey sample used is representative for population
- Carried out by unbiased person
- Anonymity
- Done written or electronic (verbally as needed)
- Results analyzed, published and used in selection of elements (8)
- Action plan prepared (as applicable)

Assessor's notes

Score 0 - 5

Rating this Client

7.   BASE-LINE ASSESSMENT

Main purpose of step

Purpose of this step is to obtain a good picture of the present situation as related to the project involved. This assessment is a foundation on which to build further.

Please consider following items for scoring (add or delete as necessary/desired):

- Base-line assessment carried out
- Adequate management system evaluation reference used
    - External reference used
    - Relation with management system subject matter
    - Including relevant elements (content/subjects)
    - Including "what is being done", "when", "by whom" and "how"
    - Including element structure to stimulate activity implementation
    - Effectiveness (results) of (element) activities considered
- Assessment done by qualified, unbiased, person(s)
- Broad participation of management in assessment
- Proper preparation by participating managers/supervisors
- Report made and properly distributed
- Included in selection and preparation of system elements/activities (8)

Assessor's notes

Score 0 - 5

Rating this Client

8.   SELECTION OF ELEMENTS/ACTIVITIES AREAS

Main purpose of step

Purpose of this step is the selection of management system activity areas or "elements" to be part of the first action plan, based on expected effectiveness and visible results.

Please consider following items for scoring (add or delete as necessary/desired):

- Elements/Activities selected, based on:
  - Results of opinion survey (6)
  - Results of base line assessment (7)
  - Established needs
  - Priorities set include effective control of system related issues
  - "Visibility", balance between efforts and (visible) results
  - Realistic time schedule to execution and reach results
  - Approved by Management Improvement Team (8) with objectives set
- Proper resourcing available

Assessor's notes

Score 0 - 5

Rating this Client

9.   INTRODUCTION TRAINING

Main purpose of step

Purpose of this step is to make sure that all management, supervision, staff, worker or trade union representations and operational personnel are aware of the improvement process, know the terminology, models, concepts, etc. To "put the noses in the same direction".

Please consider following items for scoring (add or delete as necessary/desired):

- Introduction training provided (within last 3 years)
- Program adapted to target groups
- Contents, hand-out and lesson plan appropriate for introduction:
  - Basic models, concepts, philosophies
  - Maturity profile (see appendix B on page 224)
  - Improvement process ("how to get results")
  - Objectives of process ("what results to get")
  - Main system elements and their expected results (content)
  - Opinion survey results (6)
  - Baseline assessment results (7)
  - First action plan elements selected (8)
  - Active involvement of participants stimulated
  - Follow-up included ("what will follow introduction")
- Provided by experienced instructors
- Provided to all management, supervisors, related staff and employees
- Opened by top manager

Assessor's notes

Score 0 - 6

Rating this Client

10. ELEMENT COORDINATION TEAMS

Main purpose of step

Purpose of this step is to establish coordination for development of management system elements in preparation of the implementation thereof and to see that assessment of activities and their results will be done periodically.

Please consider following items for scoring (add or delete as necessary/desired):

- Element Coordination Teams set up for each selected element (8) (16)
- To include relevant levels in organization
- Authorities and responsibilities assigned
- Staff support available for expert advice
- Proper chairperson (top-/middle managers) with adequate authority
- Task descriptions of coordinators or teams to include development and Implementation
- Clear reporting lines of coordinators or team(s)
- Regular progress reports to Management Improvement Team (3)
- Adequate resourcing available

Assessor's notes

Score 0 - 7

Rating this Client

11. ELEMENT COORDINATION TEAM TRAINING

Main purpose of step

Purpose of this step is to assure adequate knowledge and skills are available for effective element coordination, development and successful implementation.

Please consider following items for scoring (add or delete as necessary/desired):

- Training of Element Coordination Teams provided
- Contents of training:
  - Subject matter and specific element objective
  - How to develop a management system element, including:
    - Development process – 17 steps
    - Element structure
    - Element objective
    - What activities need to be established – what, why, when, by whom and how
    - Tools – forms, methods, procedures - to be developed
    - Implementation process
    - Training required for implementation (13)
    - Critical points for management support/guidance (14)
    - How to measure, monitor and review for continuous improvement
- Role of Management Improvement Team (3)
- Role of Element Coordination Team (10)
- Role of management/supervision (14)
- Provided by knowledgeable instructors
- Training handout

Assessor's notes

Score 0 - 6

Rating this Client

12.   ELEMENT DEVELOPMENT – "PLAN"

Main purpose of step

Purpose of this step is the development of selected management system elements (steps 8 and 16) and their activities by element coordination teams (steps 10 and 11), with approval by the management improvement team (step 3).

Please consider following items for scoring (add or delete as necessary/desired):

- Elements developed as selected (8) (16)
- Including input from users – opinion surveys (6) and baseline assessment (7)
- Elements developed including structure:
  - *(1) Element policy and management statement including:*
    - *Reason for element activity*
    - *Goals and objectives of element*
  - *(2) Coordination of element activities assigned*
  - *(3) Element standing plan to include what to do, by whom and when*
    - *Review of legislation/standards for minimum requirements*
    - *Additional element activities as required by other sources*
    - *Employee participation in element development*
  - *(4) Employee training to carry out element activities*
  - *(5) Employee participation in execution of activities*
  - *(6) Communication needs to internal/external parties*
    - *Data selection and analysis*
  - *(7) Standing plan assessment*
    - *Periodic evaluation of element activities*
    - *Periodic evaluation of element results in relation with objectives*
  - *(8) Review and improvement*
- Guidelines available on how to carry out standing plan activities
  - Proper detail for effective action
  - Tools/forms provided as necessary
- Element approved for implementation by the Management Improvement Team or top manager

Assessor's notes

Score 0 - 7

Rating this Client

```

```

13. ELEMENT IMPLEMENTATION TRAINING – "TRAIN"

Main purpose of step

Purpose of this step is to assure proper training for execution of the activities contained in the plan elements.

Please consider following items for scoring (add or delete as necessary/desired):

- Training provided after approval of elements (12) by the top manager or Management Improvement Team
- Training provided to people with responsibility assigned to carry out element activities
- Training to include:
  - Subject matter
  - Element activities detail and tools/forms
  - Element objectives and criteria for effectiveness measurement
  - Critical criteria for element management (14)
  - Follow-up on non-compliance issues noted during execution
- Role of Management Improvement Team (3)
- Role of Element Coordination Team (10)
- Role of management/supervision (14)
- Handout provided
- Training provided by qualified instructors
- Sufficient practice allowed during training

Assessor's notes

Score 0 - 7

Rating this Client

14.   MANAGEMENT BRIEFINGS – "DO"

Main purpose of step

Purpose of this step is briefing managers, supervisors, staff and others regarding the critical aspects of element activity execution. To enable them to evaluate, stimulate, guide and coach the implementation of the activities in their area of responsibility.

Please consider following items for scoring (add or delete as necessary/desired):

- Management briefing provided for all elements included (8) (16)
- To all top- and middle managers and supervisors
- Briefing including:
    - Purpose of briefing:
    - Critical criteria identified for element activity execution and management
    - Criteria identified for element effectiveness (result) measurement
- Provided by qualified instructors
- Handout provided

Assessor's notes

Score 0 - 6

Rating this Client

15. CARRYING OUT ELEMENT ACTIVITIES – "DO"

Main purpose of step

Purpose of this step is to carry out the activities as intended by the element plan (step 12).

Please consider following items for scoring (add or delete as necessary/desired):

- Activities assigned to responsible persons
- Activities carried out for elements developed (12)
- Activities carried out by properly trained people (13)
- Proper coaching and guiding by management/supervision using critical criteria (14)
- Periodic assessment of activities according to element plan (12)
    - By people involved in execution of activities (self-management)
    - By Element Coordination Team members (10)
    - By others, including expertise (4)
    - Assessment results provide to Management Improvement Team
- Periodic evaluation to measure effectiveness of element vs. objectives set
    - By people involved in execution of activities (self-management)
    - By Element Coordination Team members (10)
    - By others, including expertise (4)
    - Evaluation results provide to Management Improvement Team
- If element objective(s) not obtained: improvement plan(s) developed:
    - By people involved in execution of activities (self-management)
    - By Element Coordination Team (10)
    - To include adjustment and/or adding element activities
    - For review and approval by Management Improvement Team (16)

Assessor's notes

Score 0 - 10

Rating this Client

16.   REVIEW BY THE MANAGEMENT IMPROVEMENT TEAM

Main purpose of step

Purpose of this step is to review the performance and results of the management system by the management improvement team and to assure proper resourcing, development and execution of additional action plans.

Please consider following items for scoring (add or delete as necessary/desired):

- Periodic review of management system effectiveness
    - Carried out by Management Improvement Team
    - Not less than annually
- Reviews to include
    - Results of the overall management system in comparison system to objectives
    - Activities and results of all elements compared to element objectives
    - External conditions – legal, political, technical etc.
- Review and approval of plans based on element activity reviews (15)
- Action plans set up to include, as necessary
    - Adding elements if overall system objectives not obtained (7 - 16)
    - Adding elements or activities based on external requirements
    - Responsibilities assigned
    - Time path established
    - Follow-up through periodic evaluation of implementation and results (15)
- As applicable, commendation given to relevant people related to:
    - Element activities/results and action plans suggested (15)

Assessor's notes

Score 0 - 6

Rating this Client

17.   EXTEND PROJECT, CONTINUE/IMPROVE

Main purpose of step

Purpose of this step is to further extend the management system in relation to its overall goals/objectives, based on the assessments and review in step 15 and 16. Step 17 suggests repeating a number - not all - of the previous steps to bring the overall performance of the management system closer to the desired objective. Periodic evaluations need to take place to secure continuous improvement of already implemented activities.

Please consider following items for scoring (add or delete as necessary/desired):

- Extension of existing system by adding elements
    - Based on plans suggested/approved by Management Improvement Team (16)
- Continue and improve existing element activities (15) (16)

Assessor's notes

Score 0 - 8

Rating this Client

RATING THIS COMPANY

CALCULATION OF TOTAL INITIAL SCORE (TIS)

Step	Description	Score Range	Individual Step Score
1	Top Manager Leadership – **LEADERSHIP**	**0 - 4**	
2	Management Team leadership – **LEADERSHIP**	**0 - 4**	
3	Management Improvement Team – **LEADERSHIP**	**0 - 4**	
4	Internal Expertise	**0 - 5**	
5	Project Plan communicated	**0 - 5**	
6	Opinion Survey	**0 - 5**	
7	Base-line Assessment	**0 - 5**	
8	Selection of Activities	**0 - 5**	
9	Management Introduction Training	**0 - 6**	
10	Element Coordination Team(s)	**0 - 7**	
11	Element Coordination Team Training	**0 - 6**	
12	Element Development - **PLAN**	**0 - 7**	
13	Element Implementation Training – **TRAIN**	**0 - 7**	
14	Management Briefing	**0 - 6**	
15	Carrying out Element Activities -**DO**	**0 - 10**	
16	Review by Management Improvement Team	**0 - 6**	
17	Extend Project	**0 - 8**	
	Total score	**0 - 100**	
	TOTAL INITIAL SCORE (TIS)		

Date of assessment: _____

Assessor(s): _____   _____

Interdependency of steps

Using the scoring system as shown in the table, one could score each step on its own merits. The total of points would then be the score of the entire process which I call the "Total Initial Score" (TIS).

However, a (close to) maximum score may be required for certain individual steps or combination of steps before allowing (full) scoring of some other steps in the process or of the process entirely.

For example: the process can only succeed if the proper basis, in the form of leadership from the top (steps 1, 2 and 3) is there. Yet the TIS could still be 88 even if the total score of steps 1 – 3 is zero. Obviously this is not logical. How could the improvement process reach a high score when there is no or limited leadership and support from the top of the organization? The same reasoning would be true for other individual steps or combination of steps. Therefore my reasoning is that if the total score of the first three steps is less than maximal, the score of other steps may have to be reduced or even eliminated. Obviously, if step 15 is not done, the score of the entirety will be reduced to zero.

For these reasons I thought about additional scoring opportunities to allow lowering of the TIS if the scoring in specific steps or combination of steps would be less than maximal.

PLEASE NOTE. The reduction method presented below is personal and very much subject to discussion. The only reason why I present this is to show that I have thought about the interdependency of steps and combination of steps and the influence that this may have on the total score obtained. I just want to share my thoughts with you without even trying to pretend that my thoughts are close to complete. I leave it up to you to use this reduction method and apply your own percentages as you may consider proper in your situation.

I considered reduction of TIS based on less than maximum score for individual steps but decided that was too complicated – at least for me and for the time being. So I thought about doing the reduction based on a combination of steps to arrive at the TFS – the Total Final Score.

CALCULATION OF TOTAL FINAL SCORE (TFS)

I introduced the "Total Final Score" (TFS) to be based on the results of certain combinations of steps.

As you can see in the table below, I more or less combined the steps of the 17-step process based on the platform model aspects: Leadership, Plan, Train, Do and Performance level/objective.

Although the reduction of the Total Initial Score (TIS) is based on certain logic, the application of reduction percentages is rather subjective. This is why I do not suggest any percentages and leave it up to you to use the method as you see fit.

Subject group	Steps	MCS	ACS	TIS Reduction
Leadership	1, 2, 3, 5,6	22		%
Plan	7, 8, 10, 12	24		%
Train	4, 9, 11, 13	24		%
Do	14, 15	16		%
Performance level	16, 17	14		%
Totals		100		%

MCS = Maximum Combined Score of steps indicated; ACS = Actual Combined Score of steps indicated; TIS = Total Initial Score

APPENDIX G - A (safety) management system

Below is an example of the content and structure of a management system for high hazards industry. In principle, each management activity area or element includes the structure suggested. (Specific element activities are shown in italic.)

ELEMENT	ELEMENT STRUCTURE:
1. Leadership	1.1. *HSE Policy and Resources* 1.2. *HSE Management Team* 1.3. *HSE Committee* 1.4. *HSE Specialist Support & Coordination* 1.5. *Regulations, Codes and Standards* 1.6. *Permits to Operate* 1.7. *HSE Objectives and Targets* 1.8. *Written HSE System* 1.9. *Individual HSE Responsibility/Appraisal* 1.10. Management Participation 1.11. Training 1.12. Communication 1.13. Program Monitoring 1.14. Review and Improvement
2. Leadership Training	2.1. Management Statement 2.2. Coordination 2.3. Regulations, Codes and Standards 2.4. Implementation Plan 2.5. *Training Needs Identification* 2.6. *Senior Manager Program Orientation* 2.7. *Senior Manager Update Training* 2.8. *New Manager HSE Orientation/Induction* 2.9. *Formal Initial HSE Leadership Training* 2.10. *Update Training for Other Leaders* 2.11. *Implementation Team Training* 2.12. *Formal Training Program Coordinator* 2.13. *Instructor Training* 2.14. Program Monitoring 2.15. Review and Improvement

ELEMENT	ELEMENT STRUCTURE:
3. **Action Plan**	3.1. Management Statement 3.2. Coordination 3.3. Regulations, Codes and Standards 3.4. Implementation Plan *3.5. HSE Performance Targets* *3.6. Incidents* *3.7. Occupational Health* *3.8. Resource Consumption* *3.9. Emissions* *3.10. Discharges* *3.11. Waste* *3.12. Soil and Ground Water* *3.13. Land use* *3.14. Cost-Benefit Analysis* 3.15. Employee Participation 3.16. Training 3.17. Data Collection and Analysis 3.18. Communication 3.19. Program Monitoring 3.20. Review and Improvement
4. **Hiring and Placement**	4.1. Management Statement 4.2. Coordination 4.3. Regulations, Codes and Standards 4.4. Implementation Plan *4.5. Physical and Mental Requirements* *4.6. General Orientation/Induction Program* *4.7. Personnel Assignments* *4.8. Physical or Mental Incapacitation* *4.9. Employee Debriefing* 4.10. Employee Participation 4.11. Training 4.12. Data Collection and Analysis 4.13. Communication 4.14. Program Monitoring 4.15. Review and Improvement

ELEMENT	ELEMENT STRUCTURE:
5. **Personal Communications**	5.1. Management Statement 5.2. Coordination 5.3. Regulations, Codes and Standards 5.4. Implementation Plan *5.5. Job Orientation/Induction* *5.6. Task Instruction* *5.7. Planned Personal Contacts* 5.8. Employee Participation 5.9. Training 5.10. Data Collection and Analysis 5.11. Program Monitoring 5.12. Review and Improvement
6. **Technical Training**	6.1. Management Statement 6.2. Coordination 6.3. Regulations, Codes and Standards 6.4. Implementation Plan *6.5. Training Needs Analysis* *6.6. Technical Training Program* *6.7. Specialized Training Needs* 6.8. Employee Participation 6.9. Training 6.10. Data Collection and Analysis 6.11. Program Monitoring 6.12. Review and Improvement
7. Tasks and Operating Procedures	7.1. Management Statement 7.2. Coordination 7.3. Regulations, Codes and Standards 7.4. Implementation Plan *7.5. Critical Task Identification* *7.6. Critical Task Analysis* *7.7. Critical task Procedures* *7.8. Operating Procedures* *7.9. Maintenance of Procedures* *7.10. Critical Task Observation* 7.11. Employee Participation 7.12. Training 7.13. Data Collection and Analysis 7.14. Communication 7.15. Program Monitoring 7.16. Review and Improvement

ELEMENT	ELEMENT STRUCTURE:
8. **Rules and Work Permits**	8.1. Management Statement 8.2. Coordination 8.3. Regulations, Codes and Standards 8.4. Implementation Plan *8.5. General HSE Rules* *8.6. Specialized Work Rules* *8.7. Use of Signs and Color Codes* *8.8. Work Permit & Specialized Procedures System* *8.9. Compliance Efforts* *8.10. Personal Protective Equipment* *8.11. Site Security* 8.12. Employee Participation 8.13. Training 8.14. Data Collection and Analysis 8.15. Program Monitoring 8.16. Review and Improvement
9. **Hazard Identification and analysis**	9.1. Management Statement 9.2. Coordination 9.3. Regulations, Codes and Standards 9.4. Implementation Plan *9.5. Methods and Approach* *9.6. Establishing Baseline Information* *9.7. Scope of Hazards Identification* *9.8. Evaluation of Risks* *9.9. Follow-up* 9.10. Employee Participation 9.11. Training 9.12. Data Collection and Analysis 9.13. Communication 9.14. Program Monitoring 9.15. Review and Improvement

ELEMENT		ELEMENT STRUCTURE:
10.	**Engineering Controls**	10.1. Management Statement 10.2. Coordination 10.3. Regulations, Codes and Standards 10.4. Implementation Plan *10.5. Product Design* *10.6. Site Location/Lay-out* *10.7. Plant and Process Design Reviews* *10.8. Process Design Standards* *10.9. Ergonomics and Human Factors* *10.10. Construction and Pre-Startup Reviews* *10.11. Pollution Prevention* 10.12. Employee Participation 10.13. Training 10.14. Data Collection and Analysis 10.15. Communication 10.16. Program Monitoring 10.17. Review and Improvement
11.	**Maintenance and Inspection**	11.1. Management Statement 11.2. Coordination 11.3. Regulations, Codes and Standards 11.4. Implementation Plan *11.5. Policies* *11.6. General Inspections* *11.7. Critical Inspections* *11.8. Maintenance Programs* *11.9. Quality Assurance Inspection and Testing* *11.10. Follow-up* 11.11. Employee Participation 11.12. Training 11.13. Data Collection and Analysis 11.14. Communication 11.15. Program Monitoring 11.16. Review and Improvement
12.	**Management of Change**	12.1. Management Statement 12.2. Coordination 12.3. Regulations, Codes and Standards 12.4. Implementation Plan *12.5. Change Criteria* *12.6. Use of the Procedure* *12.7. Temporary Changes* 12.8. Employee Participation 12.9. Training 12.10. Data Collection and Analysis 12.11. Communication 12.12. Program Monitoring 12.13. Review and Improvement

ELEMENT	ELEMENT STRUCTURE:
13. **Product Stewardship**	13.1. Management Statement 13.2. Coordination 13.3. Regulations, Codes and Standards 13.4. Implementation Plan *13.5. Product Design* *13.6. Procurement, Handling, Storage and Shipment of Products* *13.7. Product Use and Disposal* 13.8. Employee Participation 13.9. Training 13.10. Data Collection and Analysis 13.11. Communication 13.12. Program Monitoring 13.13. Review and Improvement
14. **Contractor Management**	14.1. Management Statement 14.2. Coordination 14.3. Regulations, Codes and Standards 14.4. Implementation Plan *14.5. Pre-Selection* *14.6. Selection Process* *14.7. Contractor Introduction to Work Site* *14.8. On-Site Performance* *14.9. On-Site Performance Evaluations* 14.10. Employee Participation 14.11. Training 14.12. Data Collection and Analysis 14.13. Communication 14.14. Program Monitoring 14.15. Review and Improvement
15. **Occupational Health**	15.1. Management Statement 15.2. Coordination 15.3. Regulations, Codes and Standards 15.4. Implementation Plan *15.5. Health Hazard Identification* *15.6. Health Hazard Control* *15.7. Medical Assistance* *15.8. Personal Hygiene* 15.9. Employee Participation 15.10. Training 15.11. Data Collection and Analysis 15.12. Communication 15.13. Program Monitoring 15.14. Review and Improvement

ELEMENT	ELEMENT STRUCTURE:
16. **Internal Awareness**	16.1. Management Statement 16.2. Coordination 16.3. Regulations, Codes and Standards 16.4. Implementation Plan *16.5. Program Information Publications* *16.6. Use of Performance Statistics* *16.7. HSE Awareness Meetings* *16.8. HSE Awareness Promotion* *16.9. Promotion Campaigns* *16.10. Recognition and Award Programs* *16.11. Housekeeping Promotion* 16.12. Employee Participation 16.13. Training 16.14. Awareness Surveys 16.15. Data Collection and Analysis 16.16. Program Monitoring 16.17. Review and Improvement
17. **External Communications**	17.1. Management Statement 17.2. Coordination 17.3. Regulations, Codes and Standards 17.4. Implementation Plan *17.5. Communication with Interested Parties* *17.6. Complaints and Other Information* *17.7. Promotional Activities* *17.8. Off-the Job HSE* 17.9. Employee Participation 17.10. Training 17.11. Data Collection and Analysis 17.12. Communication 17.13. Program Monitoring 17.14. Review and Improvement

ELEMENT	ELEMENT STRUCTURE:
18. Emergency Preparedness	18.1. Management Statement 18.2. Coordination 18.3. Regulations, Codes and Standards 18.4. Implementation Plan *18.5. Identification of Potential Emergencies* *18.6. Emergency Plan* *18.7. Specific Responses* *18.8. Emergency Equipment and Facilities* *18.9. Fixed Fire Water System* *18.10. Mobile Equipment* *18.11. Emergency Communications Equipment* *18.13. Emergency Support* *18.14. Public Relations* 18.15. Employee Participation 18.16. Emergency Training 18.17. Data Collection and Analysis 18.18. Communication 18.19. Program Monitoring 18.20. Review and Improvement
19. Incident Investigation	19.1. Management Statement 19.2. Coordination 19.3. Regulations, Codes and Standards 19.4. Implementation Plan *19.5. Investigation* *19.6. Reporting* *19.7. Follow-up* 19.8. Employee Participation 19.9. Training *19.10. Incident Report Maintenance* *19.11. Property Damage Identification and Analysis* 19.12. Data Collection and Analysis 19.13. Communication 19.14. Program Monitoring 19.15. Review and Improvement

ELEMENT	ELEMENT STRUCTURE:
20. **Monitoring and Assessment**	20.1. Management Statement 20.2. Coordination 20.3. Regulations, Codes and Standards 20.4. Implementation Plan *20.5. Occupational Health Monitoring and Medical Surveillance* *20.6. Safe Behavior Monitoring* *20.7. Environmental Monitoring* *20.8. Assessment Activities* 20.9. Employee Participation 20.10. Training 20.11. Communication 20.12. Program Monitoring 20.13. Review and Improvement
21. **Management System and Process Safety Audits**	21.1. Management Statement 21.2. Coordination 21.3. Regulations, Codes and Standards 21.4. Implementation Plan *21.5. Management System Audits* *21.6. Process Safety Audits* 21.7. Employee Participation 21.8. Training 21.9. Data Collection and Analysis 21.10. Communication 21.11. Program Monitoring 21.12. Review and Improvement
22. **Process Safety Information and Document control**	22.1. Management Statement 22.2. Coordination 22.3. Regulations, Codes and Standards 22.4. Implementation Plan *22.5. Information Accessibility* *22.6. Document Control* 22.7. Employee Participation 22.8. Training 22.9. Data Collection and Analysis 22.10. Communication 22.11. Program Monitoring 22.12. Review and Improvement

APPENDIX H – A (safety) audit reference

AUDIT CHECKLIST		Maximum element score
1.	Leadership and administration	130
2.	Training of management and supervision	70
3.	Planned inspections	75
4.	Critical task control	55
5.	Accident/incident analysis/statistics	45
6.	Emergency preparedness	75
7.	Safety and health rules	50
8.	Employee induction and training	70
9.	Personal protective equipment	35
10.	Occupational health control	60
11.	Program evaluations	70
12.	Design engineering and risk assessment	100
13.	Purchasing	60
14.	Safety and health/loss control meetings	40
15.	New process/products introductions	50
16.	Environmental controls	80

PLEASE NOTE that the audit example relates only to items 3.1 – 3.2 of the recommended structure (see chapter 2.6, page 163 - 179). The example does not include the improvement loop that the structure represents.

See also page 200 where I mention the case in Spain in which the original audit version (without the structure) produced a level 8 award while the process industry version (including the structure) did not go beyond level 1. Further see the structure that is present in the ExxonMobil OIMS system mentioned on pages 167 and 168.

AUDIT CHECKLIST

1. LEADERSHIP AND ADMINISTRATION (130)

1.1. General policy (5)

1.1.1. Does the organization have a policy statement reflecting local management's commitment and support to safety/health/loss control? (2)   yes/no _____

1.1.2. Has the policy been communicated to all concerned? (3)   yes/no _____

Please provide copy of General Safety and Health Policy

1.2. Program Coordinator (10)

1.2.1. Has a person been designated as safety and health/loss control coordinator? (10)   yes/no _____

1.3. Senior and middle management participation (15)

1.3.1. Does senior and middle management make planned periodic safety and health tours? (15)   yes/no _____

Please provide planning for Safety and Health tours for this year

1.4. Established Management Performance Standards (50)

1.4.1. Do written Safety and Health performance standards exist for any of the following activities:

   1. Leadership and Administration? (3)   yes/no _____
   2. Safety/Health Training Management/Supervision?(3)   yes/no _____
   3. Safety/Health related Planned Inspections? (3)   yes/no _____
   4. Safety/Health control of Critical Tasks? (4)   yes/no _____
   5. Accident/Incident Analysis/Statistics? (4)   yes/no _____
   6. Emergency Preparedness? (3)   yes/no _____
   7. Safety/Health Rules and regulations? (3)   yes/no _____
   8. Employee Induction and Training as related to Safety/Health? (3)   yes/no _____
   9. Personal Protective Equipment? (3)   yes/no _____
   10. Occupational Health Control? (3)   yes/no _____
   11. Systematic Safety/Health Program Evaluation? (3)   yes/no _____

12. Engineering Controls as related to Safety/Health? (3)   yes/no _____
13. Purchasing Controls as related to Safety/Health? (3)   yes/no _____
14. Safety/Health related Group Communications? (3)   yes/no _____
15. New Process/products Introductions? (3)   yes/no _____
16. Environmental Controls? (3)   yes/no _____

Please provide copy of relevant standards/guidelines for performance of Management, Supervision and Staff-functions, as related to Safety and Health

1.5   Safety and Health/Loss Control at Management Meetings (10)

1.5.1.   Are regular meetings held at various levels of management, of which an extensive part is devoted to safety and health? (10)   yes/no _____

Please provide minutes of meetings.

1.6.   Safety and Health audits conducted by Management (10)

1.6.1.   Do middle and senior management levels conduct at least annual safety and health audits of the departments in their organization? (10)   yes/no _____

Please provide reports of audits carried out

1.7.   Individual Responsibility for Safety/Health & Loss Control? (20)

1.7.1.   Are safety and health/loss control responsibilities clearly defined and described for:

- all management levels? (2)   yes/no _____
- relevant staff-functions? (2)   yes/no _____
- workers? (1)   yes/no _____

Please provide representative descriptions of Safety and Health/Loss Control responsibilities of the various functions.

1.7.2.   Is safety and Health/loss control a clearly defined part of the periodic appraisals for:

- all management levels? (2)   yes/no _____
- relevant staff-functions? (2)   yes/no _____
- workers? (1)   yes/no _____

Please provide copy of appraisal forms/reports.

> 1.7.3. Have all employees been informed about their responsibility to report substandard conditions? (5)   yes/no _____

> 1.7.4. Does a formalized system exists for reporting substandard conditions/situations by employees? (5)   yes/no _____

Please provide description of system for reporting by employees of unsafe/substandard acts/conditions.

1.8. Establishment of Annual Safety/Health/Loss Control and environmental Objectives (10)

> 1.8.1. Have clear safety and health objectives been established for:

>> • the total organization or unit? (2)   yes/no _____
>> • important parts of this organization or unit? (3)   yes/no _____

Please provide description of objectives.

> 1.8.2. Have plans been prepared to obtain objectives? (5)   yes/no _____

Please provide copy of (annual) plans for Safety and Health activity.

2. TRAINING OF MANAGEMENT AND SUPERVISION (70)

2.1. Orientation/induction program for Management/supervision (5)

> 2.1.1. Is formal safety and Health/Loss Control induction or orientation given to all new members of management and supervision? (3)   yes/no _____

> 2.1.2. Is there an adequate plan to guide the orientation or induction? (2)   yes/no _____

Please provide "guide plan" for Safety and Health induction/orientation of Management and Supervision.

2.2. Formal training of management/supervision (25)

> 2.2.1. Indicate which of the following subjects are part of the formal safety and health training of management and supervision.

>> 1. management control of loss? (1)   yes/no _____

2. causes and effects of accidents? (1)   yes/no _____
3. risk management? (1)   yes/no _____
4. measurement of safety? (1)   yes/no _____
5. planned inspections? (1)   yes/no _____
6. critical tasks control? (1)   yes/no _____
7. safety/health controls in engineering? (1)   yes/no _____
8. safety/health controls in purchasing? (1)   yes/no _____
9. behavior observations? (1)   yes/no _____
10. accident/incident analysis/statistics? (1)   yes/no _____
11. employee induction and training? (1)   yes/no _____
12. rules and regulations/permit systems? (1)   yes/no _____
13. introduction to occupational health? (1)   yes/no _____
14. fire loss control? (1)   yes/no _____
15. personal and group communications? (1)   yes/no _____
16. safety and health appraisals of subordinates? (1) yes/no _____
17. emergency preparedness? (1)   yes/no _____
18. obtaining and maintaining desired performance levels? (1) yes/no _____
19. obtaining compliance with safety and health rules? (1)   yes/no _____

2.2.2. Are formal lesson plans available to guide this training? (2)   yes/no _____

Please provide "lesson plans" for course and/or subjects indicated.

2.2.3. Are adequate hand-outs provided during training? (2)   yes/no _____

Please provide course hand-outs.

2.2.4. Have all management/supervision presently in function received
        this training? (2)   yes/no _____

2.3. Formal Training of relevant staff functions (10)

2.3.1. Have relevant staff functions received a Management Safety
        training in safety and health/loss control methods and
        techniques? (6)   yes/no _____

2.3.2. Did this training include the engineering functions? (4)   yes/no _____

2.4. New process Introductions (20)

2.4.1. Are formalized instructions given for each introduction of new
        processes/products? (12)   yes/no _____

Please provide new process/products introduction procedures.

    2.4.2.   Are these instructions provided to:

- management? (2)   yes/no _____
- supervision? (2)   yes/no _____
- staff-functions? (2)   yes/no _____
- workers? (2)   yes/no _____

Please provide instruction program or meeting minutes of last new process/product introduction.

2.5.   Formal training of Safety & Health Program Coordinator (10)

    2.5.1.   Has the Safety and Health program coordinator received a basic safety and health training from a recognized organization? (6)   yes/no _____

Please provide course material, lesson plans, hand-outs, etc.

    2.5.2.   Has program coordinator received any up-date training during the last two years? (4)   yes/no _____

3.   PLANNED INSPECTIONS (75)

3.1.   Inspection Guidelines (20)

    3.1.1.   Is clearly identified which type of inspections should be carried out:

- general (housekeeping inspections)? (1)   yes/no _____
- middle and senior management tours? (1)   yes/no _____
- critical item inspections? (1)   yes/no _____
- preventive maintenance inspections? (1)   yes/no _____
- predictive maintenance inspections? (1)   yes/no _____
- pre-use inspections? (1)   yes/no _____
- legally required inspections? (1)   yes/no _____
- vendor inspections? (1)   yes/no _____
- inspections during construction? (1)   yes/no _____
- pre-start-up inspections? (1)   yes/no _____
- inspections after process/installation modifications? (1)   yes/no _____
- inspections after shut-down? (1)   yes/no _____
- permit system related inspections? (1)   yes/no _____

Please provide description of guidelines for inspections indicated.

3.1.2. Do these inspection guidelines include:

- who is responsible for initiating the inspections? (1)   yes/no _____
- who should carry out the inspections? (1)   yes/no _____
- who supervises the actual inspection being carried out? (1) yes/no _____
- the frequency of the inspections? (1)   yes/no _____
- reporting on inspection findings? (1)   yes/no _____
- use of hazard classification system? (1)   yes/no _____
- follow-up on inspections? (1)   yes/no _____

Please provide relevant guidelines with aspects indicated.

3.2. General Inspections (10)

3.2.1. Are General Inspections carried out for all areas? (3)   yes/no _____

Please provide General Inspection procedure and/or planning of inspections carried out

3.2.2. Has the frequency of these inspections been established? (1)   yes/no _____

3.2.3. Is responsibility for inspections established? (1)   yes/no _____

3.2.4. Are workers involved in this type of inspection? (2)   yes/no _____

3.2.5. Are report forms used for reporting substandard conditions? (1)   yes/no _____

Please provide sample copies of reports filled out during recent inspections.

3.2.6. Has a proper follow-up procedure been established? (2)   yes/no _____

Please provide description of General Inspection follow-up

3.3. Critical Parts Inspections (15)

3.3.1. Have critical parts been identified? (4)   yes/no _____

3.3.2. Are identified critical parts periodically inspected? (3)   yes/no _____

Provide Critical Parts Inspection procedures, planning and sample copies of reports.

3.3.3. Does a system exist for reporting substandard conditions? (3)   yes/no _____

3.3.4. Has a follow-up procedure been established to correct reported
substandard conditions? (5)   yes/no _____

3.4. Maintenance (15)

3.4.1. Are maintenance activities analyzed to indicate those repairs
and maintenance works which can be considered
abnormal? (10)   yes/no _____

3.4.2. Are these abnormal maintenance/repair activities periodically
analyzed? (5)   yes/no _____

Please provide copies of last analyses.

3.5. Hazardous Conditions Reporting (10)

3.5.1. Is there a system for all employees to report substandard
conditions/acts to a central point? (4)   yes/no _____

Please provide description of Hazardous Conditions Reporting system

3.5.2. Is this procedure known to all employees? (3)   yes/no _____

3.5.3. Is there an adequate system to ensure proper follow-up of
conditions/acts reported? (3)   yes/no _____

Please provide description of follow-up system

3.6. Regular Evaluation of Inspection Activities (5)

3.6.1. Is there a regular evaluation of inspection activities? (2)   yes/no _____

3.6.2. Does this evaluation include:

- number of inspections carried out? (1)   yes/no _____
- quality of inspections carried out? (1)   yes/no _____

Please provide last evaluation reports.

3.6.3. Are evaluation results reported to senior management for proper
follow-up? (1)   yes/no _____

4.   CRITICAL TASK CONTROL (55)

4.1.   Critical Task Control Guideline (5)

4.1.1.   Is there a management guideline on Critical Task Control? (5)   yes/no _____

Please provide copy of guideline on Critical task Control

4.2.   Critical Task Control Training (5)

4.2.1.   Have appropriate personnel been trained in the control of Critical Tasks and did this training include:

- critical task identification?   (2)   yes/no _____
- task analysis? (1)   yes/no _____
- task procedure preparation? (1)   yes/no _____
- task observation? (1)   yes/no _____

Please provide lesson plan and hand-out used during training

4.3.   Inventory of Critical Tasks (15)

4.3.1.   Have critical Tasks been identified through a systematic process including:

- listing of all functions in the operations? (5)   yes/no _____
- listing of Tasks per function? (5)   yes/no _____
- identifying the critical Tasks? (5)   yes/no _____

4.4.   Controls Established (10)

4.4.1.   Have controls been established for Critical Tasks identified? (5)   yes/no _____

4.4.2.   Have critical steps in operating procedures been identified? (5)   yes/no _____

Provide sample copies of operating procedures with critical steps identified

4.5.   Task Observation Program (15)

4.5.1.   Does a system exists for periodic planned observation of the execution of Critical Tasks and critical steps in operating procedures? (10)   yes/no _____

Please provide description of observation activities, including planning of observations.

    4.5.2. Are reports made for each observation carried out? (5)   yes/no _____

Please provide sample copies of observation reports carried out during last six (6) months.

4.6.   Critical Tasks Control System Evaluation (5)

    4.6.1. Is there a regular evaluation of Critical Task Control activities and does this include:

- review of existing procedures? (3)   yes/no _____
- observations carried out according to planning? (2)   yes/no _____
- feedback from accident reports? (1)   yes/no _____

Please provide copies of last evaluation reports

5.   ACCIDENT/INCIDENT ANALYSIS/STATISTICS (45)

5.1.   Procedure for investigating/analyzing accidents/incidents (8)

    5.1.1. Is there a procedure for reporting and analysis of accidents/incidents? (2)   yes/no _____

Please provide copy of accident/incident reporting/analysis procedures

    5.1.2. Does this procedure include:

- reporting of accidents/incidents by employees? (1)   yes/no _____
- system for evaluation of accidents in terms of potential severity and frequency of occurrence? (1)   yes/no _____
- methods to be used for analysis? (1)   yes/no _____

Please provide lesson plan and course material subject accident/incident analysis/investigation.

    5.1.3. Is this procedure made known to all managers, supervisors and workers? (2) yes/no _____

    5.1.4. Does the procedure include worker involvement in the analyzing/investigation process? (1)   yes/no _____

5.2. Training in accident analysis/investigation (5)

5.2.1. Have all people involved in accident/incident analysis/investigation been trained for this purpose? (5)   yes/no _____

5.3. Reporting/registration of accidents/incidents (8)

5.3.1. Is there a procedure for registration of accidents and incidents? (2)   yes/no _____

Please provide procedure for registration of accidents/incidents.

5.3.2. Does this registration include the form of a "log" to register all deviations from normal? (4)   yes/no _____

Please provide samples of "logs" filled out.

5.3.3. Is there an adequate form to guide the analysis and reporting of accidents/incidents identified for that purpose? (2)   yes/no _____

Please provide form(s) used to report and investigate accidents/incidents.

5.4. Action-plan and Follow-up (6)

5.4.1. Is there a procedure to properly follow-up on actions suggested to remedy the situation? (3)   yes/no _____

Please provide description of procedure.

5.4.2. Does this procedure indicate:

- who is responsible for follow-up being carried out? (1)   yes/no _____
- regular reporting on outstanding actions? (1)   yes/no _____
- final check on actions being completed? (1)   yes/no _____

5.5. Central reporting of accidents/incidents (2)

5.5.1. Are accidents/incidents identified for this purpose reported to a central point on corporate level? (2)   yes/no _____

5.6.   Injury Type Accidents (4)

5.6.1.   Are injury type accidents identified and recorded? (1)   yes/no _____

Please provide records identifying injury type accidents.

5.6.2.   Are these registrations or records periodically analyzed? (2)   yes/no _____

Please provide copies of last analyses.

5.6.3.   Are problem solving teams used to cope with identified
problems? (1)   yes/no _____

Please provide reports of problem solving teams used.

5.7.   Damage Type Accidents (4)

5.7.1.   Are repair and maintenance jobs other than normal wear and tear
identified and recorded? (1)   yes/no _____

Please provide records indicating "abnormal" maintenance jobs carried out.

5.7.2.   Are these registrations or records periodically analyzed? (2)   yes/no _____

5.7.3.   Are problem solving teams used to cope with identified
problems? (1)   yes/no _____

Please provide reports of problem solving teams used.

5.8.   Near-miss incidents (4)

5.8.1.   Are near-miss incidents identified and recorded? (1)   yes/no _____

Please provide record of near-miss incidents.

5.8.2.   Are these registrations or records periodically analyzed? (2)   yes/no _____

5.8.3.   Are problem solving teams used to cope with identified
problems? (1)   yes/no _____

Please provide reports of problem solving teams used.

5.9. Evaluation of accident/incident activities (4)

5.9.1. Is there a regular evaluation of the accident/incident report system? (2)   yes/no _____

Please provide last evaluation reports.

5.9.2. Does this include quantitative as well as qualitative criteria? (1)   yes/no _____

5.9.3. Are evaluation results shared with senior management for Proper follow-up? (1)   yes/no _____

6. EMERGENCY PREPAREDNESS (75)

6.1. Emergency Program coordination (5)

6.1.1. Has a person been appointed for overall coordination of the emergency activities? (3)   yes/no _____

6.1.2. Have persons been appointed to coordinate the actual emergency activities? (2)   yes/no _____

6.2. Emergency plan (15)

6.2.1. Is there an Emergency Plan, including:

- evacuation of people to a safe place? (1)   yes/no _____
- emergency shutdown of equipment? (1)   yes/no _____
- notification of proper emergency aid? (1)   yes/no _____
- search and rescue activities? (1)   yes/no _____
- notification of public in case of toxic releases? (1)   yes/no _____
- control of hazardous materials? (1)   yes/no _____
- control of energy sources? (1)   yes/no _____
- designation of a command post? (1)   yes/no _____
- salvage of vital equipment or documentation? (1)   yes/no _____
- "All clear" and safe re-entry procedure? (1)   yes/no _____

Provide copy of emergency plan.

6.2.2.   Are there periodic exercises to test the effectiveness of the
Emergency Plan? (5)   yes/no _____

Please provide minutes or reports of emergency plan exercises.

6.3.   Rescue Equipment (5)

6.3.1.   Has adequate rescue equipment been provided and is this
readily available to persons in need for this? (3)   yes/no _____

6.3.2.   Have relevant personnel been instructed in the proper use
of such equipment? (2)   yes/no _____

6.4.   Emergency Power (5)

6.4.1.   Is there adequate Emergency Power for:

- evacuation of people (including emergency lighting)? (1)   yes/no _____
- shutdown of equipment? (2)   yes/no _____
- use of emergency equipment (such as fire
fighting pumps)? (2)   yes/no _____

6.5.   Plant Emergency Teams (15)

6.5.1.   Are there sufficient (Plant) Emergency Teams to cope with the
probable or possible emergencies?   (5)   yes/no _____

6.5.2.   Are these teams properly trained? (5)   yes/no _____

6.5.3.   Are these teams properly equipped to fight the
emergencies expected? (5)   yes/no _____

6.6.   External Help (10)

6.6.1.   Are external Emergency Services provided with up-to-date
information covering the possible emergencies at this
location? (5)   yes/no _____

6.6.2.   Are these services familiar with the location and the areas
where goods of particular hazardous nature are kept? (3)   yes/no _____

6.6.3. Are the systems to notify these external services regularly
tested for proper operation? (2)   yes/no _____

6.7. Emergency Communication (10)

6.7.1. Are adequate means available to communicate an emergency to:

- own personnel? (3)   yes/no _____
- internal emergency services? (3)   yes/no _____
- external emergency services? (2)   yes/no _____
- the neighborhood? (2)   yes/no _____

6.8. Medical assistance and First Aid (10)

6.8.1. Is adequate medical assistance available to cope with
emergencies? (3)   yes/no _____

6.8.2. Is a sufficient number of First Aiders available at all
work hours? (2)   yes/no _____

6.8.3. Are these services familiar with special first aid needs, including
treatment of exposure to special chemicals as required, and
equipped to cope with those needs? (3)   yes/no _____

6.8.4. Are these services located such as to enable prompt response
to an emergency? (2)   yes/no _____

Indicate location of First Aid services on site plan.

7. SAFETY AND HEALTH RULES (50)

7.1. General Safety and Health Rules (7)

7.1.1. Are there general safety and health rules to guide behavior of people? (7)
yes/no _____

Please provide General Safety and Health Rule booklet or publication.

7.2. Specific Safety and Health Rules (23)

7.2.1. Has the need for specific safety and health rules been
identified in relation to specific hazards and tasks? (3)   yes/no _____

7.2.2.   Do these rules include (as applicable):

- working with chemical products? (2)   yes/no _____
- hot work? (2)   yes/no _____
- cold work? (2)   yes/no _____
- vessel entry? (2)   yes/no _____
- excavation? (2)   yes/no _____
- working at heights? (2)   yes/no _____
- electrical lock-out? (2)   yes/no _____
- opening of tanks, vessels and pipes? (2)   yes/no _____
- hoisting? (2)   yes/no _____
- any others? (2)   yes/no _____

Please provide samples of specific Safety and Health rules and forms used, as indicated.

7.3.   Review and up-dating of Rules (5)

7.3.1.   Are rules reviewed at least annually and at each process and
installation modification? (5)   yes/no _____

7.4.   Rules Instruction (10)

7.4.1.   Are people instructed in relevant rules:

- general rules at day of employment? (2)   yes/no _____
- specific rules during task instruction? (3) yes/no _____

Please provide records of instruction.

7.4.2.   Is knowledge of rules maintained and up-dated:

- through annual instructions? (2)   yes/no _____
- through safety meetings/presentations? (3)   yes/no _____

Please provide records of annual instruction and/or minutes of safety meetings.

7.5.   Rules compliance Efforts (5)

      7.5.2.   Is compliance with general and specific rules supported:

- through planned task observations? (2)   yes/no _____
- through periodic behavioral observations? (3)   yes/no _____

Provide records of planned Task Observation.
Provide reports on periodic behavioral observations.

8.   EMPLOYEE INDUCTION AND TRAINING (70)

8.1.   Induction of new employees (10)

      8.1.1.   Do new employees receive a safety and health induction
             before being put to work? (4)   yes/no _____

Please provide copy of guideline for this induction.

      8.1.2.   Is there a guideline to standardize this induction? (2)   yes/no _____

      8.1.3.   Does this induction include:

- general safety and health aspects and rules? (1)   yes/no _____
- duty to report unsafe or substandard acts/conditions? (1) yes/no _____
- security? (1)   yes/no _____
- fire safety? (1)   yes/no _____

Please provide any material normally given to new employees during Safety and Health induction.

8.2.   Instruction of new employees (10)

      8.2.1.   Do new and transferred employees receive specific safety and
             health instruction related to their job? (6)   yes/no _____

      8.2.2.   Have people providing this instruction been trained in
             instructional techniques? (4)   yes/no _____

Please provide hand-out of instructional technique training provided to persons giving Safety and Health instruction to new and transferred employees.

8.3.   Training need inventory (15)

8.3.1.   Has an inventory been made, per function or occupation to identify the need for:

- pre-hiring education and experience? (1)   yes/no _____
- additional (in-company) theoretical training? (2) yes/no _____
- additional (in-company) practical training? (2)   yes/no _____

Please provide records identifying educational and training needs per function.

8.3.2.   Does this inventory at least include:

- all normal work procedures? (1)   yes/no _____
- all special procedures, permit system, etc? (1) yes/no _____
- procedures for abnormal work, such as emergencies,
- shut-downs, etc? (1)   yes/no _____
- use of safety equipment? (1)   yes/no _____
- working with chemicals? (1)   yes/no _____

8.3.3.   Does this inventory also include:

- members of safety committees? (1)   yes/no _____
- safety coordinator? (1)   yes/no _____
- first aiders? (1)   yes/no _____
- other emergency services? (1)   yes/no _____

8.3.4.   Is this inventory regularly reviewed and, if necessary,
up-dated? (1)   yes/no _____

8.4.   Training Programs (20)

8.4.1.   Are training programs set up for all jobs or occupations
requiring such? (4)   yes/no _____

Provide list of occupations or functions with relevant educational requirement and training programs.

8.4.2.   Do these programs include:

- lesson plans? (1)   yes/no _____
- relevant text material? (1)   yes/no _____
- task procedures? (1)   yes/no _____

- visual aids, drawings, etc? (1)   yes/no _____

<u>Provide samples of lesson plans, text materials used, task procedures to guide training, etc.</u>

    8.4.3.   Do these training programs highlight:

- safety aspects of work to be carried out? (2)   yes/no _____
- health aspects of the work to be carried out? (2)   yes/no _____
- personal protection under normal work conditions? (2)   yes/no _____
- personal protection in case of emergency? (2)   yes/no _____
- permit systems? (2)   yes/no _____
- emergency actions? (2)   yes/no _____

8.5. Re-training of employees (8)

    8.5.1.   Do employees receive regular re-training? (3)   yes/no _____

    8.5.2.   Is re-training directed at the "critical" tasks or parts of the job? (5)   yes/no _____

<u>Provide samples of re-training programs.</u>

8.6. Training Program Evaluation (7)

    8.6.1.   Are training activities periodically evaluated and does this evaluation include at least:

- initial training given? (1)   yes/no _____
- re-training given? (1)   yes/no _____
- training quality? (1)   yes/no _____
- training effectiveness? (1)   yes/no _____

    8.6.2.   Do evaluation activities include:

- task observations? (1)   yes/no _____
- feed-back from accident/incident analysis? (1)   yes/no _____

    8.6.3.   Are evaluation results communicated to top-management? (1)   yes/no _____

<u>Please provide last evaluation reports.</u>

9. PERSONAL PROTECTIVE EQUIPMENT (35)

9.1. Personal Protective Equipment Rules (5)

9.1.1. Are PPE rules provided in writing and made known to all employees at their time of hiring? (2)   yes/no _____

9.1.2. Does this include:

- general PPE rules? (1)   yes/no _____
- PPE rules for specific tasks or occupations? (1)   yes/no _____
- use of PPE under emergency situations? (1)   yes/no _____

Please provide General and Specific PPE rules.

9.2. Provision of Personal Protective Equipment (8)

9.2.1. Is PPE adequately made available to all employees? (8)   yes/no _____

9.3. Maintenance of Personal Protective Equipment (4)

9.3.1. Is PPE properly maintained? (2)   yes/no _____

9.3.2. Is use and maintenance of PPE registered and periodically analyzed? (2)   yes/no _____

Please provide records covering issuance, maintenance and use of PPE.

9.4. Obtaining Compliance with rules (8)

9.4.1. Do supervisory training programs include guidelines on how to obtain compliance with PPE rules? (8)   yes/no _____

Provide training program and materials covering "how to obtain rule compliance".

9.5. Evaluation of PPE rule compliance (10)

9.5.1. Are regular observations/evaluations made to measure compliance with PPE rules? (7)   yes/no _____

Provide last observation/evaluation report.

9.5.2. Do accident/incident analyses provide feed-back on proper compliance with PPE rules? (3)   yes/no _____

<u>Provide accident investigation forms indicating relation to PPE rule compliance.</u>

10.   OCCUPATIONAL HEALTH CONTROL (60)

10.1.   Health Hazard Identification (10)

10.1.1. Have occupations and tasks been analyzed to identify existing
         and potential health hazards? (5)   yes/no _____

10.1.2. Has a standard form or checklist been used for this
         inventory? (2)   yes/no _____

<u>Please provide form used in analysis.</u>

10.1.3. Are all occupations analyzed for occupational health
         hazards? (3)   yes/no _____

10.2.   Chemical Products Exposure Inventory and Control (15)

10.2.1. Does a recent list of all chemical products used, stored
         or manufactured exists at this location to identify
         possible health exposures? (5)   yes/no _____

<u>Provide list of all chemical products handled, used, stored, manufactured and their main properties
related to risks, occupational hazards, etc.</u>

10.2.2. Is this list reviewed regularly and, if needed, up-dated? (3)   yes/no _____

10.2.3. Have adequate controls been established for the health
         hazards identified? (5)   yes/no _____

10.2.4. Do these controls include proper labeling of hazardous chemicals
         stored, manufactured and used in this location? (2)   yes/no _____

<u>Please provide system for identifying and labeling chemicals on site.</u>

10.3.   Health Hazard Information (10)

10.3.1. Are Managers and Supervisors properly informed of, and aware of
         the hazards associated with products used, manufactured and
         stored in their departments? (5)   yes/no _____

10.3.2. Are employees properly instructed in the use of products and or equipment with potential health hazards? (3)   yes/no _____

10.3.3. Is knowledge on how to deal with potential health hazards regularly tested and/or up-dated? (2)   yes/no _____

10.4. Monitoring (5)

10.4.1. Does occupational hygiene monitoring for health hazard exposures take place on a need basis? (2)   yes/no _____

10.4.2. Does this monitoring include:

- general work-place monitoring? (1)   yes/no _____
- personal monitoring? (1)   yes/no _____
- biological monitoring? (1)   yes/no _____

Please provide monitoring results of last 12 months.

10.5. Medical Examinations (12)

10.5.1. Are pre-employment medical checks carried out in relation with job exposures? (5)   yes/no _____

10.5.2. Is routine health surveillance carried out periodically depending on the potential exposure to health hazards, including those due to handling of chemicals? (7)   yes/no _____

10.6. Medical Assistance (8)

10.6.1. What medical assistance does this location have (highest score only):

- full-time medical assistance on site? (5)   yes/no _____
- part-time medical assistance on site? (4)   yes/no _____
- contract with outside medical assistance? (2)   yes/no _____
- informal relation with external office? (1)   yes/no _____

10.6.2. Is this assistance available at all work hours? (3)   yes/no _____

11. SAFETY AND HEALTH PROGRAMME EVALUATIONS (70)

11.1. Evaluation of Organizational Aspects (20)

11.1.1. Are evaluations of organizational safety and health aspects carried out on a regular basis? (15)   yes/no _____

11.1.2. Are these evaluations carried out by unbiased persons? (5)   yes/no _____

Provide checklists used in evaluation and last evaluation reports.

11.2. Evaluation of General Technical Aspects (18)

11.2.1. Are evaluations of general technical safety and health aspects carried out on a regular basis? (10)   Yes/no _____

11.2.2. If so, do these evaluations include:

- general technical safety aspects? (2)   yes/no _____
- fire safety aspects? (2)   yes/no _____
- occupational health aspects? (2)   yes/no _____

Please provide samples of checklists used in such evaluations.

11.2.3. Are these evaluations carried out by unbiased persons? (2)   yes/no _____

Provide copy of last evaluation report.

11.3. Evaluation of Process Safety Aspects (32)

11.3.1. Are evaluations of process and installation safety and health aspects carried out periodically? (10)   yes/no _____

11.3.2. Which of the following methods or aspects are included in these evaluations:

- P & I diagram reviews? (3)   yes/no _____
- Full HAZOP? (3)   yes/no _____
- Failure Mode and Effect Analysis? (3)   yes/no _____
- Evaluation Plant Fitness for Purpose? (3)   yes/no _____
- other? _____ (3)   yes/no _____

11.3.3. Are these evaluations carried out by unbiased persons? (7)   yes/no _____

12. DESIGN ENGINEERING, RISK ASSESSMENT AND CONSTRUCTION (100)

12.1. Risk Assessment (26)

12.1.1. Have risks involving this location been assessed through a systematic approach of risk identification and evaluation? (7) yes/no _____

Please provide copy of Risk Assessment records/reports.

12.1.2. Did this include both "internal" and "external" risks, including Environmental impact? (5) yes/no _____

12.1.3. Which of the following techniques or methods are, or have been used, in the design of processes and installations:

- Full Hazop? (2) yes/no _____
- Hazan? (2) yes/no _____
- Failure Mode and Effect Analysis? (2) yes/no _____
- other? _____ (2) yes/no _____

12.1.4. Have these methods/techniques been used by qualified persons in a team approach? (4) yes/no _____

12.1.5. Did this team include managers, supervisors and workers as well as staff-functions? (2) yes/no _____

Please provide records indicating persons involved in Risk Assessment.

12.2. Risk Control (18)

12.2.1. Have proper controls been set up for the risks assessed? (10) yes/no _____

12.2.2. Do these include the control of containment loss? (8) yes/no _____

12.3. Work Method/Operating Procedures (16)

12.3.1. Have work methods or operating procedures been analyzed for potential hazards or operating failures? (10) yes/no _____

12.3.2. Has this been done by qualified persons in a multi-disciplinary approach? (4) yes/no _____

12.3.3. Did this team include managers, supervisors and workers as well as staff-functions? (2)   yes/no _____

12.4.   Construction Procedures (14)

12.4.1. Do procedures for construction and process/installation
modifications including regular inspection to check
construction against (approved) plan? (14)   yes/no _____

12.5.   Process/Installation Modification Procedures (18)

12.5.1. Is there a procedure to guide process and installation
modifications and to   control potential risks? (8)   yes/no _____

Please provide construction/modification procedures.

12.5.2. Does this procedure include the use of techniques or
methods such as mini-Hazops, etc? (6)   yes/no _____

12.5.3. Does the application of this procedure involve a
multi-disciplinary approach including managers,
supervisors, workers and staff-functions? (4)   yes/no _____

12.6.   Evaluation of Procedures Application (8)

12.6.1. Is there a regular evaluation to check proper application of:

- design engineering procedures? (2)   yes/no _____
- work method/procedures preparation? (2)   yes/no _____
- process/installation modification procedures? (2)   yes/no _____
- construction procedures? (2)   yes/no _____

13.   PURCHASING (60)

13.1.   Purchasing of materials/equipment (36)

13.1.1. Are safety and health specifications set up for all regularly
purchased materials, goods, etc.? (10)   yes/no _____

Please provide samples of purchasing specifications for regular purchases.

13.1.2. Has the safety and health functions been involved in setting
up these specifications? (8)   yes/no _____

13.1.3. Is the safety and health function involved in all non-regular
purchases? (12)   yes/no _____

13.1.4. Are Material Safety Data Sheets obtained for all purchases
requiring such? (6)   yes/no _____

Please provide sample copies of Material Safety Data Sheets.

13.2. Selection and Control of Contractors/services (24)

13.2.1. Are safety and health criteria established for the selection of
contractors? (7)   yes/no _____

13.2.2. Has the safety and health function been involved in setting up
these criteria? (5)   yes/no _____

13.2.3. Do contractor selection criteria include contractor safety
program activities? (4)   yes/no _____

Please provide checklist used in contractor selection.

13.2.4. Do these criteria include selection of sub-contractor firms
by the main contractor? (2)   yes/no _____

13.2.5. Are contractor activities regularly monitored and does this include at least:

- contractor site inspections? (2)   yes/no _____
- contractor safety meetings? (2)   yes/no _____
- contractor accident reports? (2)   yes/no _____

Please provide relevant records of last major construction.

14. SAFETY AND HEALTH/LOSS CONTROL MEETINGS (40)

14.1. Safety and Health/Loss Control Meetings (25)

14.1.1. Are regular Safety and Health/Loss Control Meetings held with
all personnel at an established frequency? (12)   yes/no _____

14.1.2. Are subjects for these meetings planned well in advance? (8)   yes/no _____

Please provide subject planning for next six (6) months.

14.1.3. Are minutes made of meetings held? (5)   yes/no _____

Please provide samples of meeting minutes.

14.2.   Evaluation of Meetings held (15)

14.2.1. Are periodic evaluations made of meeting effectiveness? (8)   yes/no _____

14.2.2. Does this evaluation at least include:

- number of meetings held? (3)   yes/no _____
- quality of meetings held? (4)   yes/no _____

Please provide copy of last evaluations.

15.   NEW PROCESS/PRODUCTS INTRODUCTIONS (50)

15.1.   System for New Process Introductions (50)

15.1.1. Is there a system for the introduction of new processes,
installations, product? (20)   yes/no _____

Please provide description of system to introduce new products/processes.

15.1.2. Does this system include:

- assessment of risks involved? (10)   yes/no _____
- provision of relevant MSDS? (10)   yes/no _____
- training of managers, supervisors and workers? (10)   yes/no _____

Please provide records of last new process/product introduction.

16.   ENVIRONMENTAL CONTROLS (80)

16.1.   Assessment of Environmental exposures (25)

16.1.1. Have environmental risks been assessed? (8)   yes/no _____

Please provide copy of environmental risk assessment report.

16.1.2. Has a systematic approach been used for this purpose? (5)   yes/no _____

16.1.3. Did the assessment include:

- potential for pollution of the air? (2)   yes/no _____
- potential for pollution of ground and surface water? (2)   yes/no _____
- potential for pollution of the soil? (2)   yes/no _____

16.1.4. Did the assessment include:

- risks during normal operation? (2)   yes/no _____
- risks during abnormal of process? (2)   yes/no _____
- risks during emergency situations? (2)   yes/no _____

16.2.   Environmental Controls Established (35)

16.2.1. Are proper controls established for risks identified? (10)   yes/no _____

Please provide description of controls to prevent and limit damage to the environment.

16.2.2. Do these controls include (as needed):

- regular monitoring for typical agents? (5)   yes/no _____
- procedures for removal of normal process waste? (6)   yes/no _____
- procedures for removal of waste during emergencies? (4)   yes/no _____
- prevention of containment loss? (6)   yes/no _____
- control of spills/leakages? (4)   yes/no _____

16.3.   Environmental Emergency Procedures (20)

16.3.1. Have emergency procedures been set up in case of a
(potential) threat to the environment? (5)   yes/no _____

Please provide environmental emergency plan.

16.3.2. Do these procedures include the prompt notification of
authorities and neighborhood? (5)   yes/no _____

16.3.3. Do these procedures include adequate actions to limit
exposure during environmental emergencies? (10)   yes/no _____

APPENDIX I – Higher abstraction level audit

This appendix provides an example of a higher abstraction level audit for the element "Incident Investigation and Analysis". The assumption is that there may be no need to go into further detail regarding activities (3.1 and 3.2) when objectives are being met and the structure, representing the improvement loop, is clearly present and complete.

Element – 18 "Incident Investigation and Analysis"

Element Objectives

To assure proper investigation and analysis of individual incidents to:

- Prepare high quality investigation reports
- Make action plans such that the same or similar incidents will no longer occur
- To collect information from incidents occurred over a period of time to produce incident statistics, to uncover trends and/or common causes requiring further improvement attention.

Element Reference:

Element 18: Incident Investigation and Analysis	Response
1. Element policy and management statement The objective is to formalize, in written form, top management attitude, leadership, commitment and support to meet HSE objectives and targets identified. Reference:	Element policy and management statement are available. yes / no

1.1. Reason for element activity To explain and underline the importance of this element as part of reaching the overall management system objectives. Reference:	Reasons for element activity are properly stated. yes / no
1.2. Goals and objectives of element Goals / objectives to be obtained for this element. Reference:	Clear goals/objectives are set for this element. yes / no
2. Element coordination The objective is to assure effective coordination of the activities of this element involving proper managerial, supervisory and operational personnel such that they are properly developed, carried out, monitored and reviewed for further improvement. Reference:	Coordination of this element available and assigned. yes / no
3. Element standing plan Development of the element "standing" plan involving appropriate managerial, supervisory and operational personnel. Reference:	A standing plan for this Element is available. yes / no

3.1. **Employee participation in element development and improvement** The objective of this sub-element is to involve relevant employees (at various levels in the organization) in the development, execution and improvement of element activities. Reference:	Employees at various levels are involved in development and improvement of element activities. yes / no
3.2. **Review of legislation, Codes and Standards** To assure that all applicable regulations, codes and standards are identified and that timely actions are taken to incorporate requirements into work practices, rules, training programs, engineering standards, etc. Reference:	Review has been done and requirements are included in this element. yes / no
3.3. **Review of other sources** Review of other identified sources to assure that timely actions are taken to incorporate requirements into work practices, rules, training programs, engineering standards, etc. Reference:	Review has been done and requirements are included in this element. yes / no
4. **Employee training to carry out element activities** To provide knowledge, skills and motivation to those who are charged with carrying out the element activities, activity coordination management and coaching, monitoring evaluations and review. Reference:	Element related training identified and provided. yes / no

5. Employee participation in execution of activities Properly trained employees carrying out the element activities, including coordination, management and coaching. Reference:	Employees at various levels are involved in the execution of element activities. yes / no
6. Communication needs to internal/external parties To gather and analyze the information/data necessary for communication to identified relevant internal and external parties for the proper management of the activities. Reference:	Communication needs are identified and relevant information regarding element activities goes to identified parties. yes / no
7. Element standing plan assessment Periodic element standing plan assessments carried out by properly trained personnel. Reference:	Periodic assessment is being carried out by properly trained personnel. yes / no
7.1. Periodic evaluation of element activities Evaluation to verify whether the standing plan has been executed as planned and in accordance with the criteria set. Reference:	Element activities are periodically verified and compared to criteria set. yes / no
7.2. Periodic evaluation of element results The objective of this element is to evaluate element results against objectives set. Reference:	Element results are periodically assessed and compared with element objectives set. yes / no

8. Review and improvement	Element activities and results are periodically reviewed for possible improvement with action plans prepared.
To assure that results are being achieved - as intended and determined by changing internal and/or external conditions - and that further actions, as appropriate, are taken for further improvement. Reference:	yes / no

Possible sub-elements for inclusion in the element standing plan (3)

- Scope of the investigation activities
  - To determine which incidents need to be within the investigation and analysis activities
- Reporting System
  - To establish an effective system and methods for reporting and analysis incidents.
- Near-miss reporting
  - To establish a system to report and investigate incidents that have not actually resulted in visible loss.
- Remedial action and follow-up
  - To assure that remedial actions are being carried out as planned and in accordance with priorities set.

Also look at element 5 of appendix H (page 307) for further activities that you may want to include in the element standing plan.

Conclusions:

- Improvement loop complete   yes/no
- Element objective obtained   yes/no

Suggestions:

APPENDIX J – Protocol for learning from what goes wrong

This appendix shows an example of a protocol for reporting, registration and cause analysis of unwanted events and taking remedial actions

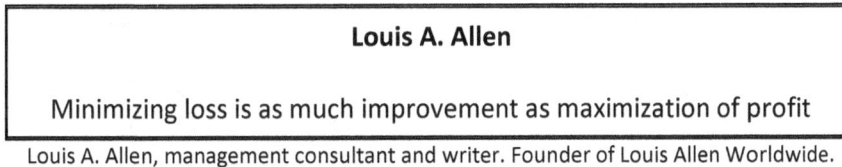

Louis A. Allen

Minimizing loss is as much improvement as maximization of profit

---

Louis A. Allen, management consultant and writer. Founder of Louis Allen Worldwide.

Definitions

Unwanted Event: an event that leads, or could lead, to unwanted consequences: harm or loss to people, property, environment or business.

Accident: an unwanted event that results in harm or loss to people, property, environment or business.

The Model

The model on which our unwanted event investigation system is based is shown below. Originally this "domino model" was set up by Heinrich/Lateiner but was upgraded by Frank E. Bird, Jr. in the late sixties of last century.

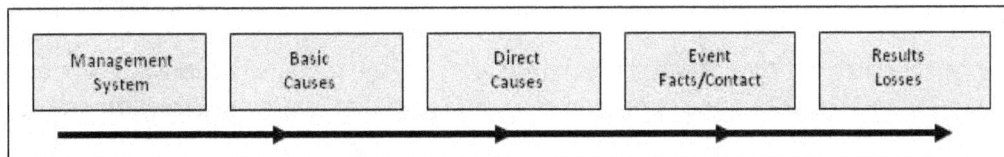

This "loss causation" model is a simplified representation of real life. It contains a dual message: (i) success is related to the quality of the management system and, (ii) unwanted events and their losses may indicate failure of that system.

Please be aware that when we mention the "management system", this is not solely related to the persons whom we refer to as "managers". Within the management system all personnel at all levels work together to obtain desired results: managers, staff, supervisory and operational personnel.

I. Purpose

The prevention of unwanted events is one of the main tasks of everyone in his/her department and a key priority within our company. Despite all preventive measures, however, they can still occur, possibly resulting in accidents. When this happens, priority must be given to any victims and ending the emergency situation. Measures should be taken to prevent a possible second (similar) incident and to restart production processes as quickly as safely possible.

In principle, all unwanted events should be investigated to at least determine the potential risk of recurrence. Not all incidents, however, need to be analyzed to determine their (root) causes. The type of event, the actual results and the potential effect, these are all part of the decision whether an analysis will be necessary - see table 3 under IV Analysis.

Accurate and timely investigation should take place to:

- Collect facts concerning the event
- Establish, based on the facts, the possible recurrence of the event and what the consequences could have been ("risk classification")
- Depending on the risk classification, allow analysis of causes for taking preventive measures
- To meet the requirements set by the authorities
- Recover any insurance payments as quickly as possible
- Establish the actual cost to production
- Capture and register correct and detailed information in case of possible future court action
- To determine the effectiveness of our management system and related activities

To record data, carry out cause analysis, generate and manage remedial actions, we use the software program UEI. Within the operation of the UEI software, there are three important roles:

- Event Owner - the person with the final responsibility of an "event", including all remedial actions
- Action Owners - the persons responsible to ensure that actions assigned to them will be properly done and on time
- Facilitator - the person designated to carry out or lead the cause analysis

Further detail about the operation of the software and related procedures can be found in the (UEI software) document.

II. Reporting and Investigation

Unwanted events to be reported and investigated are:

- Fatal accidents
- Events resulting in workdays lost
- Medical treatment accidents
- Restricted work accidents
- Vehicle accidents
- Fires and explosions
- Material damage (over € xx)
- Damage to tools (over € xx)
- Loss of material (over € xx)
- Cases of (suspected) occupational illness
- Near-accidents (events that could result in serious harm, injury or loss)
- Crime (burglary, theft, etc.)
- Accidents involving contractor or third party personnel
- Product accidents (possibly resulting product liability claims)
- Customer complaints
- Environmental incidents (above threshold value)
- Environmental incidents with possibility to surpass legal limits
- Any other unwanted event that could have a serious negative influence on company image
- All events requiring cause analysis as indicated in paragraph IV

Each unwanted event will be assigned to an "Event Owner" with vested interest. Normally this will be the head of the department where the unwanted event occurred.

III. Risk Classification

Risk classification is done by making an assessment regarding:

- The potential risk of recurrence or "failure rate" of the same or a similar unwanted event
- The likely or possible consequences, the "results", of the unwanted event should it happen again under the same or slightly different circumstances

The failure rate is divided into 5 categories 1 to 5, as indicated in the table below. Please note that the highest failure rate is at the top of the table, the lowest failure rate at the bottom.

5	Several times a year
4	1 time per year
3	1 time per 2 years
2	1 time per 5 years
1	Less than 1 time per 5 years

Table 1- Failure rate

The possible consequences are also divided into 5 categories A to E, as indicated in the table below. Please note that the most severe consequence is at the top of the table, the slightest at the bottom.

Category	Loss type	Potential consequence level
E Very High Risk	Safety	Multiple deaths
	Environment	Extensive excess of allowed emission levels. Extensive damage to the environment. Major public concerns and damage.
	Material Damage	> € 1,000,000
	Company Image	Extensive company image degradation.
D High Risk	Safety	Death of individual. Permanent disability. Serious injury of many.
	Environment	Severe excess of allowed emission levels. Damage to environment. Corrective measures required outside company boundaries.
	Material Damage	€ 100,000 to € 1,000,000
	Company Image	Serious company image degradation.
C Average Risk	Safety	Non-permanent serious injury to individual. Workdays lost. Restricted work. Minor injury to many.
	Environment	Repeated slight excess of allowed emission limits. Limited damage to environment outside company boundaries.
	Material Damage	€ 10,000 to € 100,000
	Company Image	Average company image degradation.

B **Low Risk**	Safety	Non-permanent light injury to individual. Restricted work. Pain or injury several people.
	Environment	Slight excess of allowed emissions limits. Non-permanent damage to environment.
	Material Damage	€ 1000 to € 10,000
	Company Image	Little company image degradation.
A **Minor Risk**	Safety	Pain or injury to individual. First Aid
	Environment	Emissions or pollution below allowable limits. Within company boundaries.
	Material Damage	< € 1,000
	Company Image	No company image degradation.

Table 2 – possible consequences

The risk classification is a combination of failure rate and possible consequences and is expressed in a number and letter combination such as 3C, 2A, 5B and so on.

IV.   Cause Analysis

The decision to carry out a cause analysis will be taken by the Event Owner in communication with the HSE coordinator and the person(s) authorized to carry out the cause analysis (Facilitator). If the decision turns out to be positive, it should be considered to carry out the analysis through a team effort and, if so, which functions shall take part in such team.

The analysis will be executed by or, in case of a team effort, under the direction of an authorized person.

Persons authorized to carry out and facilitate cause analyses are:

- (name)
- (name)

Cause analysis shall at least take place concerning unwanted events falling in one of the highlighted risk classes identified in the table below.

Potential Consequence	A	B	C	D	E
	Risk Class				
Failure rate					
5	5A	5B	5C	5D	5E
4	4A	4B	4C	4D	4E
3	3A	3B	3C	3D	3E
2	2A	2B	2C	2D	2E
1	1A	1B	1C	1D	1E

Table 3 – Risk Classification

NB. Unwanted events with a potential consequence over and above (indicate category) shall always be analyzed, irrespective their failure rate.

V.   Responsibilities for Investigation and Analysis

A.   Senior manager

- Designates responsibilities for developing and implementing the unwanted event investigation system
- Provides the necessary resources such that designated employees can perform their roles in a correct and efficient manner
- Takes part in the investigation and analysis of unwanted events as necessary or desirable, based on risk classification or otherwise

B.   HSE Coordinator

- Ensures that the relevant department heads and supervisors receive necessary training regarding unwanted event investigation and analysis
- Periodically reviews the operation of the unwanted event investigation program, quantitatively as well as qualitatively with reports of findings to the senior manager
- Takes part in the investigation and analysis of unwanted events as necessary or desirable, based on risk classification or otherwise

C.   Analysis by authorized person(s) - Facilitator

- Where this is considered necessary or desirable, based on risk classification or otherwise, carries out or facilitates analysis of unwanted events with the aim of identifying causes and generating preventive actions

- Maintains, as necessary, his/her knowledge concerning the cause analysis of unwanted events and the operation of the UEI software

D.   Department heads

- Ensure proper unwanted event investigation training of supervisors in their department
- Positively support reporting and investigation of unwanted events
- Ensure that unwanted events in their departments are properly reported and investigated
- Decide on investigation and cause analysis needs together with HSE coordinator and facilitator
- Assist supervisors as needed in the investigation and analysis and the implementation and follow-up of remedial actions
- Take part in the investigation and analysis of unwanted events as necessary or desirable, based on risk classification or otherwise
- Assess the quality of reports concerning unwanted events in their the department

E.   Supervisors

- As soon as possible after an unwanted event make a verbal report to his/her department head
- As soon as possible start with a preliminary investigation of unwanted events in their area of responsibility, including those involving contractor personnel or on equipment that is not owned by the company
- Evaluate the severity of unwanted event
- Complete, as far as possible, the unwanted event report using the UEI software
- Participate in the further investigation process as requested by his/her department head

F.   Employees

- Immediately report unwanted events to their supervisor
- As requested, take part in the investigation and analysis of unwanted events as requested by their supervisor

When applicable and depending on his/her assigned role in the investigation and analysis of unwanted events following responsibilities apply:

G.   Event Owner

- Ensures the smooth deployment of the entire process related to investigation of unwanted events assigned to him/her
- If necessary, initiates a cause analysis to be carried out

- Assists the person (Facilitator) authorized to carry out cause analysis of events
- Supervises and ensures the timely and proper implementation of remedial actions related to the unwanted events assigned to him/her

H.   Action Owner

- Ensures the timely and proper implementation of actions assigned to him/her
- Communicates with the Event Owner on the progress of those actions

VI.   Training

Conducting good investigations of unwanted events and follow-up of remedial actions is important and requires some basic knowledge. Supervisors and managers should be trained or instructed in:

- Investigation techniques and methods of reporting, including assessing the quality of event reports
- Their responsibilities regarding investigation, analysis, development of remedial actions and their follow-up

VII.   Investigation Team

Depending on the risk class of the unwanted event and/or the possibility of serious consequences - the Event Owner may request an investigation team to:

- Assist in the investigation of the unwanted event
- To carry out, under facilitation of the authorized person (Facilitator), the cause analysis to uncover the causes that have led to the unwanted event
- Assist in reporting and preparation of remedial actions

Team members

The supervisor(s) of the department(s) concerned will always be part of the investigation team.

Depending on the severity of the unwanted event <u>or the possible consequences</u>, the department head(s), the HSE coordinator, the Facilitator, employees, contractor and/or client representative(s) and/or others may be asked to participate in the investigation and analysis of:

- All fatal accidents
- All accidents with serious injuries (accidents, absenteeism and accidents requiring more than one visit to the doctor, the initial treatment included)
- All fires and explosions

- All material damages (over € xx)
- All environmental events with emissions above the allowed limit
- All unwanted events with the potential for serious damage or injuries
- All unwanted events involving new products, new processes/equipment, with the possibility of damage (over € xx)

The Senior Manager

The senior manager will be involved in the on location investigation of:

- All fatal accidents
- All injury accidents that require hospitalization
- All fires and explosions
- Any material damage and other incidents involving damage (over € xx)
- All unwanted events with the potential for serious damage or injuries
- All unwanted events involving new products, new processes/equipment, with the possibility of damages (over € xx)

The senior manager will also chair a monthly meeting with all department heads to review and discuss all unwanted events mentioned under Section II "Reporting and Investigation". These discussions and any decisions taken should be recorded in the minutes of these meetings.

VIII.   Contractor Unwanted events/Incidents

Unwanted events involving contractor personnel should be investigated by a project team (also see section VII) including:

- The supervisor of the department where the unwanted event occurred
- The supervisor under whose responsibility the work of the contractor took place
- The supervisor of the contractor

IX.   Timeliness of the Investigation

Investigation of unwanted events must take place as soon as possible after the unwanted event occurred and as soon as emergency help allows. Any unnecessary delay may:

- Change the circumstances under which the unwanted event occurred
- Result in loss of evidence
- Make it harder to determine the immediate and basic or "root" causes of the unwanted event

The only reason that justifies postponing the investigation is to provide assistance to any victims and securing the safety of the area.

X.   Investigation Method

As soon as possible after the unwanted event has occurred and after providing of emergency help to any victims, the investigation shall include:

- Taking notes about what happened
- Taking notes of what was done and by whom, before, during and directly after the unwanted event
- Securing names and addresses of possible witnesses for collection of testimonies
- Taking photographs of the unwanted event location or making drawings
- Securing any physical evidence considered relevant

(If it is necessary to ask "why" questions, wait till all factual information has been collected.)

- Start the investigation
- Fill out the unwanted event report form

As necessary further material should be collected to support the unwanted event investigation and reporting, including copies of procedures, articles, etc.

Photographs, drawings

If possible, photographs should be taken of the unwanted event scene and of relevant objects/materials. As needed drawings should be made of the location, including size measurements, distances, etc.

Testimonies

Collect written statements, if possibly signed, from victims and witnesses of all unwanted events resulting in:

- Serious injury
- Serious damage
- Significant environmental damage
- Significant loss of goods/materials

These statements should preferably be collected by the immediate supervisor. If not possible, this can also be done by the HSE coordinator, Facilitator or an authorized person of the Human Resources department. The signature on the statements is desirable but not essential. The interviews to obtain these statements should be kept as private as possible and take place as soon as possible after the unwanted event occurrence.

The interview should focus on what actually happened.

Investigation of vehicle unwanted events

If a vehicle is involved in an unwanted event:

- If possible: assist in helping any victims
- Contact local authorities as soon as possible
- If possible: take pictures of the event location
- Do not move the vehicle, unless required to maintain safety of other traffic
- Do not interfere with professional emergency services
- Contact your supervisor as soon as this is possible
- Collect as much information as possible to properly fill out the vehicle event report

END

APPENDIX K – Bibliography or List of English books I used to have

I used to read most of the books listed below but often only partly just to find out if there was anything new. As you can see, it is a mixture of safety books, books about risk management, about management and about behavior of people. When looking at the list, please remember that old does not necessarily mean outdated; most of what is published today is based on what was written then and the same principles often still apply.

In 2004 I gave almost all of these books to younger consultants in Belgium who were starting up their own business.

Title	Author	Publisher	Year
CAP - Common Audit Process	AEI	AEI	1997
The Management Profession	Allen, A	McGraw Hill	1964
Professional Management	Allen, A	McGraw Hill	1973
Winnie the Pooh on Management	Allen, R.E.	Methuen	1995
Profitable Risk Control	Allison	ASSE	1986
The 59 Second Employee	Andre and Ward	Houghton Mifflin	1984
Company Insurance Handbook	Association Insurance Managers	Gower	1973
Loss Prevention Controls and Concepts	Astor	Security World	1980
Global Risk Management	Baglini	RIMS	1983
Future Edge	Barker	Morrow	1992
Neanderthals at Work	Bernstein and Craft Rozen	Wiley	1992
The Nine Master Keys of Management	Bittel	McGraw Hill	1972
Damage Control	Bird, Germain	ISA	1966
Management Guide to Loss Control	Bird	Institute Press	1974
Loss Control Management	Bird, Loftus	ILCI	1976
Commitment	Bird, Germain	ILCI	1978
Practical Loss Control Leadership	Bird, Germain	ILCI	1986
Profits are in Order	Bird	ILCI	1992
Safety & The Bottom Line	Bird, Davies	FEBCO	1996
The property Damage Accident	Bird, Germain	FEBCO	1997
The Managerial Grid	Blake & Mouton	Gulf	1964
The One Minute Manager	Blanchard , Johnson	Veen	1984
Empowerment Takes more than a Minute	Blanchard, Carlos, Randolph	Berett-Koehler	1996
Putting the One Minute Manager to Work	Blanchard, Lorber	Berkley	1984
The One Minute Manager Meets the Monkey	Blanchard, Oncken, Burrows	Morrow	1989
Leadership and the One Minute Manager	Blanchard, Zigarmi & Zigarmi	Morrow	1985
Industrial Fire Brigades Training Manual	Bond and Kimball	NFPA	1968
Quantitative Methods for Managerial Decisions	Brown, ReVelle	Addison Wesley	1978
Use Your Head	Buzan	BBC	1974
Project Risk Management	Chaman and Ward	Wiley	1997

Title	Author	Publisher	Year
The Risk Ranking Technique in Decision Making	Chicken and Hayns	Pergamon Press	1989
Avoiding Surprises	Church	Boston Risk Man	1982
The Winning Performance	Clifford and Cavanagh	Bantam	1985
The Art of Winning	Conner	St. Martin's Press	1989
System Analysis Techniques	Couger, Knapp	Wiley	1974
The acceptability of Risk	Council for Science and Society	Barry Rose	1977
Hazard Evaluation Procedures	CPS	AIChE	1985
Effective Loss Prevention	Crowe, Douglas	Westprint	1976
Loss Control Management	Davis	Caftsman Press	1976
Modern Safety Practices	De Reamer	Wiley	1958
Safety Management - Improving Performance	Denton	McGraw Hill	1982
The Quality Circle Handbook	Donald Dewar	Quality Circle Inst.	1980
Quality Circle Member Manual	Donald Dewar	Quality Circle Inst.	1980
Quality Circle Leader Manual	Donald Dewar	Quality Circle Inst.	1980
Effective Management & Behavioral Sciences	Dowling	Amacom	1978
The Practice of Management	Drucker	Harper & Row	1954
Managing for Results	Drucker	Harper & Row	1964
Management	Drucker	Harper & Row	1974
Safety Performance Measurement	EPSC	IChem	1996
Modern Safety Management Practice	Everett Marcum	WSI	1978
Safety and the Executive	Findlay	Institute Press	1979
Total Loss Control	Fletcher, Douglas	ABP	1970
Management	Flippo, Munsinger	Allyn and Bacon	1975
Helping the Troubled Employee	Follmann	Amacom	1978
Coaching for Improved Work Performance	Fournies	Nostrand Reinhold	1978
Apollo Root Cause Analysis	Gano	Dean L. Gano	2003
Safety, Health and Environmental Management)	Germain, Arnold, Rowan, Roane	AEI	1997
Safety, Health, Environment and Quality	Germain, Bird, Labuschagne	IRCA	2011
Human Competence	Gilbert	McGraw Hill	1978
Product Liability	Gray	Amazon	1975
Insurance and Risk Management for Small Business	Greene	SM Association	1963
Safety management	Grimaldi, Simonds	Irwin	1975
Controlling the Controllable	Groeneweg	DSWO	1992
Managing Risk	Grose	Prentice Hall	1987
High Output Management	Grove	Veen	1984
Handbook of System and Product Safety	Hammer and Champy	Prentice Hall	1972
Reengineering the Corporation	Hammer and Champy	Nicholas Brealey	1993
Industrial Accident Prevention	Heinrich	McGraw Hill	1959
Industrial Accident Prevention	Heinrich, Peterson and Roos	McGraw Hill	1980
Successful Health and Safety Management	Health & Safety Executive (UK)	Crown	1997
The Motivation to Work	Herzberg, Mausner, Snyderman	Wiley	1959
Investigating Accidents with STEP	Hendrick, Benner	Marcel Dekker	1987

Title	Author	Publisher	Year
The Analysis of Behavior	Holland and Skinner	McGraw Hill	1961
Iacocca	Iacocca	Bantam	1984
Quality Circles Master Guide	Ingle	Prentice Hall	1982
The Management Oversight & Risk Tree - MORT	Johnson	ERDA AEC	1973
MORT Safety Assurance Systems	Johnson	Marcel Dekker	1980
One Minute for Myself	Johnson and Wilson	Avon Books	1985
Managerial Breakthrough	Juran	McGraw Hill	1964
Balanced Scorecard	Kaplan and Norton	HBS Press	1996
The Guidebook for Performance Improvement	Kaufmann etc.	Pfeiffer	1997
The Rational Manager	Kepner, Tregoe	Kepner Tregoe Inc	1965
Beyond the Quick Fix	Kilmann	Jossey-Bass	1984
MORT USR's Manual	Knox, Eicher	EG&G	1984
The Behavior Based Safety Process	Krause, Hidley, Hodson	Nostrand Reinhold	1990
Corporate Uncertainty and Risk Management	Lattey	RIMS	1982
New Patterns of Management	Likert	McGraw Hill	1961
Optimizing Human Resources	Lippitt, This, Bidwell	Addison Wesley	1971
The Challenge	Lundrigan, Borchert	North River Press	1988
Swim with the Sharks	Mackay	Sphere	1988
Safety & Health in Purchasing	Mackie and Kuhlman	Institute Press	1981
Mind Skills for Managers	Malone	Gower	1996
Loss Control Safety Guidebook	Matwes & Matwes	Nostrand Reinhold	1973
Guide for Safety in the Chemical Laboratory	MCA	Nostrand Reinhold	1972
Handbook of Ventilation for Contamination Control	Mcdermott	Ann Arbor	1977
The Human Side of the Enterprise	McGregor	McGraw Hill	1960
Self Insurance and Captive Subsidiary Concepts	McRell	Twin Coast	1973
Risk Management	Mehr and Hedges	Irwin	1974
Behavior Management	Miller	Wiley	1978
The Strategy Process	Minzberg, Quinn, Ghoshal	Prentice Hall	1995
Are You Listening?	Nichols / Stevens	McGraw Hill	1957
People, Evaluation & Achievement	Nixon	Gulf	1973
Parkinson's Law	Northcote Parkinson	Ballantine Books	1957
Accident Prevention Manual	NSC	NSC	1974
White Collar waste	Olson	Prentice Hall	1983
Theory Z	Ouchi	Avon	1981
The Peter Principle	Peter and Hull	Pan books	1969
Product Liability and Safety	Peters	Coiner	1971
Benchmarking Customer Service	Peters	Pitman	1994
In Search of Excellence	Peters & Waterman	Harper & Row	1982
A Passion for Excellence	Peters, Austin	Fontana/Collins	1985
Techniques of Safety Management	Petersen	McGraw Hill	1971
Safety Management - a Human Approach	Petersen	Aloray	1975
Safety Supervision	Petersen	Amacom	1976

Title	Author	Publisher	Year
Safety by Objectives	Petersen	Aloray	1978
Techniques of Safety Management	Petersen	McGraw Hill	1978
Analyzing Safety Performance	Petersen	Garland	1980
Human-error Reduction and Safety management	Petersen	Garland	1982
Safe Behavior Reinforcement	Petersen	Aloray	1989
Managing Employee Stress	Peterson	Aloray	1990
Quality is Free	Philip Crosby	McGraw Hill	1979
The Art of Getting Your Own Sweet Way	Philip Crosby	McGraw Hill	1981
Quality Without Tears	Philip Crosby	Plume	1984
Let's talk Quality (2X)	Philip Crosby	Plume	1989
Leading	Philip Crosby	McGraw Hill	1990
Inspection of Chemical Plant	Pilborough	Leonard Hill	1971
Trends in Management Thinking	Pollard	Gulf	1978
Planagement	Randolph	Amacom	1975
The Winner Within	Riley	Putnam	1993
Up the Organization	Robert Townsend	Fawcett Crest	1970
Leadership Secrets of Attila the Hun	Roberts	Warner Books	1985
Introduction to System Safety Engineering	Rodgers	Wiley	1971
A case study in Risk Management	Rosenbloom	Prentice Hall	1972
An anatomy of Risk	Rowe	Wiley	1977
The Knowledge Value Revolution	Sakaiya	Kodansha	1991
Office Building Security	San Luis	Security World	1973
In Pursuit of Quality, The Case Against ISO 9000	Seddon	Oak Tree Press	1997
The Fifth Discipline	Senge	Century	1992
The Fifth Discipline Field book	Senge	Nicholas Brealey	1994
Increasing Employee Productivity	Sibson	Amazon	1976
MORT Accident Investigation Manual	SSDC	DOE/SSDC	1985
The Measurement of Safety Performance	Tarrants	Garland	1980
Is This Your Day?	Thommen	Crown	1973
Biorhythms and Industrial Safety	Thumann	Fairmont Press	1977
What Went Wrong?	Trevor Kletz	Gulf	1985
Management Introduction to Total Loss Control	Tye	British Safety Council	1970
The Management Guide to Product Liability	Tye and Egan	New Commercial	1978
Business Systems Engineering	Watson	Wiley	1994
Selected Readings in Safety	Widner	Academy Press	1973
Risk Management & Insurance	Williams & Heins	McGraw Hill	1971
Practical Benchmarking	Zairi and Leonard	Chapman & Hall	1994

www.ingramcontent.com/pod-product-compliance
Lightning Source LLC
Chambersburg PA
CBHW051204200326
41519CB00025B/7001